secrets of
LEADERSHIP

Thirty Centuries of Command

secrets of LEADERSHIP

Thirty Centuries of Command

JOHN LAFFIN

SUTTON PUBLISHING

This book was first published in 1966 by
George G. Harrap & Co. Ltd.

This new edition first published in 2004 by
Sutton Publishing Limited · Phoenix Mill
Thrupp · Stroud · Gloucestershire · GL5 2BU

British Library Cataloguing in Publication Data
A catalogue record for this book is available from the British
Library.

ISBN 07509 3460 3

Typeset in 10/12pt Photina.
Typesetting amd origination by
Sutton Publishing Limited.
Printed and bound in Great Britain by
J.H. Haynes & Co. Ltd, Sparkford.

CONTENTS

AUTHOR'S NOTE

I believe that every victorious military commander has inherited something of his ability, perhaps without realizing it, from his professional predecessors. Great generals are the links in my chain of leadership, while the chain itself is made up of their collective experience, transmitted from one commander to the next by the reading, study, and appreciation of history. Many military leaders are mentioned in this book, but relatively few can be discussed at length, and they have been chosen because they are the most representative or the most outstanding of their era. Each of these generals is shown against the background of his greatest battle.

In places throughout the book I have used the term *chain of command*; this possibly needs explanation. In the Armed Forces the expression 'chain of command' is a formal term referring to the structure of command, to the channel through which orders are passed from the Supreme Command to subordinate commanders, or for any intermediate distance along this channel. It covers the whole progressive sequence of implementing a decision or command, and equally it refers to the passing back of results or information from the lower to the higher echelons. However, in a metaphorical sense the term adequately fits the chain of leadership which is the subject of this book.

ACKNOWLEDGEMENTS

My sources for this book begin with the Old Testament and end with my own war experiences and conversations with senior military commanders. Among classical and ancient writers I have referred to Tacitus, Procopius, Herodotus, Pausanias, Thucydides, Socrates (as quoted by others), Polyaenus, Plutarch, Polybius, Livy, Aelius Aristides, Aristotle, Velleius Paterculus, Strabo, and to the works of anonymous monkish chroniclers of later times.

A full list of the 500 or so books which I found helpful would make tedious reading, so for the bibiography I have selected those which were of most use and which I found most interesting. My debt to all these historians is great, but individually I have nobody to thank but my wife, whose labours on my behalf are beyond recompense, and the publisher's readers, who made some valuable suggestions.

I am grateful to various publishers and authors for permission to quote from copyright material, in particular to Faber and Faber, Ltd, in relation to writings by Sir Basil Liddell Hart and to Cassell and Co., Ltd, for permitting me to draw from my own book, *Jackboot*, for material about certain Prussian and German commanders.

ONE

THE HUNGER FOR GLORY

'Nobody who has systematically studied military science can learn much in war.' So said General Gerhard von Scharnhorst, founder of the German General Staff.

This blunt statement, apparently inviting challenge, meant that Scharnhorst believed that a leader who had studied battles and warfare of the past would find actual conflict merely a natural and unsurprising consequence of his research.

I intend to take Scharnhorst's claim even further. I believe that a distinct linking of leadership or chain of command can be clearly seen in the grand canvas of warfare throughout recorded history and that some links in this chain are so strong and so enduring that each great commander can be shown to be in the debt of outstanding soldiers of the past. Generally, they all owe something to Gideon, victor over the Midianites about 1200 BC and to David, conqueror of Goliath about 1000 BC. More specifically Miltiades, who won the Battle of Marathon in 491 BC, also won the battle of Alamein in 1942; the English bowmen who won Crécy in 1346 also won Waterloo in 1815; Hannibal, the victor of Cannae in 216 BC, was also victorious at Austerlitz in 1805; Napoleon Bonaparte, who dominated the battle of Austerlitz and who died in 1821, ruled the field at Solferino in 1859; Sabutai, the Mongol general who annihilated the Hungarian armies in 1241, was responsible for the Prussian victories against the French in 1870. Montgomery or MacArthur or von Rundstedt, who won battles during the war of 1939–45, might well win others a century or so hence. These are merely samples; other links in the chain will become evident.

Scharnhorst could have added that no commander or military historian sufficiently dedicated to his profession could possibly be surprised about any development in warfare, whether it concerns strategy and tactics, methods and weapons, equipment and uniforms, discipline and morale, civilian and political attitudes. The outcome of a war and usually of a battle is crystal clear – to anybody willing to spend fifteen years or more in close study of three thousand years of warfare and high command.

Training by the study of history has not yet reached full development except in Germany, and cannot do so until General Staffs realize that every military eventuality can be foretold by close study of the past – and 'the past' means every moment of historical time up till yesterday.

No great commander is a copyist – those commanders who have slavishly copied an earlier general have nearly always failed dismally – and the last impression I want to give is that one war can be fought on the methods of a previous one. The circumstances of war and the conditions under which the fighting takes place are never repeated, but the essence of major tactics has not changed so greatly as some writers would have us believe. The methods of their application have altered – this is the point. In essence the general tactical principles used by Britian up to the time of the Second World War can be traced back directly to those of the Romans, while those of Germany prove an equally close descent from the tactics of Alexander the Great. The chain of command, when studied, is as clear and positive as this.

A commander might be isolated in time from other commanders, but he achieves a unity with them by the historical responsibility they have shared. Most great leaders have, throughout history, studied the campaigns of their predecessors, profiting by their mistakes, capitalizing on their successes. The writings of many commanders show clearly that they have been close students of earlier great captains. A few, it is true, have been so egotistical as to go their way without reference to history, but of these men only one or two were successful, for another ingredient in the amalgam that makes a commander great is the readiness and the ability to profit from the experiences of others.

Charles James in his *Military Dictionary* of 1810 pointed out that:

the best modern generals have never lost sight of the brilliant examples that they have been left; they have never ceased to call into practice the tactics of the ancients, as far as the difference of arms and a change of manners would allow. To those who peruse the histories of the 17th and 18th centuries and read over the actions of the most celebrated generals this observation will appear peculiarly apposite. It is justified in the uniform conduct of the great Condé, Prince Eugène, Turenne, Marlborough, Marshal Saxe and Frederick the Great. . . . Impressed as it were by the result of cumulative reflection they overlook immediate occurrences, *plunge into futurity and snatch out of the womb of time the ultimate issue of events*[1] . . . Thus in the extensive field of modern and ancient military history everyone may find the particular kind and degree of instruction to which he is ambitious of arriving.

General de Gaulle was always acutely aware of the chain of command. He has no place in the battles recounted in this book, but since his ideas and ideals have been largely Napoleonic he has an assured place in the chain of command.

Writing in 1934, in *The Army of the Future*, he said:

Whatever the time and place there is a sort of philosophy of command, as unchangeable as human nature. It is the true lesson of military history. When Charles XII wept at the recital of Alexander's exploits, when Napoleon pored over Frederick the Great's campaigns, when Foch taught Napoleon's methods, it was because they were impregnated by the feeling of this permanence.

De Gaulle himself was so 'impregnated' by this feeling that he felt himself destined to lead France back to Napoloenic greatness.

One of Britain's most outstanding military writers, Colonel G.F.R. Henderson, wrote in 1905, in *The Science of War*:[2]

It can scarcely be denied that an intimate acquaintance with the processes of war, even though purely theoretical, is useful. . . . Military history offers a more comprehensive view of those processes than even active service. . . . The art of war is

1 Author's italics.
2 The book was published two years after the author's death.

crystallized in a few great principles and it is the study of military history alone that makes such principles so familiar that to apply them . . . becomes a matter of instinct. . . .

Study of the campaigns of famous predecessors must be active and not passive. . . . We may take it that in soldiering there is more to be learned from the history of great campaigns than from manoeuvres of the training ground. For instance, a man thoroughly penetrated with the spirit of Napoleon's warfare would hardly fail to make his enemy's communications his first objective; and if Wellington's tactical methods had become a second nature to him it would be strange if he were seduced into delivering a purely frontal attack. . . . Again, the study of military history results in the accumulation of facts and the knowledge of facts, however acquired, constitutes experience. The product of habit, which, as being all powerful in moments of excitement or danger, plays an even more important part in warfare than in any other phase of human affairs.

A nation loses wars and battles when its commanders have not been acutely conscious enough of the chain of command, perhaps because they were too dull, too vain, or too lazy. All the great military lapses in any nation's history can be easily explained on this principle, up to the cancerous decay of military leadership of France since 1870.

This is not to say that France has lost all military greatness. Given the right leadership, her soldiers could still fight. The Fighting French showed this against the Germans at Bir Hacheim, Libya, in 1942 and even more spectacularly in the dogged defence of the entrenched camp of Dien Bien Phu, North Vietnam, 1953–54. Communist Vo Nguyen Giap wrote that 'our combatants fought with remarkable heroism and stubbornness', before being encircled and forced into defeat. The French Expeditionary Force suffered 140,000 casualties in Indochina.

Every nation is apt to lose sight of the comparative standing of its own military leaders. To the German Frederick stands out unequalled; to the Scandinavian, Gustavus; to the Frenchman, Napoleon; to the Austrian, Prince Eugène or the Archduke Charles; to the Englishman, Marlborough, or Wellington. Only when the great leaders are studied in the perspective provided by the others can the place of each be adequately gauged. To the Englishman it probably seems outrageous to suggest that Prince Eugène was equal as a general to Marlborough. But the proof exists. Alone he conducted more successful campaigns, won more victories, and performed more first-class work than Marlborough. At Blenheim, Oudenarde, and Malplaquet he carried half the burden and won half the fame. But if a people as a whole tends to believe that its own commanders are the best, the great commander does not underestimate his foreign counterpart.

As a starting-point we could go back to the battle of Megiddo, 1479 BD, the first great clash known to us between the pastoral and agricultural civilizations, but this would be an inconvenient beginning, since information about the battle is partly conjecture, and in any case it was relatively little known and therefore had no great influence on the chain of command.

Therefore we shall start with Gideon, one of the first great captains, and discuss the general theory of the linking of leadership before progressing to the ten great battles described at length in this book, to the tumultuous centuries that separated these battles, and to the scores of colourful, dynamic, and enterprising military commanders whose writings, words, and actions prove the existence of an intangible but powerful and enduring philosophy of command. The great captains held up as examples in this book were not merely generals and commanders-in-chief; they were military craftsmen, superb artists of war.

A military force, to be effective, must live with the desire for battle, and its commanders must be hungry for 'glory' – whatever that might mean to them individually. The great captains who live in this book had that hunger – Miltiades to Montgomery, they all had it.

The chain of command is not formed with links of even length or even strength. It is an untidy chain, better looked at in perspective and better appreciated in long lengths. If we were to study only a brief period – say, a mere century – the links might not even appear to be joined.

To the sceptical I would be the first to admit that breaks exist in this chain; for example, the links were twisted and snapped by the clumsy brutal imbeciles – there were outstandingly some exceptions – who conducted the First World War. But, somehow or other, the great captains who followed these periods of military decay always managed to pick up the pieces and weld the chain into shape. And so it will always be.

It is extraordinary how few observers and historians have bothered to give a description of the field *after* a battle, yet the dying embers of conflict are often the most vivid and are always the most tragic and poignant. Perhaps many historians believe that the glory ends with the victory and prefer not to disturb their readers with the sordid details of the cleaning up. These details will be found in this book, at least in respect to some of the battles, for, human and inhuman, they restore war to a proper perspective and help rub the superficial gilt from the glory.

Yet mere acts of heroism or mere scenes of carnage do not justify a battle's being called great any more than they necessarily make a battle important. Therefore the greatest of all cavalry battles, Dorylaeum, A.D. 1097, finds no place in this book, while the only mention I can give of the Swiss piling up the rampart of ten thousand dead at St Jacob's, 1444, is here and now. So with the vain charge of Talbot, representing the dying chivalry, against cannon and earthworks at Chatillon-sur-Seine, 1475.

As General Pierre Bosquet, watching the charge of the Light Brigade, said, 'It is magnificent, but it is not war.'

For war is an art, not a trade.[3]

---

3 At this point it might be as well to distinguish between strategy and tactics, for the terms are sometimes carelessly used to mean the same thing, and most writers on war have their own definitions. The best simple definition is that strategy forms the plans of war and brings troops to the battlefield, where tactics employs them and their weapons. To put it another way, tactics is the application in the field of the strategy evolved at the War Office or at headquarters.

Two

GIDEON STARTED IT

Gideon went forth to battle because the Israelites, having suffered for several years under the incursions of the Midianites, had finally decided that their very existence depended on driving off the invaders. The Midianites, 'like a multitude of beasts, with camels as innumerable as the sands of the seashore', pitched their camp in the eastern part of the Plain of Esdraelon.[1] where their stock devoured the Israelites' crops.

With his army Gideon advanced towards the plain and reached the hills nearby. The only water available to the Israelites was at the foot of these hills and very close to the enemy. Most of the Israelites were unskilled and untrained and, heedless of the proximity of the enemy, drank deeply and carelessly. Guerrilla-like, the few veterans kept their weapon in one hand and their eyes towards the enemy while they scooped up water with their other hand.

Most modern people, brought up on mechanized warfare, are unaware of the high state of the military art in the centuries before Christ and, for that matter, in the early centuries *after* Christ. The battles of this period were not mere wild tooth-and-nail brawls between savages, but were fought by well-equipped, well-accoutred soldiers, many of them professionals.

Gideon chose his proven men – 300 of them – for combat, for he realized that his army as a whole was unfit for a pitched battle. Gideon was a very early military propagandist; he saw to it that stories spread to the Midianites about the remarkable portents and omens that marked the rise of the Israelites' new leader, and the stories fell on receptive minds.

1 This was near the modern El Afule – where, in 1917, General Allenby's British, Australian, and New Zealand horsemen cut Turkish communications.

Gideon's tactics were simple – he had to create panic in the enemy's ranks, and to this end he planned a night attack, an ambitious operation with a small, relatively inexperienced force. He formed his 300 men into three companies and sent other, less worthy troops to hold fords across the Jordan.

He then issued to each of his 300 men a trumpet, a pitcher, and a torch – which must have seemed strange weapons to his men. However, if Gideon was the commander he appears to have been he probably took them into his confidence. Born to leadership, Gideon now made a personal reconnaissance with his batman-runner, and learned that Midianite outpost men were nervous and edgy and that no enemy patrols were active.

He returned to his camp, gave battle orders and the password 'The sword of the Lord and of Gideon', a somewhat presumptuous but confident appropriation of the Almighty's aid that Cromwell, Napoleon, and Montgomery, among others, were to emulate.

The men lit their torches and hid them in the pitchers, slung their trumpets, grasped spears and swords. To strict timetable the companies moved off, quietly and well led, to their predetermined positions around the enemy's camp.

About midnight – at which time the Midianites were in the habit of changing their watch – Gideon gave his signal. His 300 men blew their trumpets and waved their torches. The result was instantaneous and spectacular as panic swept the Midianite camp. In the darkness tribe fought tribe, tents and encampments were wrecked, what discipline there was broke down. The Israelites did not need to fight; they merely stood and watched while the Midianites fled. Gideon was too able a commander to leave his victory at that. Relentlessly he pursued and relentlessly he attacked until the victory was complete in every sense.

The princples on which Gideon acted and the faithfulness with which they were recorded established lessons for many great captains who came after him. These principles, which he put into effect, are still entirely valid:

Quality is better than quantity. A small force of well-chosen, trained, and steady men is better than a semi-trained, uncertain mass.

Attention to detail and sound staff work helps greatly towards victory.

It is important for a commander to make a personal pre-battle reconnaissance.

Enemy morale can be destroyed by a surprise night attack.

Action of the component parts of an army should be thoroughly co-ordinated.

An enemy can be softened up by stories of his opponent's 'invincibility'.

A commaner must hold absolute command and must never be hampered by possibility of dispute with joint-commanders.

Choose the most suitable weapons for the action in hand.

The commander's own dominant personality and confidence will inspire confidence in his army and increase its morale.

Victory can only be complete when the pursuit is pushed to the limit and the enemy destroyed as well as demoralized. The enemy's retreat must be hampered by prior blocking of escape routes.

Troops in attack and pursuit should travel lightly.

Guile often succeeds where strength of arms could only fail.

Plans should be simple, especially for night actions.

A general must know the capabilities and limitations of his army.

Many great captains evolved maxims of their own based on Gideon's victory, and some were published – without a word of credit as to their original source – and were usually acted upon. Many of the earlier great captains and some of the later ones had certainly not read the Bible, but a large number had heard the story and must have been consciously or subconsciously impressed by it. The tactics of Gideon recur again and again, right up to Alamein.[2]

The Israelites established one principle, however, which was rarely afterwards practised. Gideon was not what we should call today a 'steady and safe' commander; in short, he was not mediocre. Thirty centuries of warfare have shown that few commanders whose abilities are limited to steadiness and safety win battles or wars. War itself is neither steady, safe, nor predictable, and therefore the original, imaginative general is the best commander to have. Unfortunately, he often appears only after a long series of defeats, rather as if somebody had said, 'Well, we've tried all the sound men, now let's give that ecentric Scipio a go.' It is one of Napoleon's marks of military greatness that he chose few of his marshals for their 'soundness' but most of them for their dash.

About two centuries after Gideon another Israelite army faced an army of Philistines. As their chosen representative the Philistines sent forth Goliath, a well-armed giant of a man with a coat of mail said to weigh 5,000 shekels of brass – a confident, veteran soldier, scoffing at his opponent, the young David. David, nimble but quite unarmoured and armed only with a sling, picked up a stone and fired it at Goliath 'and smote the Philistine and slew him'. Then, with a borrowed sword, he cut off the big man's head.

Stones were hardly new as weapons – they must have been among the very first weapons man used – but in his fight David formally introduced the missile into warfare, and showed that the best way to overcome an enemy is not to rush at him with sword or spear or to protect oneself with enveloping armour, but to kill him with an accurate bullet from a distance. Thus he established one of the first tactical principles of war. By cutting off Goliath's head David showed that for a victory to be complete the enemy must not only be felled but destroyed and his comrades demoralized. The Prussian Clausewitz (1780–1831), the greatest philosopher of war, restated with startling clarity the principle illustrated by David's victory.

2 Gideon was an enterprising commander in his own right, but it is tantalizing to speculate on the possibility that his ruse was partly influenced by memories of Joshua's trumpets at Jericho.

One of the major links of leadership is that the great captains have realized that tactics and developmental innovations must be *thought out in advance*, as Gideon and David showed. We can begin with Epaminondas and his 'oblique order' in the fourth century BC and end with Guderian's panzers in 1940 and the Polaris submarines of the nineteen-sixties, and in the intervening centuries we can point, successively, to Hannibal's grasp of surprise tactics, Claudius Nero's use of interior lines, Scipio's use of a planned reserve, all in the third century BC, English longbow stand-off tactics at Crécy, 1346, Gustavus' 'combinations' in the Cromwell's use of battle discipline as a tactical weapon in the seventeenth century, Marlborough's ingenuity of manoeuvre early in the eighteenth century, Frederick's oblique attacking order during the middle years of the same century. Late in the eighteenth century and progressively through the nineteenth and twentieth centuries we have Napoleon's rapid concentrations and tactical ambushes. Wellington's mastery of the defensive-offensive, Moore's astonishing British light infantry, so spartan in their toughness, Scharnhorst's Prussian military machine, Moltke's Prusso-German General Staff war-by-rail-and-telegraph system, Allenby's bluff and deception, the will-o'-the-wisp tactics practised in Africa by the German Colonel von Lettow-Vorbeck 1914–18, Montgomery's attitude of 'change the plan to fit the situation' in the nineteen-forties. These men won victories very largely because they looked ahead, and, even more significantly, they *looked back* and saw that their precedessors had looked ahead.

While battle was limited to sheer muscular action of men and horses the leader's skill lay in keeping his forces in such a relation to the enemy, the field, and the sun as to be able to use his army rapier-style – cut, thrust, and parry. Resolution was paramount, for the determined soldier, company, or army could paralyse the enemy with fear. Hence the commander had to inspire his subordinates with enthusiasm and so increase their drive.

Every leader had a direct view over the whole field of the engagement; it is astonishing how frequently both commanders in an action managed to find a windmill or a tower of some sort, a mansion roof or a mound from which to observe and direct battle. Often enough the commander could give orders without needing intermediaries, and could by his presence and personal conduct influence the behaviour of his men. Tactics depended on a quick eye and quick reactions. Hannibal won his victories because he had both, backed by oustanding personal example.

In contrast to this in one way only has high command changed through the centuries – the commander's duties have become more complex. But we shall see at the end of this book that even in this respect warfare is turning full circle.

Ideally, military command at any level is a rich compound of many ingredients. Foresight and anticipation. Leadership and example. Direction and control. Decision and daring. It presupposes superior knowledge and ability, and it is nearly always accompanied by loneliness, which increases in proportion to rank. Few men reach high command, and of those who do fewer still relish it, for with it comes awful responsibility. Fortunately for the peace of mind of those who hold high command, by the time they have attained it most are also attuned to it.

Socrates (470–399 BC), himself a soldier for several years, was one of the first to summarize the qualities required by a general. His assessment, as quoted by others, made an impression on many commanders up to as recent a leader as Wavell, who quoted Socrates' sayings as a foreword to one of his own books.

> The general must know how to get his men their rations and every other kind of stores needed in war. He must have imagination to originate plans, practical sense and energy to see them through. He must be observant, untiring, shrewd, kindly and cruel, simple and crafty, a watchman and robber, lavish and miserly, generous and stingy, rash and conservative. All these and many other qualities, natural and acquired, he must have. He should also, as a matter of course, know his tactics; for a disorderly mob is no more an army than a heap of building materials is a house.

Socrates was giving a blueprint for the most complex, challenging, and frighteningly responsible job known to man.[3] Most of the great captains of history can be measured against it.

3 Nockhern de Schorn in his *Idées Raisonnées sur un Système Général* wrote that the life of man is not sufficient for the acquirement and full possession of the science of war in all its parts and branches.

There are always those who fail when put to a sharp or immense test, though not necessarily because of their own deficiencies; for defeat may be the result solely of insufficient strength in relation to the power of the enemy. Napoleon did not fail the test at Waterloo, despite his defeat; Hannibal did not fail in any way at Zama, 202 BC, although Scipio defeated him decisively. His brother, Hasdrubal, was killed and had his army decimated at the Metaurus, 207 BC, but he did everything that a great commander could do. History has known victorious commanders who had smaller quantities of the ingredients of high command than did the men they vanquished; on the day of the test circumstances simply happened to fall their way. Hindenburg won the battle of Tannenberg in 1914, not so much by superior skill, as because he happened to get hold of a copy of the Russian field cipher.

Command, and especially high command, calls for the ability to show compassion on one occasion and ruthlessness on another. Scipio Africanus showed both on practically the same day in 209 BC He terrorized New Carthage by sacking the town and then behaved kindly to the Spanish hostages he found there and loaded them with presents. This had a profound influence on winning the goodwill of the people.

Sympathy and understanding are vital qualities in a commander, and only through them can he gain real co-operation. Arbitrary control will stand up for a time, but, being no more than voice control, it breaks down sooner or later, as it did for Hitler.

Some soldiers have originated tactics which have echoed down the centuries. A prime example is the Athenian Xenophon, the greatest rearguard commander in history. After the defeat of Cyrus the Younger by Artaxerxes at Cunaxa in 401 BC Xenophon commnaded the rearguard of the Ten Thousand in their march to the Euxine. He carried out this controlled and disciplined retreat for fourteen months and marched more than 4,000 miles. He was the originator of all rearguard tactics, and no similar action in modern times reveals any tactic not employed by Xenophon. Modern rearguard actions directly attributable to the Xenophon method include: Moreau's rearguard offensive against pursuing Austrians in 1796; the gallant rearguard actions by Sir John Moore's troops at the defile of Constantino and at Calcabellos in 1809 to check the French; Ney's protection of Massena's retreat from the line of Torres Vedras in 1811; the holding of El Boden heights and village by Wellington to cover his withdrawal in 1811; Ney's superb rearguard actions during the French retreat from Moscow in 1812; Lee's use of two brigades and thirty guns to cover his retreat from Sharpsburg in 1862; Johnston's series of actions to delay Sherman's advance, 1864; the covering of the First Austrian Corps at Müchengratz in 1866; the spirited infantry, artillery, and cavalry rearguard defence during the retreat from Mons in 1914; Townshend's covering of his retreat from Ctesiphon in 1915; Rommel's splendid delaying actions against Montgomery after Alamein in 1942.

The outstanding military pioneer of the seventeenth century, Gustavus Adolphus, the creator of the first 'modern army', revealed that he prized the teaching of Xenophon. The *Cyropaedia*, Xenophon's book, was for Gustavus his military Bible, as it was for the great captains of the ancient world.

A study of Gustavus's tactical formations clearly shows that they were adapted from the Roman legion and its manoeuverable maniples.

Not all leaders have learnt from the successes or failures of their predecessors. At the battle of Pydna (Macedonia) in 168 BC Perseus, commanding the Macedonians, apparently had no conception of the tactics employed by Alexander the Great, who had built the Macedonian and Hellenistic empires. Alexander won his greatest victory, Arbela, in 331 BC by taking advantage of a big gap in the Persian front. At Pydna it was the Roman leader, Aemilus Paullus, who clearly has learned how to exploit such an opportunity. When several small gaps appeared in the Macedonian phalanx of pikemen Paullus quickly ordered units of his force to infiltrate these gaps, thus leading to the collapse of the Macedonian army, with the loss of 20,000 killed. Had Alexander's front become full of holes he would have pushed forward all his cavalry and light infantry against the Romans – who, as it happened, were badly shaken at that moment – and under their protection would have reformed his front of pikemen. Perseus's failure to apply Alexandrian tactics destroyed the empire of Alexander, 155 years after his death.

Again and again one finds contemporary historians referring to 'new strategy', 'new tactics', 'new methods'. There are 'new types of generals', and 'revolutionary advances in mobility, mechanization, and military engineering'. They even talk of 'new principles of war'. Strictly speaking, there are not even any new weapons, for no entirely new weapon has much influenced the course of any war; the decisive weapon in a war has always been known in a previous war, although it might have then been in only a crude form. There was nothing new about the German rocket bombs of the Second World War; rockets as military projectiles had been invented by Sir William Congreve almost 150 years earlier. The atom bomb was new only in its vastly increased destructiveness.

Frederick the Great has been credited – and not only by Prussian and German historians – with having invented the oblique order of battle, discussed in the account of the battle of Leuthen (Chapter Twelve). But Frederick, an educated man, had read about the battle of Leuctra, which took place in 371 BC, when Epaminondas with 6,000 Thebans defeated 11,000 Spartans by the oblique battle-order.

Alexander the Great's army provided other lessons for Frederick, two thousand years later. Alexander's army not only had its major and basic cavalry and phalanx, but many lightly equipped units, archers, javelin-men, slingers, horsemen. This swarm of irregulars foraged for the main body and protected it while on the march and in battle co-operated with it.

Frederick copied these tactics, using Pandours, Croats, and Tyrolese riflemen. True guerrillas, they spread in all frontal directions, adding weight to the more deliberately moving professionals they protected. As the mass neared the enemy the light soldiers would usually edge round the flanks to the rear. When the enemy was defeated they would harass his withdrawal and hold captured ground. Sometimes they would swarm – and 'swarm' really is the word – around the enemy's flanks, not giving battle, but acutely embarrassing him. If their own army was beaten they would provide a difficult-to-get-at-rearguard.

Hitler the would-be Great used truck-borne infantry, motorcycle infantry, and motorized artillery in just the same way. Their tactics were irregular and were based on opportunism, mobility, and independence just as were those of the Greeks, and the earlier Prussians.

'Hitler has organized a brand-new kind of private army', wrote a newspaper correspondent in 1936. Private armies were not new even when the Emperor Augustus came to power, but in 27 BC he organized one of the most efficient private armies – the Praetorian Guard. During the last years of the Roman Republic many commanders had raised special bodyguards – *cohortes praetoriae*, so named because the general's camp headquarters was called the *praetorium*. When Augustus restored the republic he kept these guards and organized them into nine cohorts, each of 1,000 men. The whole principle underlying the formation, retention, and use of the Praetorian Guard was copied by Hitler, with his Brownshirts and S.S., though both these organizations assumed larger proportions and wider duties than did the Praetorian Guard. The Life Guards of Britain were a very similar formation to the Praetorian Guard, although they were not used to support a military autocracy as the Praetorian Guard was.

Caesar (102–44 BC) left a considerable contribution to military leadership, though in the intervening years he has become larger than life. Fine leader and efficient soldier that he was, he does not equal Napoleon, Gustavus Adolphus, or Frederick the Great as an all-round leader.

He was certainly the soul of his army, and in this he equals, for example, Alexander and Hannibal in ancient times and General Moore (of Light Division fame), the Americans Sherman and Lee, von Lettow-Vorbeck, Montgomery, and Rommel of more recent times. Caesar was constantly interested in his soldiers' well-being, though the Roman historian Suetonius notes that he valued his soldiers neither for their personal character nor their fortune, but solely for their prowess. In this he was like Wellington, who did not give a damn for his soldiers as human beings. A later historian, Mommsen, said that Caesar treated his soldiers 'as men who are entitled to demand and were able to endure the truth'. Montgomery certainly emulated Caesar in this respect. When Caesar and Montgomery were with their men defeat never entered their head.

Caesar had four great qualities as a leader of armies. His confidence in his own genius was immense, and he was an outstanding organizer: he had a true conception of war in his own era, and was thus able to visualize a grand strategy clearly: he could foresee his enemy's intentions: he had that streak of audacity and bold self-confidence that made him immune to the fears and apprehensions that beset lesser leaders and tied them down.

Alexander, Hannibal, and Scipio had much the same qualities, but Alexander and Hannibal had actually hammered into shape the type of army that fitted their own genius. Scipio and Caesar inherited their army system, though Caesar improved on what was left to him.

Many generals have followed Caesar in having faith in their own genius, and even if that genius was nothing more than a hyperbolic term for extreme thoroughness the faith they had in it served its purpose. Since most great generals studied Caesar and his campaigns at some time of their earlier military career it is reasonable to suppose that they were influenced by him. In modern times Cromwell, Marlborough, Napoleon, Massena (one of Napoleon's marshals), Frederick, Gustavus, Clive, Sherman, Wellington, Moltke, 'Gordon of Khartoum", Kitchener, Eisenhower, Patton, MacArthur, Montgomery, the Australians Monash and Morshead – all these men, though of differing stature, had great faith in their own genius.

Most of them, and others, had Caesarian audacity, too. Chief of those who inherited this are Charles XII of Sweden; Frederick the Great; the Englishmen Marlborough, Wolfe, Clive, Beresford, Elles; the Frenchmen Soult and Ney; the American Sherman; the German general Guderian; and Morshead.

THREE

THE MORAL ELEMENT AND MOBILITY

In Napoleon, perhaps more than in any other military commander, can be clearly seen the result of intensive study of military history, of which he is the arch-advocate. Many generals have learned from their own mistakes; Napoleon tried to avoid making mistakes; he learned from the mistakes and from the triumphs of others. His only major mistakes occurred when he had no lessons from history to guide him. Had an earlier commander made a disastrous march to Moscow Napoleon would never have done so. Napoleon was familiar with every great battle ever fought, and though no battle can ever be a copy of an earlier one, he applied the strategy and tactics of his military forebears to his own campaigns.

'Read, re-read the history of the eighty-eight campaigns of Alexander, Hannibal, Caesar, Gustavus, Turenne, Eugène, and Frederick' Napoleon said emphatically.

His debt to these previous great captains and to others is discussed in detail elsewhere in this book. But what did he find in the history of the campaigns of Alexander, Hannibal and Julius Caesar? He found a record of marches and manoeuvres and of the general principles of attack and defence, but all this was mechanical and elementary. What he found most valuable was a complete study of human nature under war conditions – details of men under discipline, affected by fear, hunger, lack of confidence, over-confidence by distrust, shock, patriotism, political interests, the oppression of responsibility, physical, emotional, mental, moral, and sexual stress.

He was no imitator; no great general can be, for no campaign or battle can have its exact prototype in history. But from history

Napoleon learned the vast value of the moral element, and his use of his knowledge became instinctive. He was able to work on the minds and emotions of his own men and of his enemies – at long distance and close range – with a subtlety and skill that few generals have equalled and none have surpassed.

A great general, as distinct from merely a competent one, can penetrate his opponent's brain – and his study of history as much as his own ability has helped him to do this. All the great captains had this faculty. By getting into his opponent's brain Miltiades defeated Datis, Arminius defeated Varus, Cromwell defeated the Royalists, Turenne, Frederick, and Napoleon defeated all and sundry, and Montgomery defeated Rommel.

War is, or should be, more of a struggle between two human intelligences than between two masses of armed men.[1]

'It is to be ignorant and blind', wrote Hannibal's Grecian biographer, 'in the science of commanding armies, to think that a general has anything more important to do than to apply himself to learning the inclinations and the character of his adversary.' He ascribes Hannibal's astonishing victories to his observance of this maxim.

When Napoleon's baggage was captured during the retreat from Moscow the Russians found among his private papers biographies of all the Russian generals opposed to him.

Wellington closely studied the French marshals, so that on one occasion when facing Soult he was able to observe that Soult 'is a very cautious commander' and based his tactics on this fact.

Up till 1815 at least the French made a more careful study of military history in all its facets than any other nation. All military papers, records and correspondence since 1661 in the time of Louvois were kept in the War Department in Paris and with such splendid system that anything could be referred to in a moment. When the expedition which sailed for Bantry Bay in 1796 was fitted out it was done entirely from papers found in the War Department; they had been there since 1689, the year in which

---

1 As Liddell Hart pointed out in 1929 in *Thoughts on War*, 'the profoundest truth of war is that the issue of battles is usually decided in the minds of the opposing commanders, not in the bodies of their men.'

action took place between the French and English fleets in the Bay. From these papers, which were in such immaculate order they might have been placed there the day before, detailed instructions were given to every senior officer.

The British have never had such a fine system, which perhaps is why they always lose at the beginning', even if it does not explain why 'they always win in the end'.[2]

All the generals of the American Civil War paid close attention to the moral aspect of war, and the Southern General Lee especially so. He studied his opponent, knew his peculiarities, and adapted himself to them. His military secretary revealed that he had 'one method with McLellan, another with Pope, another with Hooker, and yet another with Grant'.

It is no puzzle to realize that the Russian Skobeleff (or Skobelev) was the first European general to master the problem of the offensive. As he said, he 'knew the American War by heart', and in his successful assault on the Turkish redoubts at Plevna in 1877 he followed the plan of the American generals on both sides when attempting to carry such positions. He followed up the assaulting column with fresh troops without waiting for the first to be repulsed. But the Americans had learned these methods from the British; there is a strong similarity between the tactics of the American Civil War and those taught in the British Field Exercises. And the British had learned from Napoleon, who never kept a reserve 'for tomorrow'.

The blitzkrieg – the lightning war – is another supposedly new method of wafare. The word is new, but the tactics are ancient. The keynote of all reforms had been 'increase of mobility', and all the more enlightened leaders strove for it. This is evident in any study of men like Gustavus, Cromwell, Marlborough, Frederick and Napoleon. From the advent of mechanization mobility has

2 In August or September 1794 the British Army occupied ground near Bois le Duc that had been occupied by the Duke of Cumberland in 1747, and a search was made for records of that campaign, but nothing could be found, not even a sketch map. Marlborough had operated over the same country for several weeks during 1703, but to have expected to find records would have been futile.

been pushed to what I should be inclined to call the limit, did not history show that there is no apparent limit.

The real break-through with mobility arrived in Europe with the Mongols in the twelfth and thirteenth centuries. With armies of quality, highly mobile, the Mongols' tactics were flexible in execution, and their moves were made with clockwork precision. They combined fire and shock tactics – disorganizing the enemy by fire and then charging him with relentless, ordered speed, while they sought out soft spots.

When necessary the Mongol horse-archers would ride as close as possible to the enemy and then go to ground to give covering fire while other horsemen, armed with lance or sword, charged the enemy. If necessary they could withdraw to the protection of their covering-fire position. This leap-frogging process would go on until the enemy was overcome.

The Germans based their mechanized and armoured tactics precisely upon those of the Mongols. Light armour or motorized infantry would test the enemy's defence, and if they found it strong would take reasonable cover and engage the enemy while the heavy tanks or bombers came up.[3]

Deceit too is supposed to be something fairly new in war, although it is something that the enemy uses, but never oneself, never the side on which God is fighting. There is nothing new about deception. Gideon used it effectively. Polyaenus made a collection of more than 900 stratagems for the use of Roman emperors in the war against Parthia in the second century A.D. Verus and Antonius thought that no deceit was too bad to serve as a good precedent for the conduct of war, and every soldier, from private to field-marshal, at some time or another makes use of deception, even if only in order to survive. In ancient times deceit was fairly straightforward. A besieging general would offer the defenders of a town safe conduct if they laid down their arms; then, as they filed weaponless out of the gates, they would be slaughtered. Today, with increased intellectualism, deceit is much more complex and subtle, and ranges from unfounded atrocity stories – 'the Germans are throwing babies

3 A fuller account of these tactics will be found in Chapters Eight, Twenty-one, and Twenty-two.

on to bayonets' – to letters allegedly found on dead enemy soldiers purporting to tell of their despair and their bestialities. Faked photographs on hundreds of different subjects were a deceit-refinement used in the Second World War.

The chain of command has impressed itself into strategy as well as into tactics, but tactics are given much greater weight than strategy in this book because they are more usually the province of individual commanders, while strategy is the business of what we might term the 'base staff'.

However, it is necessary to refer to the so-called strategy of 'indirect approach'. Alexander showed by his overthrow of Persia and Scipio by his defeat of Carthage that when fighting a major enemy supported by minor enemies it is more efficient to crush the major ones first and individually than to attack the major power. The Romans and the Macedonians built their empires on this system, and later Napoleon followed it assiduously. The British Empire was built on the same pattern, and the United States climbed to positive power in much the same way. In a way the strategy was used against Nazi Germany, when her satellite limbs were hacked off one by one – Libya, Tunisia, Sicily, Italy, Holland, the Eastern countries, and so on. It might well be argued that since Germany had buffers in all directions she could not be directly attacked except by air, but I believe that, no matter what her geographical position might have been, the strategy of indirect approach would have been the only feasible way of defeating her. That Germany could not be knocked out by the smashing, continual blows from the air appears to prove this belief.

Of the roughly 300 campaigns of the 30 major wars covered by the period of this book, in only 6, up to 1939, was a decisive result achieved by a direct strategic approach to the main army of the enemy. The most recent of them up to 1939 were Wagram, 1809, Sadowa, 1866, and Sedan, 1870. Between 1939 and 1945 Stalingrad and Alamein were the only two purely military victories achieved in this direct manner.

It would be possible to point to many wars and battles where the result might well have been reversed had the senior commanders of the defeated side been more conscious of the chain of command and had they 'read' and 're-read' those eighty-eight campaigns and others as well. Two modern examples will be sufficient.

Study of previous wars and campaigns would have helped the Japanese in their war with Russia in 1904. Indeed, they had studied recent campaigns, but they should have gone farther back, to Turenne, Marlborough, Napoleon, Sherman. Inanely, the Japanese concentrated their strength and threw it straight at the Russian Army. No Japanese general, it appeared, had intelligence enough to study a map or to reflect that the Russian army, far, far removed from its bases, depended for its day-to-day existence on the trans-Siberian railway. By cutting this single-line track the Japanese could quickly have strangled the Russians into submission. Instead they exhausted themselves in a series of bloody, stand-off brawls and were lucky to be able to make peace.

A decade later military command began to ebb towards its lowest watermark. The generals were given a blank cheque in lives, equipment, and money. Inevitably this led to extravagance, and it killed any sense of improvisation and enterprise. In any case, these generals had never learned the supreme lesson of the study of military history – that the past enables a commander to forecast the future. They had made no realistic plans in advance.

Liddell Hart, in *Thoughts on War*, emphasized that 'there are over two thousand years of experience to tell us that the only thing harder than getting a new idea into the military mind is to get an old one out'. This biting comment is unfortunately only too true – of second-class commanders. The Great Captains have not been so inhibited, as Liddell Hart himself directly observed 'Throughout military history the hallmark of the Great Captains has been that they stripped the art of war of the coils of customs that . . . like ivy drain the sap from the tree of commonsense.'

During 1914–18 the generals apparently thought little or nothing of mountains of butchered men. Manpower and shell-fire seemed inexhaustible, so blind force replaced surprise and mobility. Very few leaders of the thousands who functioned in 1914–18 were able to break through the doctrine of force and to use their brains.[4]

If they had no outstanding mental capacity of their own they could have used or taken notice of the several accurate, detailed forecasts published in English and in their own time about the

4 They are named in Chapter Twenty.

trend of war. As early as 1817 one of Napoleon's generals, Rogniat, in his *On the Art of War*, made some pertinent comments about the way war was bound to develop, as indeed it had already developed in some of Napoleon's later campaigns.

Rogniat noted that it was wrong to place excessive reliance on artillery, and claimed that the number of guns should be in inverse proportion to the excellence of the troops. If a commander relied chiefly on artillery, Rogniat reasoned, he was tied to the good roads, for only on them could he advance his guns and his munitions wagons. In the battle he mounted his guns to command the enemy's lines, so that the infantry merely supported the guns. 'Therefore the engagement merely degenerates into an artillery duel at long range, little or no pursuit is possible and the whole thing becomes a cruel game which wastes men's lives without results and leads to the endless prolongation of the war.'

The influence of history and of various great captains is shown in the maxims published in the British Army's *Field Service Regulations*. Their appearance here is to be commended, but it seems a pity that the originators of the maxims are not credited.

Here are some samples:

Moral qualities are the soul of victory. *Said by several commanders. Napoleon especially.*

There must exist unity of direction and control of the armed forces. *Clausewitz.*

Impersonal, passive or weak command inevitably results in loss of morale, in want of resolution and ultimately in failure. *Found in military writings as far back as those of Caesar.*

The full power of an army can be exerted only when all its parts combine in action. *Napoleon.*

A commander [when acting on the offensive] must be clear in his own mind as to what he has to do in order to achieve his object and be determined to succeed in his task. His plan, conceived in accordance with the principles of war [which is tantamount to saying that the commander must be well read], must be simple and based on the best information possible; it must be understood by subordinates and carried through by them with resolution. *Noted by dozens of great captains and military writers.*

It is by superior fire-power and not by men's bodies that success is own. *Put into practice by the Biblical David, exercised at Crécy, stated by Mahomet (among others) in the fifteenth century, and finally regurgitated, inter alios, by Churchill.*

In order to achieve victory a commander must sooner or later assume the offensive. *This goes back to the Chinese General Sun Tzŭ, the earliest known military commentator.*[5] Its truth is so obvious that many great captains have not bothered to re-state it, but have merely put the principle into practice. However, Bernhardi, a leading German military thinker of the last generation, said bluntly, 'The offensive is the stronger form of war and has even gained in superiority.'[6]

'The offensive is the stronger form of war.' We shall see this illustrated by Miltiades at Marathon.

5 He wrote *The Art of War* five hundred years before Christ. See Appendix.
6 Supporters of the defensive quote Clausewitz's statement – 'The defensive form of war is in itself stronger than the offensive', but fail to appreciate the qualification of the phrase *in itself*, and apparently have not read a few lines farther where Clausewitz says that 'We must make use of it [the defensive] only as long as our weakness compels us to do so.'

FOUR

UNORTHODOXY AT MARATHON

Early in the afternoon of a September day in the year 491 BC an Athenian general, Miltiades, gave to his small but compact army the command to prepare for battle. This was a momentous order, for it led to the shaping of history, and the battle that followed provided a model which many a general would follow in the centuries to come.[1]

No battle could better serve as a starting-point for a study of the links of leadership, because the victor was the weaker numerically, because he had his opponent at a psychological disadvantage before the battle, because he dared to take the intiative, and because the fruit of the victory was the birth of Europe, from where most of the great generals of history were to come.

Properly to understand Marathon we must retreat briefly to 522 BC, the year of the death of the Persian ruler Cambyses – when the Persian Empire stretched from the borders of India to the Aegean Sea, from Nubia to the Black Sea, and from the Indian Ocean to the Caspian Sea. The Persians, in thirty violent, victorious years, had swallowed up four great kingdoms – Media, Babylonia (Chaldea), Lydia, and Egypt. Heir to this great but still unconsolidated empire was Hystaspes, but while he procrastinated

---

1 I must admit that some historians claim the importance of Marathon to be exaggerated. Liddell Hart believes that the Greeks exaggerated it because of the impression the victory made on their imagination and that, through them, Europeans in all subsequent ages over-valued it. But he does admit that by 'reduction of its importance to juster proportions its strategical significance is increased'.

a pretender seized the throne, only to be killed by Darius (521–483 BC), son of Hystaspes.

Darius assumed sovereignty and organized the empire, dividing it into twenty regions, each ruled by a capable governor. He created a strong fleet to command the Eastern Mediterranean and built a system of roads to link the regions with his capital Susa – also known as Suster or Shushan. One of the first rulers to see the necessity for rapid communications, he established a posting station and inns every 14 miles along his roads so that a messenger could cover the 1,600 miles from Sardis to Susa in less than a week.

A thoughtful, thorough, systematic general, Darius put his army on a divisional basis. Each division had 10,000 men, formed into ten battalions of ten companies, each company having ten sections. Most of his senior officers and garrison commanders were Persian or Medes, while his royal bodyguard – the 10,000 'Immortals' – was exclusively Persian. His cavalry too was wholly Persian. His organization must have been extremely efficient and was indeed an outstanding achievement of the epoch.

With an eye capable equally of appreciating the petty and the important, Darius set out to secure his empire from attack. After a series of campaigns in the East he pushed his frontier beyond the Indus, using this great river and the mountains west of it like some great moat and wall. This task was relatively easy; securing the western frontier was difficult. Darius recognized that the gap between the Caspian Sea and the Hindu Kush was a weakness on his frontier, but this he could block if necessary. In practice his weakest frontier was along the shores of the Aegean and the Sea of Marmara. Darius believed that, because the peoples on either side of these seas were of kindred race and therefore likely to help each other in adversity, he must force his frontier westward until all the many Greek states were behind it.

About the year 512 BC he crossed the Bosphorus, sailed up the Danube a little way and made a foray north. Eventually he withdrew to Sardis, leaving behind his lieutenant, Megabazus, and a powerful army to reduce Thrace from the Sea of Marmara to the Struma river. Megabazus tried to reduce Macedonia, too, and though he failed, its king, Alexander, acknowledged allegiance to Darius.

This was the real beginning of a two hundred years' war between Greece and Persia, the first recorded conflict between

Europe and Asia. The historic struggle between East and West, still in progress, began at that point.

It is possible that at this date Darius had never heard of the existence of insignificant Athens, although Athenians had certainly found their way to some of the Persian dominions in Asia Minor to plead for armed assistance against their fellow-countrymen. Chief of the refugees was Hippias, the tyrannical ruler of Athens, who had been driven out in 510 BC The Athenians sent envoys to Sardis to urge the Persians not to take up the quarrel of the Athenian refugees, but Artaphernes, Darius's governor at Sardis, bluntly told the envoys that the Athenians must take back Hippias if they wanted to be secure.

While this crisis mounted the Ionian Greeks pleaded with several cities and states for help to regain their independence from Persia. Athens and the city of Eretria in Euboea – the large island off the coast of South-east Greece – were the only ones to give help. Twenty Athenian galleys and five Eretrian crossed the Aegean Sea, and the troops they carried made a bold surprise attack on Sardis, capturing it from the domineering Artaphernes. The startled Persians rallied, and the small Greek force was forced back and then defeated before it reached the coast.

Heredotus graphically describes Darius's reaction:

When it was told to King Darius that Sardis had been taken and burnt by the Athenians and Ionians he took small heed of the Ionians . . . but he asked who, and what manner of men, the Athenians were. And when he had been told he called for his bow . . . let the arrow fly towards heaven . . . and said, 'O Supreme God! Grant me that I may avenge myself on the Athenians'. And when he had said this he appointed one of his servants to say to him every day as he sat at meat, 'Sire, remember the Athenians'.[2]

Darius's fury is understandable when we realize that dozens of kingdoms were in his power – among them such powerful races as the Syrians, Assyrians, Chaldees, Phoenicians, Babylonians,

2 'Remember Pearl Harbor!'

28

Armenians, Palestinians, Bactrians, Phrygians, Parthians, Lydians, Medes.[3] The Medes ranked next to native Persians in honour, and the empire was frequently spoken of as that of the Medes and Persians. It was to be a Mede whom Darius would choose to exact vengeance on the Athenians.

After he had completely reduced Ionia, Darius ordered his victorious forces to punish Athens and Eretria and to conquer European Greece. In 492 BC his son-in-law, Mardonius, reduced Thrace, compelled Alexander of Macedonia again to submit to Persia, and was about to advance into Greece when his fleet was wrecked by a storm off the Acte Peninsula, near Mount Athos. Darius ordered a larger army to be collected and sent to all the maritime cities of the Persian empire for ships to carry cavalry and infantry across the Aegean. Heralds toured the Grecian cities demanding submission to Persia. Nearly all the continental Greeks and islanders submitted, but Athens and Sparta – the Greek warrior-state – spiritedly refused, and underlined their decision by beating the Persian envoys.

In the summer of 491 BC[4] the invasion army was assembled in the Aleian Plain of Cilicia and embarked on a fleet of 600 galleys and many transports. Darius placed command of the force jointly with Datis, a Median general, and to Artaphernes, a son of the governor of Sardis. Datis held the effectual command, with special instructions from Darius to take Athens and Eretria and to bring all the inhabitants away as slaves.

After some minor actions Artaphernes attacked Eretria, to which Athens had sent 4,000 troops to help in the defence, but they heard in time that Eretria was to be betrayed by some leading Eretrians and hastened back to defend their own city. Datis crossed to the Attic coast at Marathon, 25 miles northeast of Athens, where he drew up his galleys on the shelving beach. His rear was entirely secure, for he held all the islands and on many of them, especially Euboea, provisions and military stores.

3 In one inscription which has survived Darius describes himself as 'Darius the Great King, King of Kings, the King of the many-peopled countries, the supporter also of this great world'.
4 490 BC is the traditional date for the battle, but modern belief is that the correct year was 491 BC

Datis's decision to land at Marathon was largely influenced by the renegade Athenian Hippias, who was in touch with a group of would-be traitors in Athens – the powerful and noble Alcmaeonidae family – who, to obtain pardon for the Athenian part in the Ionian revolt, were willing to take orders from the Persians. These traitors suggested that if the Athenian Army could be lured away from Athens while another Persian force was landed at Phaleron, near Athens, to support the Alcmaeonidae, Athens could be carried by revolt instead of by ruinous battle.

Hippias had another reason for suggesting Marathon; 47 years previously he and his father had won an easy victory over their Athenian enemies on that very plain.

But Hippias made a serious mistake in proposing Marathon as a battlefield, a mistake so serious that it gave the Athenians a distinct psychological advantage, and one Miltiades was astute enough to be aware of. Marathon itself was a region sacred to Hercules; the plain was the scene of the exploits of the Athenian national hero, Theseus. Also, according to old legends, on this plain the Athenians and the Heraclidae had beaten the invader, Eurystheus. In short, the plain of Marathon was almost holy ground for the Athenians, and men will fight especially hard for their own holy ground.

The Athenians sent a messenger to Sparta asking for help, and also one to Plataea, on the Gulf of Corinth. It is doubtful if this messenger's duty was to do more than give news of the invasion, for Plataea was a weak state. Nevertheless, the Plataeans at once equipped and sent 1,000 men to help the Athenians, a generous gesture to repay Athenian help to Plataea in a similar crisis a few years before.

The courier to Sparta covered the 150 miles in 48 hours, arriving on September 9th. The Spartans, the finest soldiers in Greece, at once promised aid, but they had religious scruples about moving before the night of the full moon on September 19th–20th when a particular festival was held. They would send help the moment this festival was over they said.

The Athenians took the Persian bait and probably realized that it was a bait. They no more wanted battle in the city than the traitors did. About 10,000 strong, the army marched north from Athens, wheeled towards Marathon, and camped in the valley of Avlona near the shrine of Hercules. The Persian Army was by this time ashore, camping under the protection of the Great Marsh. South of the marsh lay the Plain of Marathon, cut practically in half by the Charadra river. On the southern flank of the plain was the Little Marsh. The entire plain between the Great Marsh and the Little Marsh, and edged by the rugged limestone hills which overlooked it on the west, covered no more than eight square miles.

The Persians had had time to occupy the passes leading from the plain to Athens, but had not done so, hence it was obvious that they did not intend to make an overland march on Athens. The wise course for the Greeks appeared to be a wait until the Spartans could join them, and for eight days the opposing armies warily watched each other.

At this point news came through that Eretria had fallen through treachery and the inhabitants were bound for shipment to the Persian Gulf as slaves. Artaphernes could now move by sea to Athens and capture the city while Datis held the Athenian Army impotent at Marathon.

A council of war, momentous as it happened, was summoned to the slope of Mount Agrieliki, overlooking the plain. The system of Athenian command is now obscure, but basically the army had a polemarch or war-ruler who held command for a year – Callimachus at the time of Marathon – under whom were ten generals, each a tribal leader and each holding tactical command for a day at a time. On the day that the news arrived that Artaphernes was embarking his troops the general of the day was Miltiades, and it was he who dominated the council of war. Two of the eleven generals present were Themistocles, the future founder of the Athenian Navy and the victor of Salamis, and Aristides, who later led the Athenian troops at the battle of Plataea.

Miltiades wanted an immediate attack on the Persians. The idea was put to the vote, which resulted in five generals against Miltiades and four with him.

The five who did not favour battle based their objections on the Persians' numerical strength, which has been much debated over the centuries. Between 100,000 and 150,000 sailed from the Persian bases, but Datis's effective strength at Marathon was probably no more than 20,000.

Everything now depended on the vote Callimachus cast. Herodotus, who spoke to veterans of Marathon, records what Miltiades said to the polemarch.

> It now rests with you, Callimachus, either to enslave Athens or, by ensuring her freedom, to win yourself immortality or fame. . . . For never since the Athenians were a people were they in such danger as at this moment. . . . If Athens comes victorious out of this contest she has it in her to become the first city in Greece. If we do not bring on a battle presently some factious intrigue will disunite the Athenians and the city will be betrayed. . . . But if we fight, before there is anything rotten in the state of Athens, I believe that, provided the Gods give fair play and no favour, we are able to get the best of it in an engagement.[5]

Apart from indulging in this poetic extravagance Miltiades must have pointed out, more practically, that as the Athenians were occupying an unattackable position the Persians clearly had no intention of attacking them. The obvious conclusion was that dirty work was afoot.

Callimachus voted for attack, and the other generals conceded Miltiades their days of command to him.

Miltiades was the right man on hand at the right moment. Miltiades had been ruler of the Chersonese (the Gallipoli peninsula), but when the Persians extended their power to this region Miltiades had been forced to submit to Darius, and he was one of the many tributary rulers who led contingents to serve in the Persian Army. He turned against Darius, who became bitterly vengeful, and in 494 BC he sent a strong squadron of Phoenician galleys against the Chersonese. Knowing that resistance was hopeless, Miltiades loaded five galleys with treasure and escaped to Athens. His enemies there had him tried for tyrannical government of the Chersonese, but Miltiades rode high in public favour and was not convicted.

Probably on September 21st Miltiades drew up the Athenian Army and marched his 10,000 men in two parallel columns, each

---

5 I am intrigued to know if Montgomery had read Herodotus at the time of Alamein. 'The Lord Mighty in Battle. . . '; '. . . we will hit the enemy for six . . . '; etc

about half a mile in length, on to the plain, where he wheeled them into line. The Persians at once deployed their army between the right bank of the Charadra and the Little Marsh, so that they were parallel to the shore. On a mile front and with slightly less than a mile between them the armies stood and waited.

Nearly all of the men on the battlefield had seen action and many of them much action. The Persians and their supporting troops were soldiers by trade, accustomed to pre-battle tension, to the fury of combat, and the inevitable post-battle pillage and rape. Every free Greek was trained for military duty, and because of the incessant wars between the states few Greeks reached manhood without having seen active service. The muster-roll of free Athenians of military age never exceeded 30,000, and at the time of Marathon was probably only 20,000.

The Greeks, with fast-beating hearts, eyed the massive Persian array and murmured to one another about the odds. According to old national custom the soldiers of each tribe went into battle together – another psychological advantage – and, being close in this way, they spoke freely and intimately as they waited for orders.

Miltiades or Callimachus reduced the Green centre to four ranks, lengthening his line and maintaining eight on the flanks so that the Persian front would not overlap the Athenian line. Callimachus led the right wing, the post of honour; the 1,000 Plataeans were on the left. Miltiades was somewhere near the centre at the head of his own tribal regiment, while Themistocles and Aristides led the centre.

Miltiades faced a serious tactical difficulty, one that must have been obvious to every man in the Greek ranks. The bulk of the Persian infantry consisted of archers; the Athenians had no archers. The Persians had at least 1,000 cavalry; the Athenians had no cavalry.

In fact, the entire effective Greek force was composed of hoplites – the heavy infantry – although there were some thousands of irregular, lightly armed troops. But the Greeks, until the time of Iphicrates, early in the fourth century BC, did not use lightly armed soldiers in a pitched battle, keeping them for skirmishes or for pursuit of a broken enemy. Each regular soldier was attended in the camp by one or more slaves, who were also lightly armed.

To compensate for Persian power and variety of weapons Miltiades had to depend on discipline, confidence, leadership – and unity.

In the Persian Army there was no common creed, language, or race. It was a splendid but motley army – magnificent horsemen from the Khorassan steppes, archers from Ethiopia, swordsmen from Egypt, the Indus, the Euphrates, and the Oxus, mountain men from Afghanistan and Hyrcania. They were united only as tried fighting men and by the example and drive of their leaders.

At close quarters the Persian Army was a fascinating spectacle, for the troops of the various nationalities which comprised it wore different uniforms. The Persians and Medes wore felt turbans which they called tiaras, sleeved tunics of various colours, corslets of iron or steel made of rows of metal scales sewn on leather or linen. Their shields, or *gerrhes*, were made of wickerwork, and on their right side they carried large bows, cane arrows, and short darts.

The Assyrians were easily distinguished by their helms of brass mail and by their tunics of flax, formed of about eighteen strips of woven flax, glued together one above the other. They could resist quite a heavy blow from an edged weapon, but were easily pierced by a sword or spear. The Egyptians also wore these tunics. The Ethiopians, in skins of lions or leopards, used 600 bows of palm-wood and long cane arrows tipped with sharp pieces of stone and darts with the pointed horns of roebucks. The Lydians in their arms and armour resembled the Greeks, while the Phrygians used the shield and axe, the double edged *bipennis*, often combined with a hook or hammer.

The Greek hoplites wore a strong leather tunic, and sometimes a breastplate, a helm, shield, and greaves. The shield was generally round or elliptical but there was a variety of helms. The one most favoured was the 'Boeotian helm' – with deep head-piece and with nose, neck, and cheek guards, the whole wrought into a simple solid piece. Eventually all hoplites wore this helm.

The greaves of this period were of bronze – a development since the Homeric age, when they were of pewter. Made to individual measurements, they were fitted to the legs below the knee and, because of the pliability of the metal, could be worn without any clasp or fastening.

The hoplite or man-at-arms never went into action except in his own proper place in the phalanx.[6] At different periods the number of men comprising a phalanx varied greatly. In its earliest form it had no more than 200. During the Persian wars the number rose to 5,000; still later, in the wars of the Greeks with the Romans, the phalanx embodied an army 16,000 strong. Miltiades used all his 11,000 men in one phalanx. The hoplites stood firmly pressed one against the other, shields partly covering one another, spears protruding menacingly in front.[7] Thus equipped, the phalanx usually advanced slowly and steadily into action. Miltiades could rely on such a powerful mass breaking the Persian front, but first of all he had to reach that front. He was in the position of a modern leader trying to take a position with the bayonet without any covering fire. From about 250 yards from the Persian archers the Athenians must assault at the double before too many arrows find their mark. But no phalanx a mile long, however drilled and disciplined, however fit and athletic its members might be, could maintain its dressing. Disorder had to be risked.

The initial hum died away. Sun glinting on their armour, the Athenian troops waited while the army augurers prepared their sacrifices and announced that the aspects were propitious for victory. The trumpet sounded for action, and, chanting a battle-hymn, the Athenians moved towards the motionless Persians. Behind the soldiers, on the mountain slopes, many civilians had gathered, apprehensive and excited, shouting support to their troops. They might have been enjoying sports at a picnic, as they gathered under the cedars, pines, and olive-trees, with the scent of myrtle and arbutus permeating the warm autumn air. Many of the men were armed with javelins, swords, and shields, and were ready to join in the battle if necessary.

6 Until Philip of Macedon reorganized the phalanx the Greek word 'phalanx' indicated no special unit of hoplites but merely the hoplite army, often quite small, of a Greek state.

7 The phalanx as evolved by Philip and used by him and by his son, Alexander, was a fearsome sight. The *sarissa*, the Macedonian spear, was much longer than the earlier Greek spear – it measured up to 24 feet in fact. In phalanx formation the points of the front rank projected at least 16 feet in advance of the line, while those of the second, third, fourth, fifth, and sixth ranks projected, respectively, about 13, 10, 7, 4, and 2 feet. At the head of each file protruded a layer of six points.

The tragic poet Aeschylus, who fought at Marathon, records that the civilians said: 'On, sons of the Greeks. Strike for the freedom of your country; strike for the freedom of your children and your wives – for the shrines of your fathers' gods and the sepulchres of your sires.'

Right from the beginning the Athenian attack was faster than usual. Miltiades wanted to be close to the enemy before the Asiatic cavalry could mount and manoeuvre against him.

Until the battles of Leuctra and Mantinea, more than a century after Marathon, there is no other instance of a Greek general deviating from the standard way of committing a phalanx of spearmen into action.

It seems likely that although the Greeks advertised their projected attack, the Persians were not fully prepared to receive it. Nevertheless, they waited confidently for the assault, reasonably certain that the Greeks could not cross the zone beaten by arrows and that their own cavalry would soon be attacking the enemy rear. Herodotus said that the Persians thought the Athenians 'a set of madmen rushing upon certain destruction'.

But the Athenians crossed the dangerous zone in good order, and the front attack of the Persian Army was speared and trampled underfoot. As was only to be expected in a long charge by a long line, the wings swept forward faster than the centre and the Greek line became concave. At the weaker centre the Persians broke the line and drove back the regiments led by Aristides and Themistocles. This spirited Persian defence turned into a counter-attack, and the Athenian centre was chased back over the plain and into the valley, where the Greek leaders checked the retreat and re-formed their men.

The Persian success in the centre was partly their own undoing, for it drew their front into a convex shape, automatically reduced the length of the front, and presented the Greeks with flanks to attack. The Athenian wings brought about a double envelopment and reduced many of the Persian regiments to panic. It is not possible to say for certain if Miltiades planned this manoeuvre.[8]

---

8 Three hundred years later Hannibal won Cannae by a deliberate double envelopment.

After great success on the flanks Miltiades linked his two wings together – a difficult movement during such a battle – and led the Athenians against the Persian centre as Aristides and Themistocles also came back into the fight with their re-formed troops.

While the Persian archers in the rear kept up a hail of arrows over the heads of their comrades the leading Persian infantry rushed forward many times, sometimes singly, sometimes in small groups, trying to force a break in the phalanx, but most of these brave men had no chance to use their swords and daggers before being impaled on an enemy spear.

The apparent inaction of the Persian cavalry is puzzling. Oriental cavalry has always taken an embarrassingly long time to prepare for a charge, but the battle at Marathon lasted some hours, and the Persian horse could easily have harassed the Greek rear. Certainly the Greek line took up the entire breadth of the practicable ground of the plain, and the flanking marshes were wet at this time of year, but when the Greek centre was broken the Persian cavalry could have followed their own infantry through the breach. There is no historical evidence that this happened, but I think it is a reasonable assumption. It is also reasonable to assume that although the horsemen were able to drive away part of the phalanx for a time, neither they nor their horses could face the wall of spikes presented to them. The people of Marathon have told me firmly that this is what happened, and there is often good ground for local belief, even two and a half thousand years after the event.

Miltiades, who had thorough first-hand knowledge of the organization and capabilities of Persian armies – he had, after all, served with them – obviously did not worry too much about the threat the Persian cavalry represented.[9]

Time was passing and evening was approaching. The Greeks were tired, but they scented victory. Then, almost suddenly, the Persian Army broke and fled towards the boats. A fierce fight took place on the shore as the Persians struggled desperately to get their galleys into the water. The Greeks lost more men here than

9 Some historians have doubted if the Persian cavalry was ashore that day, and suggest that it had been sent back to Euboea for forage, but Miltiades' own tactics strongly indicate that the cavalry was present.

during the main battle. Callimachus was killed, as well as Stenislaus, another general, and the scholar Cynaegeirus, who grasped the ornamental work on the stern of a galley and had his hand axed off.

Datis lost only seven ships, but he left behind at Marathon 6,400 dead soldiers of the Persian Army. The Athenians, according to the reliable testimony of Herodotus, lost only 192 men killed, a loss as disproportionate as in any battle in history. The contrast is quite unbelievable, for the Persians simply could not get to grips with the Greeks, whose armour protected them from the arrows.

Soon after the battle 2,000 Lacedaemonian spearmen from Sparta arrived. Starting immediately after the full moon, they had marched the 150 miles in three days. They inspected the battlefield and the masses of enemy dead, praised the Athenians for their victory, and departed.

Datis, still trying to achieve a victory, and in obedience to a signal flashed from a shield by someone on Mount Pentelicon, sailed quickly for Athens, hoping to find it unprotected and to gain possession of it from Hippias' supporters. But Miltiades, leaving Aristides and his regiment on the field, led his Athenians in a rapid night-march back to Athens. When the Persian fleet sailed into Piraeus harbour next morning Datis could clearly see on the heights the long spears of the troops who had beaten him only hours before, and he made no attempt to land. The Persian giant had been humbled by the Athenian dwarf; a vast empire by a tiny republic of 700 square miles.

It was customary for all Athenians slain in battle to be interred in a public sepulchre near Athens, but everybody felt that a distinction should be made for the dead of Marathon, so they were buried under a mound on the plain. The Greeks built ten monumental columns on the spot – one for each Athenian tribe – on which were engraved the names of the fallen. These columns, some of the first war memorials, existed for many centuries. At the end of the first century A.D. the historian Pausanias read the names of the dead on the columns, which have long since crumbled into dust, although the mound remains.

Another monument was built in honour of Miltiades, and numerous memorials erected in Athens and elsewhere. The battle was sculptured also on the Temple of Victory in the Acropolis.

Even more importantly, the Athenians deified the spirits of the men who had fallen in the battle.

The gallant Plataeans, who had risked so much without prospects of reward, were made, in effect, honorary Athenian citizens, and at all sacrifices in Athens the blessing of Heaven was asked for the Athenians and the Plataeans jointly.

Greece never forgot Marathon. The significance of the battle endured through the country's greatness and through her decline and fall. Many much larger Greek-Persian battles followed Marathon – Artemisium, Salamis, Thermopylae, Plataea, Eurymedon, but none has the significance of Marathon, which was a critical day in history. Until this day the Persians had been invincible, and other races were paralyzed by their acceptance of this invincibility. Marathon started a chain reaction which was to inspire the Greeks to beat back Xerxes, Darius's son and avenger, and which led on men like Xenophon, Agesilaus, and Alexander in their Asiatic campaigns.

Strategy was in its infancy at this time, so the Persian strategical plan was startling in its inventiveness. Few generals were astute enough in those times to evolve a triple plan of campaign as Datis did: to subdue Eretria and terrify the Athenians; to lure an army away from its natural object of defence; to encourage a fifth column in the city scheduled for capture. Datis left a strategical legacy no less than Miltiades' tactical one. Miltiades showed that a national army with high morale could defeat a larger, heterogeneous army that had no national will; that a psychological advantage was a military weapon.[10] He showed that bold tactics could triumph over military disadvantage; that armour was vital against missiles and that disciplined obedience to command could win the day. That day at Marathon Miltiades forged one of the first recorded links in the chain of command.

10 Examples of other battles where the victor had his opponent at a psychological disadvantage are Salamis, 480 BC; Aegospotami, 450 BC; Mantinea, 362 BC; Ipsus, 302 B.C; Cannae, 216 BC; Metaurus, 207 BC; Zama, 202 BC; Preston, 1648; Dunbar, 1650; Blenheim, 1704; Oudenarde, 1708; Quebec, 1757; Rivoli, 1797; Austerlitz, 1805; Jena, 1806; Vicksburg 1863; Königgrätz, 1886; Sedan, 1870; the battle for France 1940; Singapore 1941; the Australian defence of Tobruk, 1941; Alamein, 1942.

It is important to remember that the soldiers Miltiades led were tough and physically fit, for all Greeks had an almost religious reverence for athleticism. I believe that Hannibal, much later, was influenced by the remarkable strength and stamina of the Spartans when he insisted that his army be trained to high physical fitness. His Spanish troops were especially sound in body. Many subsequent commanders were aware of the need for strong, healthy bodies, but, oddly enough, few introduced regular physical training, though the Turkish Janissaries, enlisted in boyhood, were well developed physically by planned exercises. Napoleon's army was remarkably tough, but this was due to the way the men were forced to live rather than to any systematic exercises. The fittest soldiers in modern times have undoubtedly been the Germans, New Zealanders, and Australians of the Second World War. The soldiers of all three races were outstandingly physically developed according to a predetermined system. Still there was a distinct difference in the approach to fitness between the Anzacs and the Germans. The Germans were fanatically keen on *gesundheit*, and, like the Greeks, went at it with religious fervour. They trained not only the body but the mind as well. The Anzacs simply happened to like to be fit; their approach was systematic, but their attitude was casual, and since it *was* casual, it was not so necessary to devote so much attention to making their minds fit. A casual mind is less likely to suffer from modern battle strain than an intense one.

FIVE

CLAUDIUS NERO'S MARCH TO THE METAURUS

The battle of the Metaurus in 207 BC has fascinated many a scholar, historian, and commander, though possibly for different reasons. Byron, who recognized a military feat when he saw one, commented that the 'unequalled march' made by Nero[1] 'deceived Hannibal and defeated Hasdrubal, thereby accomplishing an achievement almost unrivalled in military annals'. In fact, but for Nero's victory his imperial namesake might never have been able to reign at all.

The river which gave its name to the battle is today called the Metauro, and it reaches the Adriatic about midway between Rimini and Ancona. We do not know exactly where the battle took place, but I believe, from a study of the ground and of historical records, that it occurred along the ravine of S. Angelo, which joins the Metauro itself.

A battle between Hasdrubal's army and the Roman legions was inevitable, but that it took place exactly where it did was pure chance. This was unusual in ancient times, when the place of battle was almost entirely predictable. The reason why Hasdrubal was brought to battle at the Metaurus and why he was defeated and killed there makes one of the most interesting battle accounts of history – as well as one of the most momentous. The links in the chain of command forged here have endured to modern times.

Immediately before the Second Punic War Rome was young and ambitious, but had two great powers to contend with – in the

---

1 The consul, not the infamous emperor.

east Macedonia and in the south Carthage, a great city built on the Gulf of Tunis by the Phoenicians in the ninth century BC

If Rome were to be secure she had to eliminate these powers, or at least she had to create unattackable frontiers – the so-called 'Alexandrian drive', named after the principle propounded by the great Greek commander.

In Spain – the land approach to Carthage – there was no such frontier, for the Ebro river was no barrier at all. Rome, ever the intriguer, was greedy for the Spanish silver-mines and Spanish markets, and to strengthen her hold on them fostered into power a political party in Saguntum (now Sagunto, north of Valencia). This party attacked the Torboletae people, who were subjects of Carthage. Hannibal, in justifiable retaliation, attacked and took Saguntum, in 219 BC, after an eight months' siege. The following year Rome demanded the surrender of Hannibal, and when this was refused war broke out.

Both sides welcomed the war. Hannibal, an astute man, realised that Rome was not yet unified and that she was vulnerable, especially as the Gauls in Northern Italy were permanently antagonistic to her. Hannibal, too, was a master of cavalry, which was little understood by the Romans. Hannibal approached the impending war somewhat impetuously, wanting to strike hard and quickly to remove the Roman menace.

The Roman senators arrived at their decision with reasoned deliberation. The Gauls had been beaten and colonies established to control them; southern ports had been garrissoned, and command of the seas was in Roman hands. As Rome held Sicily she could mount a direct attack against Carthage. With all these advantages the Roman senators were extremely confident, but war often produces the unexpected, and while a nation can be evaluated its leaders cannot always be accurtaely measured. The Romans measured Hannibal short. Because of him the war on which they were embarking would last sixteen years and be tremendously costly. In the end, as we shall see, Hannibal's link in the chain of leadership would pass to Rome, but nobody knew that in 218 BC

Hannibal was born in 247 BC and at the age of nine left Carthage with his father, the great Hamilcar Barca, for Spain. Well educated, supremely fit, alertly intelligent, and simple in his tastes, he was esentially a soldier from his early days. In 218 BC, when he set out from New Carthage (now Cartagena) for the Ebro, he planned to break up the Italian confederacy and force Rome to make peace. Seeing himself as a liberator rather than a conqueror, he moved into France to what is now Perpignan with 12,000 cavalry, 37 elephants, and 90,000 infantry. He reached Avignon, forded the Rhône, and crossed the Maritime Alps, somewhere near the Little St Bernard Pass, losing many of his men to attacks by the mountain people. He reached the plains of Cisalpine Gaul with about 6,000 cavalry and 20,000 infantry.

In December 218 BC he tricked Tiberius Sempronius into battle, held him in the front, and sent half his cavalry to outflank and attack the Romans in the rear. The result was a rout, followed by another in April the following year, when he deliberately placed himself between the armies of Servilius and Flaminius and practically annihilated Flaminius's army.

On August 2nd, 216 BC, near Cannae, he faced an immense Roman army and drew his own force into crescent formation, with strong cavalry forces on each wing of his infantry line. He routed the Roman infantry, and allowed them to press back the Carthaginian crescent until it became concave. Naturally, the Romans became very confident. At the critical moment Hannibal ordered his African infantry on the flanks to wheel rapidly inward, thus practically sealing the Romans into a bag, which was finally closed by the cavalry. The Roman Army was smashed to pieces. They lost 70,000 infantry killed and practically all their cavalry. Another 10,000 men not engaged in the battle were taken prisoner. Hannibal had 5,700 casualties.[2] One Roman who escaped the slaughter was Scipio, later known as Scipio Africanus. A young officer at Cannae, Scipio became one of the great generals of history and defeated Hannibal at Zama.

This success was the most perfect tactical victory in history, and was not to be rivalled until Napoleon's victory at Austerlitz in 1805. The modern parallel is the Russian encirclement of the German forces at Stalingrad.

2 These are the figures given by Polybius and are probably correct.

Cannae was a personal victory for Hannibal. Without detracting from his brilliance it must be said that the Romans' own stodgy conception of war materially helped him. The Romans had practically no idea of tactics, and their generals, usually chosen from political motives, had no imagination or foresight.

The Romans depended purely on discipline, drill, and valour, a useful formula against a rabble-like enemy, but not against good troops brilliantly led. In 1870 and again in 1914 the French made precisely the same mistake as the Romans, believing that the valour and drill of their brightly uniformed soldiers would prevail against mechanized might.

Polybius said that

> of all that befell the Romans and Carthaginians, good or bad, the cause was one man and one mind, Hannibal. . . . For sixteen years he maintained the war with Rome in Italy, without once releasing his army from service in the field, but keeping those vast numbers under control . . . without any sign of disaffection towards himself or towards one another . . . though he had troops who were not even of the same race.

This in itself was a great feat of leadership. Many nations in later years kept their soldiers in the field for longer periods – the Dorsetshire Regiment of the British Army once spent more than thirty years in India – but Hannibal's army spent longer cut off from their homelands than any other in history.

Hannibal's one material weakness was that he had no siege-train, and his only personal failing was that he was not as brilliant in assaulting a fortress-city as he was in the field. He could have taken Rome immediately after Cannae, but when he delayed it was too late, and though he took the greater part of Southern Italy his war became a series of field engagements, marches, counter-marches.

In Spain Hannibal's brothers, Hasdrubal and Mago, were successful against the Roman forces there, and the only Roman victory was the taking of Syracuse, a Sicilian city allied with Carthage, but even here the Syracusans held out for four years until their city was betrayed to the enemy in 211 BC. Scipio Africanus was appointed to command the Roman armies in Spain, and so able was his leadership that by the summer of 206 BC the whole of Spain had submitted to Rome.[3]

However, in the spring of 208 BC Hasdrubal had cleverly disentangled himself from the Roman forces and crossed the western Pyrenees, outwitting Scipio, who had hoped to catch him in the eastern mountains. With strong Spanish infantry, African troops, some elephants, and much money, he made for Auvergne, where he spent the winter and recruited large numbers of Gauls to fight with him against the Romans.

The Romans were now scared to death. With Hannibal on the loose in the South and Hasdrubal soon to be rampaging in the North Rome would be crushed between them. The prospect of two such men campaigning around the hills of Rome was appalling, and the senators looked hurriedly for able leaders of their own. They recommended as consul Gaius Claudius Nero, a patrician who had fought against Hannibal in Italy and against Hasdrubal in Spain. He had no great reputation in the sense of having a string of victories to his credit, but the public elected him on the senators' recommendation.

Choice of plebeian consul – Roman law stipulated that there must be one patrician, one plebeian consul – was very difficult, for so many plebeian generals had already perished in the war. The elderly Marcus Livius was an obvious choice – Livius had been consul in the year before the beginning of the war with Carthage and had beaten the Illyrians. But after this success he had been unjustly accused and found guilty of peculation and unfair division of the spoils among his soldiers. Still bitter and resentful, he ironically mocked the senators when they asked him to lead an army against the Carthaginians, especially as he and Nero hated each other, but eventually he swallowed his pride – as the senators had already done – and consented.

Hasdrubal passed through the Alps without any of the difficulty his brother had experienced, using Hannibal's engineering works and recruiting men for his army in every

---

3 General Fuller believes that Scipio's continuous success was due to his 'Hellenic open-mindedness'. This is certainly true, for he had a mental elasticity and tolerance that was certainly not an attribute of Romans at that time.

settlement through which he passed. In Liguria many trained soldiers joined him. He crossed the Po and for a time fruitlessly besieged Placentia, which he had planned to use as a base.

All this time the Romans worked frantically to get their six armies into shape. The fifteen legions were made up of 70,000 Romans and about the same number of Italian allies. With another 30,000 soldiers in Spain, Sicily, and Sardinia, Rome's military manpower was stretched to the limit, for she had already lost well over 100,000 men during the war.

Three armies were sent north, one to threaten the restless Etruscans, one to check Hasdrubal's vanguard, and the main force, under Livius's direct command, to move more slowly to battle. The 42,500 men of the three armies of the South were under Nero, chosen to face Hannibal.

Luck plays a big part in war, and Hasdrubal and Hannibal now had some bad luck. Hasdrubal had sent a patrol of six with a letter to Hannibal, telling him that he intended to cross the Apennines and would meet him in the district of Umbria, north-east of Rome, the direction from which Rome could be best attacked. The patrol expected to find Hannibal at Tarentum, which, in fact, was a Roman stronghold. Hannibal had been in winter quarters in Bruttium in the south-west and had gone north to Canusium, near which the patrol must have passed in their long and dangerous journey. The Carthaginians' quite heroic ride behind enemy lines ended in disaster – they were captured by some Roman foragers, and the vital letter they carried was sent on to Nero, not far away at Venusia. Hannibal had heard that his brother was in Italy, but could make no firm plans until he could contact him. He did, however, know much about the Roman movements because he had an efficient intelligence system. Nero reacted to Hasdrubal's letter as one would expect from a great commander, as distinct from one of ordinary attainments. He had orders, as had all consuls, to keep within his own province, to operate only on orders from Rome, and to make war only on a direct instruction from Rome. Nero, however, had the courage to act on his own initiative. He sent the captured letter to Rome, together with one of his own, reporting that while Hannibal remained in doubtful inaction he intended to lead 6,000 picked infantry and 1,000 cavalry north to reinforce the northern armies. He suggested that a legion at Capua should be moved to Rome and that the troops in Rome should be moved to Narni. The brothers, Nero realized, were within 200 miles of each other, and if Rome were to be saved they must not meet. Hasdrubal at this time was at Sena, south-east of the Metaurus.

With the fine eye of a quartermaster Nero sent messengers ahead on his road of march with orders to local leaders to see that provisions, horses, mules, and carts were ready by the wayside for his soldiers to use.

After leaving camp Nero took another rather unusual step: he halted his army and told his 7,000 chosen troops what he planned to do. It seemed an audacious project, he said, but actually it was militarily sound. He was leading them to certain victory, and they would get full credit for it. The reception they would receive on the way to battle would prove how high their fortunes stood.

Meanwhile Nero's message to Rome had had the effect of a bomb thrown among pigeons. There was instant panic. Nero was called irresponsible and rash; his action was labelled traitorous. He had left his large army without proper leadership, and Hannibal would push it aside and begin his ravages against Rome once more. Two consuls had been lost in battle the previous year, now Nero seemed bent on suicide, for if the speed and success with which Hasdrubal had crossed the Alps and moved down Italy was any indication, then he was an even better general than Hannibal. The city seethed with rumour, speculation, and terror. After so many years of living under his shadow his very name frightened the Romans.

But Nero was confident, and the districts through which he passed along the Adriatic coast responded magnificently to his call. In the warm April sun farmers, traders, and their families flocked to the roadside in thousands, bringing food and drink, flowers and prayers. The army marched night and day, resting in relays in the carts provided by the country people.

Livius and another leader, Porcius, had their camp near Sena, only half a mile from that of Hasdrubal. In collusion with Livius, Nero timed his approach so that he would enter Livius's camp by night – without any noisy reception – and so that the reinforcement would not be noticed he arranged for his officers and men to double up with men from Livius's army and to share their tents. It was a masterly piece of deception, similar in effect to that practised by Montgomery at Alamein.

Nero arrived at Sena with considerably more than the 7,000 men he set out with, for along the road he had enlisted many volunteers, especially veterans of former campaigns.

Next morning Livius called a council of war, at which it was proposed that Nero's men be given time to rest after their gruelling march. According to Livy, Nero emphatically opposed the delay. He said,

Who is for giving time for my men to rest is for giving time to Hannibal to attack my men in camp in Apulia. He is for giving time to Hannibal and Hasdrubal to discover my march and to manoeuvre for a junction . . . at their leisure. We must fight instantly, while both the foe here and the foe in the South are ignorant of our movements. We must destroy this Hasdrubal, and I must be back in Apulia before Hannibal awakes from his torpor.

His arguments prevailed, and it was decided to fight. The red ensign, the signal for immediate battle, was hoisted, and the Roman army was drawn up outside the camp.

Hasdrubal up to this point was equally anxious for battle, but had not thought it wise to attack the Romans in their lines. When they offered battle he too arrayed his troops. But, for all their precautions, the Romans had been careless in one detail. One of Hasdrubal's patrols reported that the trumpet, which gave the signal to Roman legions, had sounded once in Porcius's camp but twice in that of Livius – a strong hint that a third superior officer was present. As Hasdrubal rode forward to observe the enemy line he thought that their numbers seemed to have increased. Some of the horses, too, appeared out of condition, as if they had made a strenuous forced march. He deduced that both consuls faced him.

Doubtful and apprehensive because he had not heard from his brother, concerned about the greater numbers of Romans – although, in fact, he outnumbered them – Hasdrubal decided not to fight after all and ordered his troops back to camp. Throughout the day both forces watched each other warily, but when night fell Hasdrubal led his men out of camp, planning to retreat to the friendly region of Insubrian Gaul and to make further attempts to contact his brother.

He moved quietly up the Metaurus river valley towards the Via Flaminia, but he never did reach this road because his guides either deserted him or lost their way, and neither Hasdrubal nor his officers could find a ford across the river, so he had to halt for the night. The night's confusion did its inevitable evil work, and in the morning Hasdrubal found that many of his Gallic supporters were helplessly drunk and that even some of his own men had lost their sense of discipline and purpose.

His cavalry screen reported that the Romans were coming up steadily, and Hasdrubal knew that he could not continue his retreat; the Romans would simply walk over his army. He was forced to prepare for battle. His dispositions were as sound as possible, considering that he was caught on ground he had not chosen. He put his Ligurians in the centre and protected and heartened them with his ten elephants; he posted the Gauls, with their long javelins, great broadswords, and big shields, on high ground on the left flank, overlooking a ravine. He himself took charge of the Spaniards, his best troops, on the right flank.

These veterans, protected by helmets and shields and armed with short cut-and-thrust swords, he could count on for desperate action. His front covered about five miles, but had big gaps between centre and flank forces. Hasdrubal's tactics were sound. He hoped that the ravine and rough country on the Roman side of it would delay the Romans in coming to grips with the Gauls, who were undisciplined barbarians. With his fine Spanish troops he would smash the Roman left and try to roll up the Roman line. He could depend on the Ligurians at least to hold the centre.

The Romans were capable troops, well led, but at this date they had not reached the perfection of manoeuvre acquired a century later. The formation of a legion differed in various periods, but at this time each legion had two main divisions of troops – the *hastati* and the *principes*. Each legionary wore a breastplate of mail, bronze greaves, and a bronze helmet with a proud crest of scarlet or black feathers – and very martial he looked. He had a large oval shield and two javelins – one light for throwing, the other strong and with a four-foot iron blade for thrusting and not usually for throwing. On his right thigh he carried a short cut-and-thrust sword.

The *hastati* formed the first ten ranks of the legion and the *principes* the second ten ranks, with about three feet between files and between ranks – a vast difference from the phalanx system. In immediate battle-order each even-numbered rank took a pace and a half to the right, so that the legion assumed the quincunx pattern and the troops looked rather like pieces on a draughtboard. In this formation the men did not hinder one another's movements, and a battered front rank or one which had thrown its javelins could be moved to the rear withut confusion or disorder.

When the Romans, in this formation, clashed with other well-trained troops the fight was no mere hacking, untidy brawl, but a fairly orderly collection of single combats going on up and down the line. Unless many men fell the dressing of the lines remained remarkably uniform.

The third division of the legion was the *triarii* – a reserve of 600 veterans – ready in an emergency to move to any part of the legion's front. *Hastati, principes,* and *triarii* were not arranged in continuous ranks but in maniples of 120 men each, which were separated from each other and were themselves arranged in the quincunx formation. Each legion also had some lightly accoutred skirmishers and a troup of 300 cavalry. Altogether, the legion was a hard-hitting, compact, practically self-contained unit, akin to a brigade group in some modern armies.

The elephants took the initiative, and in their charge broke the Roman lines, causing gaps in several places. Despite this minor setback the Romans under Livius and Porcius attacked determinedly, to be met by stubborn resistance from the Ligurians and Spaniards. They made no headway, and Hasdrubal, seeing that Nero could not come to grips with the Gauls, urged his men on more fiercely. Livius himself must have wondered if he had taken on more than he could handle.

Nero, on the Roman right, became very restive. His men were struggling over very difficult ground, and the Gauls were obviously commanded by officers who had orders to refuse battle and merely to keep the Roman right occupied. Acting once more completely out of character for a Roman consul, Nero decided to take a hand in the fight on his left. He moved some of his best troops – possibly 2,000 – in a rapid march along the rear of the Roman army. Livius and Porcius, had they looked rearwards, must have been astonished at this unorthodox manoeuvre. Then, with perfect surprise, Nero led his men in a violent charge on the flank and rear of Hasdrubal's force.[4] The impact and shock were too great; the Spaniards and Africans who fought with them were thrown back on the Ligurians and overwhelmed, while the Gauls, at last brought to bay, were butchered in thousands. The Carthaginians lost 10,000 dead in all, the Romans 2,000.

As always, the battlefield was a shambles, made even worse than usual in this case by the maddened elephants, now out of control and trumpeting around the battlefield. Most were killed by their mahouts, who were equipped with a hammer and long spike which was driven into the animal's spinal column.

Hasdrubal knew he had lost the battle, and probably had time to reflect that but for the surprise assault from the flank and rear he might well have fought a stand-off battle. He knew, too, that as a captive he would be treated with cruelty and contempt and paraded in chains through the streets of Rome. As the son of Hamilcar and brother of Hannibal he could expect no mercy. Sword in hand he charged into the middle of a cohort of Romans – a force of 450 men – and died fighting.

Nero did not rest on his laurels, but again force-marched his troops, back to his lines in Apulia. He was facing Hannibal's Carthaginians before they became aware that he had been absent. He took with him from the Metaurus a grisly trophy of his victory – Hasdrubal's head.[5] He had a rider throw it into Hannibal's camp, and a Carthaginian soldier hurried with it to his commander. Hannibal, who had not seen his brother for eleven years, said in his distress that he now recognized his country's destiny and that Rome would become mistress of the world. The battle of the Metaurus certainly ensured a further 200 years of Roman military conquest.

Nevertheless, the Romans still dared not attack Hannibal, even though the initiative had passed into their hands. Eventually he was recalled to Carthage to oppose Scipio, but was defeated by him at the battle of Zama (south-west of Carthage) in 202 BC. One of

4 Marlborough did this at the battle of Ramillies in 1706.
5 This was a savage, barbarous act, but typically Roman at that time.

the great turning-points in history, Zama established the undisputed authority of Rome over the Western Mediterranean and reduced Carthage to a mere defenceless mercantile town. But Carthage's road to ruin began on a lonely ravine in Italy.

Political consequences apart, Nero's approach march was a splendid military achievement, as outstanding as his decision to make it in the first place. Marlborough might well have been influenced by it when he made his long, dynamic march from Flanders to the Danube to win the battle of Blenheim in 1704. The Archduke Charles emulated Nero in 1796 when he marched a long distance to defeat the French under Jourdan and then drove Moreau through the Black Forest and across the Rhine. This freed Germany from French invasion for a time, though not so enduringly as Nero had freed Rome. But if Nero's feat has been equalled it has not been surpassed.

At the battle itself his quick unorthodox decision to change position and attack on the flank had a profound influence on military thought, both in his time and many centuries later when accounts of his actions began to be read by commanders. Nero's contribution to leadership has been one of the most enduring.

SIX

TEUTOBURGER WALD, THE FIRST GERMAN BATTLE OF ANNIHILATION

Judged alone by its long-term consequences to Britain, the battle of the Teutoburger Wald in the year AD 9 deserves a special place in history, but, oddly enough, few Britons have ever been aware of these consequences. In Victorian times the great historian Arnold drew attention to them, and went so far as to say that but for the German victory over the Romans 'our German ancestors would have been enslaved or exterminated along the Eider and the Elbe; this island would never have borne the name of England and we, this great English nation . . . would have been utterly cut off from existence.'

Sir Edward Creasy, writing in 1851, claimed that Arminius, the German victor at the Teutoburger Wald, 'is far more truly one of our national heroes than Caractacus and it was our own primeval fatherland the brave German rescued when he slaughtered the Roman legions . . . in the marshy glens between the Lippe and the Ems.'

'An Englishman', said Creasy, 'is entitled to claim a closer degree of relationship with Arminius than can be claimed by any German of modern Germany.' Exploiting the theme mercilessly, Creasy further referred to the English as 'being the nearest heirs to the glory of Arminius'.

These historians and others have exaggerated the situation, for if Arminius had not provided Britain with German ancestors somebody else certainly would have done so. Arminius merely happened to be the man on the spot. Still, his military achievement cannot be denied, even if its glory was particularly savage. And Germans, despite Creasy's rather offhand reference to their relationship with Arminius, have perpetuated his achievement.

The Germans had been involved with Rome since the end of the second century BC and initially had caused as great a panic in Rome as had the Gauls and Carthaginians. Finally, in 101 BC the brilliant but brutal general Marius, with the help of Catulus, defeated them in the great battle of Vercellae.

Marius, seven times elected consul, made profound changes in Roman military organization, changes which influenced strategy and politics. About 104 BC Marius scrapped the old militia system and opened the army to volunteers outside the propertied class, and later recruited men from the servant and even criminal classes. More than this, he employed foreigners in Rome's army. He reorganized the legion into cohorts, each cohort having 3 maniples of 200 men each. A maniple had 2 centuries of 100 men each. All distinction between *hastati*, *principes*, and *triarii* disappeared and the tactical unit grew from 120 to 600 soldiers. Since the legion had ten cohorts – four in the first line, three in the second, and three in the third, the legion's strength rose from 4,500 to 6,000 men. The legionary cavalry was done away with and foreign cavalry took their place. The legion was used in a different way, too, for the spaces between cohorts was shortened until the old phalanx order re-evolved itself.

The Roman Army was now a professional one, rather imbued with a mercenary spirit – a fact which had a bearing on the circumstances which brought about the battle of the Teutoburger Wald.

In earlier days the soldier had sworn allegiance to the Republic; now he swore it to his general. If the army had well-educated, skilful generals the army was successful; when they were inadequate discipline suffered. Julius Caesar inherited this military system and probably changed its basic structure little. However, he increased the numbers of light infantry, bowmen, and slingers and greatly improved cavalry, artillery, and engineers. Catapults and *ballistae* were in close support to the infantry, and sometime between Caesar's day and AD 9 each legion had an 'artillery' train of sixty *ballistae* and ten catapults – the equivalent of today's field guns and howitzers – to fire darts and stones.

Because of these developments the defensive became the stronger form of war and the least expensive in casualties, although at this date heavy casualties were accepted as a necessary concomitant of war, and if generals were worried about them they have left no evidence that this was so.

Caesar made the Rhine the eastern frontier of Central and Northern Gaul, and to establish it as such conquered the Belgic tribes, most of which were of German origin, living roughly in what is today's Belgium. In 57 BC Caesar defeated the Nervii and gained control of the left bank of the Rhine below Cologne, and a few years later had secured all the Rhine from Xanten to Belfort. He bridged the Rhine south of Coblenz and made a terrifying demonstration against the semi-nomadic Germans to cow them into submission.

They were interesting people, fierce in battle, but with only the semblance of military organization. They carried short spears, with a narrow and small but sharp head. Most mounted men had a shield, but very few infantry possessed such a luxury. It might have been an impediment anyway, as the infantry moved rapidly enough to fight with their own cavalry. Tacitus recorded, significantly, that 'on the field of battle it is disgraceful for a chief's companions not to equal him and that to aid him, protect him and by their own gallant actions add to his glory, were their most sacred engagements.'

With the help of the German General Staff both the Kaiser and Hitler taught their followers the same creed 2,000 years later.

Augustus, the first Roman emperor, had serious strategical problems connected with the area north of the Danube and east and west of the Rhine, and he decided to solve many of them by pushing the Rhine frontier 200 to 250 miles eastward, first to the Weser and then to the Elbe. He would then have a roughly straight frontier from Hamburg to Vienna, with a line of communications linking these two centres via Prague and Leipzig. The great advantage of the new frontier would be to create a buffer than would make it much harder for the Germans to attack Gaul, which Augustus viewed as a great supply centre.

Napoleon in 1806 emulated Augustus's sound strategy when he created the Confederation of the Rhine as a similar buffer between France and Austria and Prussia.

Two competent Roman generals – first Drusus, then his brother Tiberius – carried out Augustus's plan and pacified Germany to such an extent that the barbarians began to learn Roman ways.

The Romans' policy was to cause disputes and wars among the Germans themselves, and all Roman generals and governors were under orders to do just this when it was necessary to weaken resistance to Rome.

Arminius and his brother, sons of Sigimer, chief of the Cherusci tribe, were among those accorded Roman citizenship and made members of the equestrian order. Honours and wealth meant nothing to Arminius, but they warped his brother, who turned renegade, adopted the Roman name of Flavius, and fought for the Romans in their wars against the Germans.

In AD 6 Publius Quinctilius Varus, former governor of Syria, and husband of a grand-niece of Augustus, was put in charge of Rome's Germanic region. The frontier was quiet, the garrison soldiers had become soft and lazy, and many of the Germans were trusted. The ancient historian Strabo wrote, 'Against these people mistrust was the surest defence, for those who were trusted effected the most mischief.' Varus did not learn this lesson until too late.

The Romans were causing their own kind of mischief. Varus had some qualities, but he had neither morals nor principles and was licentious and rapacious. In Syria this excited no comment, for there he lived in an immoral, debased cowardly community, but somebody should have told him that he could not act this way in Germany. The Germans, barbarians though some of them still were, were decent and virtuous. Chastity was honoured and respected. Varus treated the Germans as slaves and indulged in brutal orgies and was soon copied by his officers and men; no common German home was safe from outrage, and a sense of bitter resentment pervaded the Germanic tribes.

Some of the leading Germans had been carefully brainwashed by the Romans. Cleverly the Romans conferred rank and privileges on the younger members of prominent families. Varus demanded heavy taxes and tributes, and precious metals, mainly used among the Germans for making ornaments, were steadily drained away. If Varus had financial advisers with him they did Rome a disservice by not attempting to curb his greed.

Arminius, aged twenty-six, became the leader of a secret resistance movement, which he fired with his own spirit and sustained with his determination. But the Romans would not be easy to attack. Varus had about 14,000 Roman infantry, 1,000 Roman cavalry, and equivalent numbers of foreign infantry and cavalry. Elsewhere in Gernany were numerous detachments, building roads, making bridges, and clearing ground.

Arminius had little respect for Varus as a general, but he had a profound respect indeed for Roman officers and men and their military prowess. A pitched battle, no matter how suddenly sprung on the Romans, could only lead to a slaughter of Germans.

Nobody who had yet defied the might of Rome had been successful. Some had had their minor triumphs – as had Vercingetorix when he threatened Caesar at Alesia – but in the end all had succumbed.

Like Miltiades, who had fought with his enemies before he fought against them, Arminius had seen action in Pannonia and Illyricum as a member of a Cheruscan contingent serving with the Romans. His familiarity with Roman tactics gave him an opportunity to devise a way of beating them.

He complicated his own plans by falling in love with Thusnelda, daughter of a chieftain named Segestes, a collaborator, who stopped the girl from seeing Arminius. They eloped, and the furious Segestes reported the elopement to Varus, giving him the bonus information that Arminius was planning treason. He suggested that he and his fellow-conspirators be chained. Varus believed that Segestes' accusation was made in spite and refused to believe it.

Arminius and his comrades, frequently in Varus's company, deceived the Roman into believing that they respected and admired him as a judge and orator. Also, they saw to it that the summer of that year was quiet and uneventful and that Varus was left in peace. September arrived and Varus planned to move from his summer quarters near Minden to winter quarters at Aliso, on the upper Lippe river.

At this point messages arrived to say that tribes near the Weser and the Ems had risen in open revolt. This was Arminius's cleverly laid bait, for the 'revolt' was being carefully stage-managed.

The Germans close to Varus pointed out that this rising must be put down at once and by him personally. They must have been persuasive, for Varus decided to return to winter camp at Aliso by way of the rebellious area, but apparently he thought the rising would be easily crushed for he took with him the garrison's women and children. This was his first violation of Roman generalship; his second was to clutter his column with a great train of baggage-wagons and camp-followers. Perhaps he intended to hold all these encumbrances back when he entered hostile territory.

The first part of his journey lay through friendly country, but soon the track led away from firm, ground into marshes, forests, and ravines. The engineers were constantly busy, felling trees, building small bridges, and laying planks for roadways through the marshes. All this time Arminius remained with Varus, and once again Segestes warned Varus that he was heading into a trap. Still Varus ignored him.

Then, one evening, Arminius and his associates vanished from the Roman camp. Next day reports came that outpost dettachments of soldiers had been overwhelmed and killed. Varus apparently at last realized that Segestes' reports had been true, and he headed for the road which travelled through the Doren pass to Aliso. He was in a dangerous situation, but other Roman leaders had been in just such a predicament – Caesar and Drusus, for example – and had extricated themselves. Varus, unfortunately, was not the dedicated professional that these men were.

Varus's light infantry, the foreign auxiliaries, had now deserted, and the country was very difficult for normal Roman tactics. That day the Germans showered spears from the flanks into the struggling, disordered column. Under this harassing attack the Romans beat their way to the most open and firm place they could find and formed camp, barricading it and entrenching it. These garrison troops might have been soft but they were still Roman soldiers. Unfortunately they did not have the same sense of devoted service to their Republic as had the men who served under Nero.

Next morning the Romans burned most of their wagons, which were impeding their progress, and marched once more, to be again harassed by spears from the forest. Probably every Roman soldier from Varus to legionary hoped the Germans would form line-of-battle, but Arminius was too astute to court defeat like that. After a fairly secure night the column marched the next morning – right into a heavy rainstorm. Miserably wet and thoroughly apprehensive, the Romans approached a high, forested ridge, where Arminius had built tree barricades to make the Romans' progress more difficult.

All wagons had to be abandoned now, and soldiers clustered around them, retrieving their belongings. Tired and discouraged, they reacted slowly to the orders of their officers. This could never have happened under a competent, strong commander. The column was near enough to chaos for Arminius to give the signal for battle. He had detailed a party to spear the Roman horses, and the wounded animals, throwing their riders, bolted through the column, compounding the confusion. Numonius Vala, the cavalry commander, abandoned the infantry, and with most of the other cavalry scrambled for safety. They did not find it. Unable to keep together and bogged in the mud, the Roman horsemen were slaughtered to a man.

Varus ordered the column to counter-march in the hope of reaching the nearest Roman post on the Lippe, but this was only an indication of his panic. Such a movement was impossible. Varus himself was wounded and committed suicide to escape capture. Some reports say that all his leading officers also took their own lives, but it would be more pleasant to believe the story that one of his two chief aides died fighting.

The Roman column nevertheless held together for some time before the incessant German attacks broke it to pieces. Even then the Romans fought well wherever they could form an island of resistance. One group retreated to a mound, where they formed a ring, dug a pitiful trench, and resisted throughout the day and night. Then, exhausted, hungry, thirsty, and wounded, they were overwhelmed. Some fleeing Romans drowned in the swamps; others, throwing away their armour, escaped some distance before they were picked off by the enemy. A few got away to carry the news of the bloody battle.[1]

1 The exact place in the Teutoburger Wald where the battle took place is impossible to say because a very large area fits the description of the battlefield. However, I believe as did Sir Edward Creasy, that it is somewhere between the modern towns of Bielefeld and Driburg. Some German historians place the battlefield near Munster or Detmold.

The Germans spared nobody, for in those days it was rare to show mercy to a fallen foe or respect for a brave enemy. The Germans, too, were reacting to years of oppression, and in many cases were bent on personal vengeance. The Romans who were killed in the battle were fortunate; their end was swifter and less painful than that of those who were captured and cruelly sacrificed or buried alive. Thus perished three Roman legions.

The one bright spot in the disaster was the defence of Aliso by Lucius Caedicius. The Germans made several attacks on his camp, but he beat back every one, mainly by intelligent use of his archers. When the Germans besieged his camp he broke out on a dark night and, though handicapped by many women and children, got his force through to Vetera, where he linked with two legions under Asprenas. Arminius did not further molest the Romans; perhaps he knew that he had already secured the independence of his race.

The disaster shocked Rome and Augustus, who feared a German invasion, though neither Arminius nor any other German leader contemplated invasion. Augustus sent the efficient Tiberius to take over again the command in Germany. In AD 13 Germanicus, his successor, disembarking at the mouth of the Ems, marched to the Weser, and camped somewhere near Minden. The next day Arminius won a minor action against the Romans, but the following day he was seriously wounded in a major battle in which the German infantry was mauled. The horsemen of both sides fought a stand-off battle, but Germanicus claimed a complete victory. How complete it was may be gauged by the fact that the Romans soon left the area and retreated to the left bank of the Rhine.

The Roman campaigns were mere superficial shows of a superiority that no longer existed, and Augustus and his successors – Tiberius was the first of them – abandoned all hope of permanent conquest.

Nevertheless, Rome retaliated against Arminius in one of the cruellest ways possible. Segestes surrendered to Germanicus and tricked his daughter into their hands as well. Pregnant, she was sent to Ravenna, where her son was born. At the age of four the boy was led captive through the streets of Rome; in this despicable way the Romans avenged themselves on Arminius, who never again saw his wife and child. He waged a second successful war of independence, but was assassinated at the age of thirty-seven by some of his own kinsmen.

Tacitus called him 'the liberator and incendiary of Germany', and in this he was not far wrong. To reflect on what might have been had history gone another way is an evocative pastime. Arnold and Creasy praised Arminius more or less as the prefounder of the British race. General Fuller points out more soberly that had Germany been Romanized for a further 400 years – the Roman Empire endured for this period after Teutoburg Wald – there would have been no Franco-German problem, no Charlemagne, no Louis XIV, no Napoleon, no Kaiser Wilhelm II, and no Hitler. So in more ways than one Arminius's victory was far-reaching.

His military legacy was equally momentous, but so far no historian has gauged it. Other commanders before and after Arminius have sought to take their opponent off-balance, but rarely with such success. The utter destruction of the British Army in its retreat from Kabul, Afghanistan, in 1842 is a modern parallel. Only one man got through the Afghan trap to reach Jellalabad.

Arminius's technique of deception has been copied with frightening faithfulness by later German leaders such as Frederick and especially Hitler. Hitler, too, pretended to be friendly while he laid his trap; Hitler, too, swallowed up nations and their armies by Arminian tactics and Arminian lightning blows. The word 'blitzkrieg' was not coined until the Second World War, but Arminius used its principle 1,930 years before. Like Arminius, but with far less excuse, Hitler was a wholesale butcher, and both practised the policy of separation-annihilation. Like Arminius, Hitler could sway crowds and had an innate political sense. Both men managed to keep their schemes secret from their enemies until the moment for action arrived. Both had the utmost contempt for their enemies. The parallel does not end there, for, like Arminius, Hitler suffered at the hands of his own people.

Only two real differences existed between them: Hitler's armies were trained and had first-rate equipment; those of Arminius were not trained and had no military stores. And Arminius's motive for his actions was independence; Hitler's was domination.

Velleius Paterculus, the most reliable ancient historian of Rome's German campaigns, said that Arminius made use of

Varus's negligence as an opportunity for treachery, 'sagaciously seeing that no one could be more quickly overpowered than the man who feared nothing, and that the most common beginning of disaster was a sense of security.' Could Hitler have read Velleius on Arminius and applied his theory to his earlier conquests? If he did the chain of command came full circle.

SEVEN

COMMAND FROM 378 (ADRIANOPLE) TO 732 (TOURS)

Most military historians have 'skipped' the long period between the Roman wars and medieval times for the good reason that the sources for our knowledge of this period are less reliable and more fragmentary than those of earlier or later times. However, much martial activity occurred during the first thousand years AD and as some of it has a direct bearing on the sequence of leadership a summary of it must be attempted. For the purposes of this study the first important battle after that of the Teutoburger Wald was the battle of Adrianople in AD 378. It was as salutary in its way and in its time as the firing of the first musket or the dropping of the first atomic bomb. Fought between the Romans and the Goths, it showed that the old tactics of phalanx and legion were finished, that bravery was the fundamental aspect of shock warfare, and that cavalry was even more in the ascendant.

Infantry never had much to fear from cavalry provided it kept its order, but with the great increase in the use of missiles order was practically impossible. The acute problem was how to combine defence against cavalry with missile power. Many men worked at this problem, but, as we shall see, another 1,300 years would pass before even a partial solution was found.

The Goths of this era used a laager, or wagon-fort – they themselves called it a wagon-city – as an integral part of any tactical scheme. They would form their wagons into a circle and use it either as a mobile or as a stationary fortress from which their fast, impetuous cavalry would make fierce raids. If pushed back by a superior force they would retreat into the safety of their laager, which was practically unassailable. The Huns used the same method. In the fifteenth century John Zisca, the Hussite leader, copied it, and in the nineteenth century the Boers used it most efficiently against the British and Zulus. Many wagon trains crossing the American prairies during the nineteenth century formed a laager when threatened with Indian attack, but, having no cavalry which could emerge to fight off or harass the enemy, these American wagon-forts were often overwhelmed.

In the year 378 the Goths and other nomadic bands were so militant and martial that they challenged the power of Rome in the East, where Valens, then co-emperor with his nephew Gratian, commanded. The Roman soldiers of this period – at least those in the East – were pathetically inferior to the men of earlier times; those under Valens were downright effeminate and soft, although Sebastianus, a competent general appointed by Valens as commander-in-chief, tried to salvage something from the wreck. His appointment came too late.

Had matters been left to Sebastianus there would have been no battle of Adrianople, but Valens was ill-advised by others and attacked the army led by Fridigern, the Goth general. Fridigern cunningly played for time so that his cavalry, then absent, could come up to support his well-placed laager. This cavalry drove the Roman horse from the field, and the unsupported infantry was fiercely attacked. Blinded by swirling dust, suffering intensely from thirst on a scorching August day, the Romans huddled impotently together as arrows hissed into their ranks. Fridigern now unleashed his infantry from the laager, and in a bloody struggle the main Roman force was stamped into the dust. Valens himself was mortally wounded later in the day. With him died nearly every officer in the army and about 40,000 men.

Adrianople might almost have been a general signal for war. The Goths and Vandals and other barbarian hordes attacked the Roman Empire; in the next forty years Rome suffered as never before or since, and the Vandals swept over Gaul to occupy Paris.

In 410 came the final indignity: Alaric the Goth, having twice before besieged Rome, took it and sacked it. The great captains of the past and their efficient soldiery would have turned in their graves to see all that they had built up crumble to ruin. If ever there was an object-lesson to prove that the price of liberty consists of eternal vigilance and a powerful deterrant this was it.

The Huns also caused much devastation in the next century. They were led in their most victorious days by Rua and then by his nephew Attila, who has often been stupidly held up as a great soldier but was in fact nothing more than a robber and gangster. His conquests were not due to any military skill or even to superiority of numbers, but merely to the extreme mobility of his bands of horse-archers and their Hun ability to exist under arduous conditions. The Hun hordes swept through an area like a hurricane, utterly destroying it and its people.

Early in 451 Attila, with a huge army of Huns, Ostrogoths, Gepids, and a dozen other tribes, swept westwards from the Rhine, ravaging with unsurpassed fury an enormous area and sacking and burning such towns as Rheims, Metz, Arras, Mainz, Strasbourg, Cologne, Trier. They besieged Orleans, which was saved by the arrival of the combined Roman-Gothic army under the Roman general Aëtius and King Theodoric I of the Visigoths. They forced Attila to retreat, and late in June, at the battle of Châlons, near Troyes, defeated him.

Theodoric was killed but Attila escaped, or very possibly was allowed to escape. But one thing that all victors should learn is that an enemy leader must be made harmless – for good and all – especially if he is the ever-restless, strife-causing type. The allies who fought against Napoleon learned this lesson in the end, and later the Kaiser was similarly rendered impotent. These were political decisions and not made by generals.

In 452 Attila invaded Italy, wiped out some cities, damaged others, massacred whole populations, and carried off others as slaves. Fortunately for humanity Attila died of his excesses the following year.

Châlons had been represented as a victory which saved the West from extinction by the Asiatics. This is too great a claim. Even had the Romans and Goths been beaten at Châlons Attila's empire would have fallen to pieces on his death, for it was a personal empire without any national, religious, intellectual, moral, or political basis.

Less than a century later Rome was again in the middle of strife, this time under Justinian the Great, who through two competent generals, Belisarius and Narses, again established Roman supremacy. The main battles of twenty years of almost constant warfare were Tricameron, 533, and Taginae, 552, at which battle, on an Apennine plain, the eunuch tactician Narses defeated the Goths by the first experiment in the use of bow and pike.

Narses had an infantry, phalanx-like front, with inward-facing flanks of archers. With the Goths facing him in force, Narses gave strict orders that no man could sit down to eat, go to sleep, remove his cuirass, or unbridle his horse. Similar commnads, leading to instant readiness, have won many battles, big and small.

Narses allowed the Goths to take the initiative, for his tactics depended on their doing so. They charged the pikemen, could not break through, and were raked from the flanks by the Roman archers, while a free-striking force of 1,000 cavalry attacked the enemy rear. After some hours, when the Goths were worn down, the Romans advanced and routed them. Narses' flanks-forward formation was to be copied many times, sometimes with modifications, but it was such an obvious trap that no general worth his job would be deluded into attacking straight against the centre.

By 534 the Mediterranean was again a Roman lake, with the exception of a few isolated parts of the coast, but Italy was ruined by her twenty years of war and unable to withstand the assaults and invasions of other races, notably the Lombards. Rome reconquered North Africa from the Vandals, but was unable to keep the Moors in check as the Vandals had done, and Africa reverted once more to barbarism, and the area fell easily to the Saracens in the following century. Justinian was no doubt pleased with his victory at Taginae, but it was the greatest Pyrrhic victory in history, for it was the climax by which Rome became a back-number in world affairs.

By the year 630 the Romans and the Persians had exhausted each other and had been further wasted by other wars over the previous century. In that year, by no mere coincidence, began a struggle which was to last a thousand years. This was the year in which Islam as a power began to rise. By 652 the Moslems had taken Syria, Persia, Egypt, Iraq, Mesopotamia, Ecbatana, the Persian Gulf, and Khorasan, annihilating Roman and Persian and Byzantine armies in the process. In following years the Arabs many times tried to capture Constantinople,[1] and in the years 717–18 they laid siege to it. The man who defended it, a professional soldier called Leo the Isaurian – although he cane from North-east Sicily, not Isauria – created a new empire which was to become Europe's buffer against Asia for seven centuries.

Leo's defence of Constantinople was a classic of its type, and in many ways was a precursor to the Battle of Britain. Constantinople was an almost impregnable fortress, with strong walls well equipped and manned largely by steady Anatolian troops. It was not practicable to storm the city – at least until the advent of gunpowder – so the Saracens attempted to storm it by sea – bringing a squadron of large ships, each with 100 armed men aboard, against the sea-wall.[2] After the assault failed the Saracens realized that blockade was the only feasible way of reducing the fortress.

Leo's survival had therefore to depend on his fleet's being able to break the blockade, just as Britain's survival depended in the Second World War. But Leo's fleet was numerically much inferior to the Moslems'.

He defended his harbour by a great boom chain hanging between two towers, and on one occasion, seizing an opportunity, he had the chain lowered and made a lightning raid on an enemy fleet, destroying twenty with 'Greek fire'[3] and capturing others.

He was even more successful when he left the protection of his boom, caught the Moslem fleet unprepared – he had a good espionage system – and rammed or burnt many vessels in a one-sided battle. Exploiting his success, Leo ferried a commando force across to the Asiatic shore and inflicted a sharp defeat on a Moslem army.

1 Named after the Emperor Constantine, who inaugurated the city on May 11th, 330, and took up residence there. It was often called New Rome.
2 Five hundred years later the Venetian Doge Dandolo captured Constantinople by a similar assault against the sea-wall.
3 Greek fire was probaly made from naphtha, sulphur, and quicklime, and ignited spontaneously when wetted. Similar compositions had been in use for centuries, and many commanders tried to improve on their predecessors' efforts to use fire as a weapon. It was early used as an offensive weapon at sea, and could also be used in defence of a fortress, but its use by mobile troops was delayed until the Great War.

This was one of the first examples of combined operations. It was also one of the first instances of a general instantly following up a victory with another. Apparently, few commanders before Leo had even considered such a thing. When they won a battle they slaughtered their enemy until their blood-lust was satisfied and then rested on their laurels. Leo's idea of exploitation had a profound effect on many leaders who studied his battles. His twelve months' defence of Constantinople was a military achievement of the first order and a significant historical act. Had Britain fallen to Hitler in 1940 the results would have been vast enough to defy conjecture. Had the Byzantines lost Constantinople in 718 the Moslems would have surged through Europe and probably have stamped out of existence the crystallizing kingdom and empire of the Franks.

Militarily the Byzantines were centuries ahead of the West. The Byzantine Empire was originally the East Roman Empire, so all its developments were built on foundations laid by the Romans; in fact, nothing in Byzantium is more truly the heir of Rome than her military policy. The first half of the seventh century is the distinctive period in which the historian would be inclined to place the rise of a 'Byzantine Empire', but the Byzantine Army had been well established for years. It had excellent military textbooks more than eight centuries before the Western world, so not surprisingly the army itself was one of the most advanced in the world.

The Byzantine emperors divided their realm into army districts, each protected by fortresses, linked by good roads. A Byzantine general rarely sought battle. When threatened he simply retired to a fortress, well provisioned against a siege. Eventually the besiegers had to raise the siege to find food, and while they were doing this the Byzantines would emerge and destroy them.

The Byzantine Army had two clear divisions – fighting troops and administrative soldiers. In this too they were centuries ahead of their time. The administrative section included a supply column, field engineers, a baggage column, and even an ambulance corps – probably the first of its type. The fighting troops were in three separate commands – infantry, cavalry, and artillery. Never before and only rarely since have troops been so well equipped and organized. Detailed movements had been evolved to counter every possible form of attack, and all officers were expected to study these movements.

Alone in Byzantine, in the Euorpe of the Middle Ages, the business of war was treated with scientific deliberation, each generation facing new problems and solving them by sustained study. Not numbers, but reasoned skill carried a battle, which was no mere *mêlée* but the disciplined co-operation of many units. Byzantine generals could never afford to indulge in quixotic chivalry, for too much depended on the preservation of their small forces. They used every possible subtlety – feigned flight, night attacks, ambushes, false messages designed to fall into enemy hands. The Byzantines believed that a general who relied on force when he could achieve his object or objective by enterprise was a fool. The characteristics of the Byzantine soldier – as his leaders never ceased to tell him – were training, bravery, discipline, and pride in his profession.

Byzantine engineers studied in detail all the natural difficulties which might be encountered during a campaign. In the West an army might march for days to find a ford across a river. The Byzantines built sectional boats, which were numbered and then carried by mules. When a stream was reached the sections were quickly put together and caulked.

I can find no direct evidence which might prove that later generals of other nations, except those of the Ottoman Empire, followed the many examples of efficiency set by the Byzantine leaders – the Byzantine military textbooks were not translated for several centuries – but I think it possible that von Moltke, the great Prussian strategist responsible for the victories of 1866 and 1870, profited from them. It is possible, too, that Isabella of Spain, one of the first great army quartermasters, knew of Byzantine methods.[4]

At Constantinople in 718 the Byzantine had stopped a mass cross-country invasion of Europe, but, reaching the western end of the Mediterranean by sea, the Moslems and Moors had already plundered Aquitaine and Burgundy, Narbonne, occupied Carcassonne and Nîmes, and had even reached the Vosges. Despite a defeat at Toulouse, the Moslems were practically undisputed in

4 Unfortunately for the Byzantines, their empire was rotten with moral and spiritual decay, and it was this inner weakness which largely led to their defeat by the Turks at the battle of Manzikert in 1071 and to the end of the magnificent Byzantine Army.

their progress through Southern France because the one man who might have stopped them, Charles (or Karl) Martel, son of Pepin II, was enjoying a war on the Danube to secure his north-east frontier before he set out to bind the whole of Gaul into an empire. Gaul at this time was a mere conglomeration of impermanent barbaric kingdoms. The great bulk of the people consisted of Romanized Celts, the Germans sprinkled among them and usually dominant over them. The Teutonic Franks, too, had a pronounced superiority over the other conquerors of the great region.

The local leader in the most dangerous position at the time of the Moslem incursion was Duke Eudo of Aquitaine, with the Moslems menacing him in Spain and the Franks on his north-east. Duke Eudo wanted at least one secure frontier, so he made an alliance with a Berber chief, Othman ben abi Neza, who ruled an area on the northern side of the Pyrenees. In this Eudo was merely doing what many leaders have done, so that he could concentrate his forces against one enemy, not two. He married Othman's daughter and strengthened the alliance. The Moslem governor of Spain, Abd-ar-Rahman, was incensed at Othman's 'traitorous step' and chased him into the mountains, where Othman either jumped from a precipice or was pushed from it.

Abd-ar-Rahman turned his attention now to Acquitaine. His main intention in invading the region was plunder, but he also wanted revenge for the killing of some Moslem detachments north of the Pyrenees. The possible conquest of France was incidental but no doubt considered by Abd-ar-Rahman, who was a competent and experienced general. He seems to have been highly popular with his troops, probably because he allowed them unlimited plunder, which is a dangerous way to buy popularity.

In the summer of 732 Abd-ar-Rahman crossed into France near Irun, at the Bay of Biscay end of the Pyrenees, and moved into Gascony. How many men he had is conjectural. Arab writers say he had 80,000, while Christian historians of the era say 'many hundreds of thousands'. Moslem armies were always large, but never so large as this, and I think the figure was probably under 100,000, mostly mounted, with a strong detachment of skilled Berber cavalry.

Some monks who recorded the Saracen invasion say that the Moslems brought their wives and children with them as well as their belongings, as if planning to settle in France. This may account for the 'many hundreds of thousands'. It was natural for the figure to be exaggerated because the Saracens terrified the people of France. Time and again flourishes of horsemen would swoop upon a settlement or farming community to plunder, rape, and burn.

The size of the army would have appeared larger, too, because of the great number of mules, some to carry supplies but mostly to carry plunder. Behind the army proper, mingled with the camp-followers, came a horde of petty but vicious criminals who depended for their living on what the troops left them or threw to them.

Abd-ar-Rahman had nothing to fear from his rear; nevertheless, further to terrorize Acquitaine, he detached a force to strike due east to Arles, near Marseilles, while he took the army due north.

Abd-ar-Rahman's earlier successes had been largely due to his care in protecting his rear, which he did more by threat of action than by action itself. It is impossible to assess how much these tactics influenced later generals since it is only common sense to defend the rear of a column in enemy country, but some generals have suffered disastrously from not using such common sense.

Duke Eudo threw whatever forces he could scrape together into Bordeaux, but they were overwhelmed and the prosperous city was stormed, looted, and burnt. As always, the helpless civilian populace was cruelly maltreated, but in that era they looked on such suffering as inevitable. No matter to what race soldiers belonged they looted, raped, and burnt.

Abd-ar-Rahman crossed the Dordogne river and passed through the fertile countryside, ever plundering – massacring people as the whim took him, which was often. There was no escape for the people in the path of his army, for the cavalry ranged far and wide, prodding peasants out of their hiding-places so that they could be slaughtered.

Charles, successful in the east, was now south of Paris. He crossed the Loire and caused almost as much havoc in the region of Berri as the Saracen general was causing farther south. Eudo, Duke of Aquitaine, and Charles were deadly enemies, but Eudo was forced to swallow his pride and appeal to Charles for help. And Charles readily agreed to give it on condition that Eudo submit to Frankish control.

Meanwhile Abd-ar-Rahman had invested Poitiers, about sixty

miles south of Tours, and was moving on to Tours to sack the abbey, which he had heard contained great treasures. Like his men, Abd-ar-Rahman had an insatiable appetite for spoil.

Moslem tactics – if tactics they can be called – were very wasteful, for they were nothing more than furious, ill-conceived charges. Tragically, this link in the chain of command seemed to be picked up and used again during the Great War. It is doubtful if many Allied generals of the Great War had read of Abd-ar-Rahman, but they must have read of the Saracens, and historical literature, much of it legendary, has painted the Saracens as invincible horsemen. *Ipso facto* – perhaps a certain type of modern military mind reasoned – the Saracen *tactics* must be sound and invincible. But the Saracens won most of their battles because they were lightning fast while their enemies were laboriously slow; they were efficient schemers, but they knew little of tactics.

Their main weapons were the lance and sword, with which they were adept. The Moslems had very few archers. They relied on their speed for defence and seldom wore armour.

Charles's army was formed almost entirely of infantry; even the nobles used horses only on the march and rarely in battle. The only professionals were the men of Charles's own private force – this applied to any Frankish general – while the rest of the army was made up by militia levies, ill trained and ill equipped. The one force which kept a Frankish army together was food, and if the general could not see it was provided he could say goodbye to his army. The professionals mostly had armour – which was again coming into fashion – and all the men carried a shield. Their weapons were swords, javelins, daggers, a battle-axe, and a throwing axe; a skilled axeman could split a skull at fifty yards. There seems to have been no systematic organization into units of the various types of arms.

Charles's great quality was that he always understood his enemy because he made a point of studying him. Any good general has always done the same. Charles's letter to Eudo illustrates this quality:

Follow my advice and do not interrupt their march nor precipitate your attack. They are like a torrent, which it is dangerous to stem in its career. The thirst of riches and the consciousness of success redouble their valour, and valour is of more avail than arms or numbers. Be patient till they have loaded themselves with their encumbrances of wealth. . . . This will divide their counsels and assure your victory.

An Arab writer said that Abd-ar-Rahman attacked Tours with great ferocity, 'almost before the eyes of the army that came to save it; and the fury and cruelty of the Moslems towards the inhabitants of the city were like the fury and cruelty of raging tigers.' He ascribed the subsequent downfall of the Moslems to their excesses.

If Charles were aware of what was happening in Tours – and he probably was – he must have needed great will to hold himself in check and not to attempt to drive the Moslems from the city. This would have been militarily rash. Nevertheless his approach did force the Moslems to withdraw from the city, and they were so hampered by their loot that they were no longer mobile. The two armies now confronted each other for seven days. General Fuller believes that in this time Charles was waiting for reinforcements to arrive while Abd-ar-Rahman was sending his plunder to the rear. It is sound conjecture, particularly as it concerns Charles, but Abd-ar-Rahman would have found it impossible to induce his soldiers to trust their plunder to anybody else. The human jackals who followed the army would have taken it and spirited it away to Spain. Neither could Abd-ar-Rahman order the plunder to be abandoned, for his men would not have obeyed him.

Probably the armies had a few fringe combats near Tours, after which Abd-ar-Rahman fell back towards Poitiers and somewhere near this town decided to accept battle – perhaps from pride, perhaps to cover the withdrawal of his loot, most probaby because he did not want to be caught with the river Dordogne at his back without room to manoeuvre.

Charles did indeed understand his enemy. Once brought to battle the Moslems must attack; they had no option, because they had no defensive ability. Charles therefore arranged his army in phalanx and waited for the inevitable wild cavalry charge, which was not long in coming. The Moslems charged many times – this was ideal cavalry country – but Martel's army stood 'like a belt of ice frozen together', as one ancient chronicler put it. As evening approached Duke Eudo and his Acquitainians turned one of the enemy's flanks and attacked Abd-ar-Rahman's camp, thus forcing the Moslems to fall back; their loot was in the camp, and they were fearful for its safety. There is some doubt whether Abd-ar-Rahman was killed on the first day or the second, but the former seems most likely. According to one record he was speared to death while trying to rally his retiring troops, while a more heroic chronicler claims that he was killed as he charged into the midst of the phalanx.

Probably fighting occurred on the second day, but some authorities say that during the night the Moslems abandoned their camp and much of their loot and fled south. In either case the Franks had won a decisive victory. Pursuit was out of the question, for Charles had no cavalry, and being shrewd, he would not have wanted Eudo to feel perfectly safe from further Saracen aggression; for so long as Aquitaine needed Frank protection the Franks could control Lorraine. As it happened, the Saracens made no further serious attacks beyond the Pyrenees.

Casualties at Tours are beyond computation. They range from as high as 360,000 Moslems killed to as few as 1,500 Franks killed. The Moslems certainly lost more than the Franks, and their losses would have been increased by attacks on their camp-followers in their retreat to the Pyrenees. The one really sour note in Charles's victory is that he took Abd-ar-Rahman's loot for himself, but this was an act in accord with his era.

Charles's feat supplemented – indeed, complemented that of Leo. Between them they had saved France. In later years Charles forced the Moslems to withdraw from the Rhône valley. He was no doubt ironically grateful to Abd-ar-Rahman, for his defeat of the Saracen gave him a tremendous reputation and enabled him to build his empire and to found an imperialistic dynasty, to be inherited in 768 by his grandson, Charles the Great – Charlemagne.

The contributions to the military leadership left by Charles Martel – known as 'the hammer' – are those of the wisdom of studying an enemy before fighting him, of holding back until the right moment, even at the expense of suffering on the part of friendly people, of the superiority of sober valour over impetuous courage, of method over dash. It is not without significance that Charles was Duke of the Austrasian Franks, the bravest and most thoroughly Germanic part of the nation. The military qualities he showed at Tours are more Germanic than French, which is perhaps why he was the subject of frequent lectures to officer cadets of the Prussian and German Armies from the time of Scharnhorst onward. His place in military leadership is more prominent than it appears to be.

EIGHT

CHARLEMAGNE; GENGHIZ KHAN AND SABUTAI; EDWARD III, CRÉCY

Charlemagne's work as a military commander stands as an island of sanity in a sea of stupidity, for the Middle Ages provide few examples of genuine art in war.

Charlemagne was one of the first generals to organize an army highly. He wanted an army of quality, not quantity, and when he called upon his nobles to supply men he ordered that each horseman must come equipped with shield, lance, sword, and bow, and that foot-soldiers must carry sword, spear, and bow.

He wanted his army mobile, but this was impossible if it had to rely for subsistence on what it could forage, so he organized a supply-train as well as a siege-train. Because he ruled such a vast area he established what were really forts at strategic points in his domains. Oddly enough, though this seems obvious military strategy, it had been neglected for many centuries.

It was about this time, too, that warfare was given a great boost by the growing attitude that it was noble to fight in defence of freedom and liberty – though no two definitions about freedom and liberty coincided. The Church recognized that war could, indeed, be righteous.

In the year 990, for the first time, rules and regulations for warfare were laid down in the *Pax Dei* ('Peace of God'). This code aimed at protecting women, clerics, peasants, church buildings, cattle, and agricultural implements from the soldiery. Men guilty of breaking the code faced excommunication, but the threat was not as successful as its exponents hoped.

Between 850 and 900 the Scandinavians – the Vikings – left

their mark on martial development. During this half-century they raided the whole of Western Europe, forcing their victims to employ professional soldiers and to build strongholds. This meant that military power passed into the hands of the nobility. In the end many nobles had armies which were stronger than those owned by monarchs, thus giving rise to further warfare.

Continental countries relied on cavalry to beat the Vikings, but in England King Alfred tried something different. He built a fleet and beat the Vikings on their own element. On land he relied on infantry and took no steps to raise cavalry.

Infantry was well developed in England by King Harold's day. At the Battle of Hastings, 1066, his men were armed with spear, javelin, two-edged sword, and the unwiedly Danish axe, but bows were not popular at this time in Britain. The hostile Normans carried lance, sword, and mace, and a short Norman bow or the crossbow.

Harold's formation at Hastings was probably that of the shieldwall, the best possible one against the Norman infantry and cavalry. For a long time during the battle this formation, the stolidity of the English, and the fierceness of their fighting blocked the Normans. Had Harold maintained his position he may not have lost the battle, but William lured his enemy from their positions by means of a feint retreat – an old stratagem from the Orient, as we have seen.

Finally he ordered his archers to fire at a high angle so that the English would have to raise their shields. Harold himself was hit in the eye, and when he fell the English disintegrated.[1]

William the Conqueror's invasion of England in 1066 was a masterpiece of clever strategy and tactics, and probably he was the inspiration and model by which Norman arms were so remarkably successful for the next century.

Some weapons, like the crossbow, were becoming more 'scientific' – so much so that in 1139 the Second Lateran Council outlawed the crossbow, describing it as 'a weapon fateful to God and unfit for Christians'. The Council held, in fact, that long distance or missile warfare was unchristian.

1 The death of the commander-in-chief in battle still meant the defeat of his whole army, so great was his control and his power so great a symbol.

The crossbow did not require the same muscular strength to operate as the longbow, but it was much more complicated and was spanned (loaded) by various systems of leverage. Some types were wound up. In action the archer sheltered behind a high wooden shield known as a pavise, which rested on the ground supported by a prop.

The Lateran edict did not keep the crossbow out of war, but it did have the effect of further ennobling warfare, thus giving it romantic qualities which appealed to chivalrous men of birth.

During this period Earl 'Strongbow' and his 200 or so Welsh knights gave a splendid example of commando tactics, by conquering the greater part of Ireland and repulsing a powerful Norse invasion. Strongbow's small but efficient hard-hitting force were masters of every commando tactic and trick, and they achieved as much as Otto Skorzeny and his hand-picked Nazis in North-west Europe in 1944–5.

Prince Edward, later Edward I (1272–1307), left some strategic lessons for later commanders. His solution to subdue the Welsh – a hardy, fierce race – was to build castles at strategic points, the legacy of Charlemagne. He connected them by roads, and by keeping the enemy on the move he wore them down. The British used these tactics 600 years later in various parts of the Indian subcontinent.

In the East Genghiz Khan made his impressive contribution to military history; by clever use of three armies in combination he broke up the powerful Kin Empire. In 1241 Genghiz Khan's leading general, Sabutai, took two armies into Europe in as devastating and dynamic a military sweep as any in history. He split his main army into three widely separated columns and pierced as many holes in Hungary to the Danube – cleverly keeping the flank columns well ahead of the central column, the main striking force. His second army all this time was guarding his northern flank, decisively beating Bohemian, German, and Polish armies. Near Gran the Hungarians had assembled on the far bank of the Danube and were in far too strong a position to be attacked. Sabutai staged a careful and convincing 'retirement', which deluded the Hungarians and lured them after the Mongols. In an action as clever as it was violent Sabutai wiped out the Hungarian army, to become undisputed master of Europe's central plains. What might have happened had the Mongols stayed on their conquered soil – nobody could have thrown them out – provides fascinating conjecture. Strangely, they left a year later.

It is difficult to resist the conclusion that von Moltke was directly influenced by the Mongol strategy and tactics in his campaigns of 1866 and 1870. The point will be amplified later in the book.

Great military changes took place in the thirteenth and fourteenth centuries. It was during the thirteenth that body armour reached twin peaks of effectiveness and absurdity. A knight wore such a weight of armour that he suffered torment in a hot sun. Many a knight needed two footmen to hoist him into the saddle, and if he were struck from his horse during combat he was useless; he might even be unable to rise to avoid being trampled by horses or clubbed to death by infantry.

By adding flaps, hinges, and over-pieces knights tried to cover up every possible chink through which an adversary might prick them with dart, arrow, sword, or lance. Under his armour the knight wore a thick quilted garment, while over it and the additional plates he wore his surcoat with belts. With his shield and weapons he could well be carrying a load twice his own weight.

Saracen armour was much more practical. It was of ring- or chain-mail, strong, light, and flexible, and much more comfortable. The Saracens played havoc with the Christian knights – crusaders – many of whom were burnt to death inside their armour by Greek fire.

When they returned home the knights of the West brought something with them from the East – memories of the magnificent castles of the East – in Palestine, for instance. This led to a rash of castle-building in Central and Western Europe, and before long every district was dominated by a castle, to which peasants in the area looked for protection.

By a process of military evolution there came into being city militias, then specialist mercenary soldiers who were very well paid. Late in the thirteenth century, too, France and England and later Italy began to pay all soldiers, even the short-service ones. Soldiering was becoming a regular profession in Europe.

Some mercenary bands, selling their services to the highest bidder, were superb soldiers. Others were mere opportunists and became brigands when there was no war.

During the first half of the fourteenth century France was hopelessly in the grip of chivalry. Battles were fought by 'men of quality' on horseback. A knight thought it below his dignity to attack infantry, who were more concerned with taking prisoner opposing knights and holding them for ransom than with killing them. At the battle of Courtrai in 1302 the French nobility imagined itself to be the best fighting force in the world, but it was little more than a gallant but undisciplined mob. The French knight considered himself far superior to any common soldier, especially if the soldier happened to be on foot. He regarded the appearance on the field of battle of spearmen, crossbowmen, or others as an insult. He had no more regard for his own common soldiers than he had for the enemy.

It was unfortunate for France that this was the period of Edward III, one of the first 'modern' generals, and whose tactics so deeply offended the French. Edward's battle of Crécy has a definite place in the British chain of command, for with this victory came England's foundation as a military nation. That this should be is somewhat paradoxical, for Edward III had got himself into a most dangerous situation at Crécy, and his victory was due largely to the French being even more rash and so allowing themselves to become the vanquished in one of the most decisive battles in history.

At the time of Crécy the English Army was raised by ordering all landowners to provide men-at-arms, spearmen, or archers according to a set scheme approved by the English Parliament in 1345.

The men-at-arms wore armour and carried the lance, sword, dagger, and a shield. Most of them were trained from early youth, perhaps as boys of no more than ten or eleven. The cavalry were called pauncenars, from the German *Panzer*, meaning a coat of mail. These lance-armed warriors were not so well equipped with defensive armour, but they did wear a sleeveless coat of chainmail known as the habergeon. The lighter cavalry wore an iron helmet, a thickly padded doublet, iron gloves, and a sword.

The infantry consisted of Welsh spearmen who wore no armour. Every man was given – at the King's expense – a tunic and a mantle made of the same material and of the same colour. This early battle-dress was first issued in 1337.

The archers were the backbone of any English military force of the period. Some were mounted, but they used their horses merely to hurry from one place to another. The archers wore only iron caps for protection, but sometimes they had large shields pointed at the bottom, which could be driven into the earth. The English archers were extremely skilful. Their bows were usually of yew and were 6 feet 4 inches long, the arrows being of several lengths but generally described as cloth-yard shafts. The arrows were fitted with a pointed barb of iron and fledged with goose or peacock feathers. They could pierce oak to a depth of two or more inches.

A good archer could fire six aimed shots a minute with an effective range up to 240 yards and an extreme one of 340 yards. Volley firing was devastating and demoralizing even to well-trained troops – as other British troops were to show at Mons in 1914.

One advantage of the longbow over the crossbow – which was used by French Genoese mercenaries – was that it was held perpendicularly to the ground, and not horizontally like the crossbow, so that the bowmen could stand closer together and concentrate their fire.

Another formidable English weapon was the bill – evolved from an agricultural implement – a staff weapon with a hook, spike, and blade. A foot-soldier could drag a horseman from his saddle with the hook, then kill him with the spike or blade. The blade could be used, axe-like, for wide and vicious swinging. The pole-axe was also in use. Only a brave man would tackle a soldier wielding this long-staffed fiercesome weapon.

Edward disembarked his army at La Hogue between July 12th and 17th, 1346, reached Caen on July 26th, and here ordered that all the men so far wounded and all the booty taken should be put aboard the ships. But the crews had mutinied and had returned to England, forcing Edward to make drastic changes in his plans. Without communications he could not stay at Caen, but if he headed south he would clash with the superior army of the Duke of Normandy. Therefore he marched east, following the Seine towards Paris, which he approached on August 13th, leaving a trail of devastation in his wake.

Peasants and farmers who were unfortunate enough to live on the line of an invading army's march rarely had warning of its approach. Suddenly soldiers would appear, rough, crude men who took everything that was eatable or portable and fired anything that was not. They often assaulted women and would kill any man who interfered. If they felt high-spirited they would fire the fields of grain, trample their horses through the vegetable patches, or hack down fruit-trees until they tired. A 'friendly' army was only a little less cruel than a foreign one.

Edward's men plundered and burnt town after town, and even abbeys were destroyed, though on one occasion when this happened Edward hanged twenty of his officers for permitting the outrage.

Leaving the Paris area, Edward now pushed north and by August 21st had reached Airaines, south of the Somme river. Philip of France was now at Amiens with an army growing larger by the day. Edward had great difficulty in finding a ford across the Somme, but a big reward brought forward a French traitor who led the English to a crossing-place ten miles below Abbeville. Despite fierce opposition from a French force of 2,000 the army got across on the 24th, an hour before the French army came up – only to be stopped from fording the river by the rising tide.

At Crécy Edward decided to fight. His reasons for selecting the site have been much discussed. Edward has been praised for anticipating that Philip would advance by the Abbeville–Hesdin road, but such anticipation required no great intellect. Edward knew that Philip could chase him by two roads only, and one of these roads was practically barred to the French because of the only thick wood for miles around.

Similarly he has been praised for realizing that the French would attack frontally; there was no other way they *could* attack, for their blind instinct of chivalry demanded a frontal attack. The French military mind of this period could not have conceived the idea of a flank attack. The position that Edward chose fitted his tactics and his strength, but many other such positions existed in the area. He fought at Crécy because he was tired of running before the French, because – as Froissart says – he had reached the area which was the inheritance of his grandmother, and pride insisted that he defend it. More than that, Edward was enclosed in a triangle – with the sea, the Somme, and the French army for its sides.

The country around Crécy is of rolling downs falling to two small streams, the Maye and Authie. The English lay on the sloping banks of the Maye above the little town of Crécy.

Edward gave a supper for his senior officers – a fine meal, for wine was to be had for the taking, and the country was rich in game and farm produce. The carts and carriages that followed the English Army were loaded with plenty of provisions – all looted. Edward then prayed at the altar of his oratory, a portable chapel. It was midnight before he retired to sleep.

Philip stayed at Abbeville, and that night he too gave a supper for all his dukes, barons, and other nobles. After supper he asked that there should be no quarrelling among them, for his nobles were very touchy about their pride and honour.

At daybreak on August 26th Edward and his son, the Prince of Wales – the young Black Prince – as well as many others, heard Mass and were confessed and given communion. This over, Edward commanded every man to proceed to the field of battle. He ordered a park to be made by the woodside behind the army, and in this were put all the carts, carriages, and horses; the King had decided that all would fight on foot. The only entry to the park was guarded by picked men.

Edward placed two of his three divisions in the forward slope of the rise east of the Crécy–Wadicourt road and the third in the rear. The Prince of Wales, aged seventeen, nominally commanded the right-front division – consisting of about 800 men-at-arms, 2,000 archers, and 1,000 Welshmen – but the actual commanders were Warwick the Earl Marshal and the Earls of Oxford and Harcourt. Northampton and the Earl of Arundel commanded the left division of 700 men-at-arms and 1,200 archers, while Edward himself commanded the 700 men-at-arms and 2,000 archers of the rear division. Edward's headquarters were at a windmill from which he could see the entire field of battle.

His dispositions finished, Edward mounted a pony, and with a white rod in one hand and flanked by his marshals, he rode slowly along the ranks encouraging his men. They had their midday meal, then again formed battle-order, but sensibly were told to sit and rest in ranks, with their helmets and bows in front of them.

Philip now had his army assembled at Abbeville – 8,000 men-at-arms supported by 4,000 foot and adorned by an extraordinarily illustrious collection of royalty and nobility. No fewer than three kings fought with him – the half-blind King John of Bohemia, John's son Charles, King of the Romans, and King James III of Majorca. Also were present many dukes and most of the chivalry of France.

Early on August 26th Philip set out on the Abbeville–Hesdin road with four knights forward as a reconnaissance patrol. These knights discovered the English positions, and on their return suggested to Philip that the army should halt for the night, so that the whole army would be ordered for an attack on the following morning.

Philip gave orders to this effect, but now occurred one of the lamentable incidents which have so often marred French arms. The leading French troops had halted, but the nobles leading the following men refused to halt until they too were at the front. The front men, turning and seeing the rear men still pushing forward, resumed their march. The King and his generals tried in vain to stop the army, which pressed forward in confused order until they saw the English army drawn up. The sight was so unnerving that the leading ranks turned about, alarming the men following. A short but violent storm now occurred, after which bright sun appeared again, shining in the face of the French. Many English archers lay on their bowstrings to keep them dry during this storm.

The Count of Flanders and the Count of Alençon had by now marshalled the Genoese into better order and marched them forward into the Vallée des Clercs. The Genoese were ordered to shout so as to frighten the English, and they tried this three times, but, as Froissart records, 'the English never moved'.

They left the first aggressive move to the Genoese, who opened fire with their crossbows; their bolts fell short. The English archers then took one deliberate step forward and commenced volley-fire. The effect was instantaneously devastating; many Genoese were hit, and others cut their bowstrings or threw their bows away and ran. Philip ordered that the deserters be killed at once to save his army from mass panic.

The French knights needed no urging to fight; they trampled down the Genoese and hacked at them with their swords in their eagerness to get into battle, though English arrows were now falling among them. As shafts bit into man and horse, nailing helmet and armour to skull and flesh, chaos creased the French front ranks and many knights were thrown by their rearing mounts. A disciplined division, having been repulsed, would have cleared its front so that the second division had a clear run to the assault, but this did not happen at Crécy, and the second French division collided with the wreckage of the first. On the Prince of

Wales's front the situation was dangerous for a time because a portion of the French force dashed against it, though more from the horses' fright than by military design. Edward sent the Bishop of Durham – the ecclesiastics of this period were enthusiastic fighting men – and 30 knights to reinforce his son's division. To a messenger who had come from the Earl of Warwick, Edward asked, 'Is my son dead or hurt or felled to the earth?'

'No, sire,' was the reply, 'but he is hard-pressed and needs your aid.'

Froissart quotes the King's reply: 'Well, return to him and to them that sent you and say to them that they send no more to me . . . as long as my son is alive; and also say to them that they suffer him this day to win his spurs; for if God be pleased, I will that this journey be his, and the honour thereof.'

While this was happening Northampton, probably under Edward's orders, was wheeling his division so as to attack the flank of the French who were charging the English right division. The French were bloodily repulsed and fell back into the ranks of their third division, led by Philip himself. Fifteen times the French assaulted and every time without any preconceived plan. No Japanese *banzai* charge was more fanatic than that of the French chivalry; for them 'Death before dishonour' were no mere words.

The Welsh troops worsened the enemy's confusion, for whenever the French men-at-arms fell back the Welshmen rushed forward and slaughtered many fallen nobles – to the bitter fury of Edward and his chief lieutenants; they could not get ransom for a dead man.

Philip himself, wounded, and now with fewer than 70 lances to guard him, rode frantically about the field, trying to mount yet one more desperate charge against the English lines. In the end the Count of Hainault made the King see reason and induced him to withdraw.

The French were routed, but pursuit was out of the question, for dusk had now fallen and Edward had no effective cavalry. But he was a competent enough commander to keep his men under arms, and next morning, when the French reinforcements came up, not knowing that their army had been defeated, the English scattered them with heavy loss. After that, in a clearing mist, the English troops were allowed to break ranks and gather in the loot, which meant stripping the dead of everything they had. Even bloody clothing was useful to the poorer soldiery.

Not until the dead were examined by the three heralds sent on to the field by Edward, and the few prisoners questioned, was it known that the King of Bohemia, the Duke of Lorraine, 10 counts, and 1,542 knights and squires had been killed. At least 10,000 common soldiers were dead on the field, a scene of concentrated butchery if ever there was one. According to report the English casualties were fewer than 75 and included only 2 knights, but such a slight loss cannot be believed.

Among the French prisoners were the Bishop of Noyen, the Archdeacon of Paris, and the Counts of Aumale, Montbeliard, and Rosenberg.

Ordinary soldiers were buried on the spot, some being found in bushes and in hedges as well as in the open, but Edward sent the bodies of French nobles to Montreuil to be buried in holy ground. He also declared a truce for three days so that the peasants around Crécy could search for and bury any bodies they found.

Crécy will always hold its pre-eminent place in military history. It was to the English what Marathon was to the Greeks or Anzac to the Australians. English troops had beaten the Scots and the Welsh, but these campaigns had passed unnoticed in Continental Europe. The English had fought under Henry III and Edward I in France, but their actions had been mediocre and their achievements few. Now, after Crécy and its sequel – the seige and capture of Calais – English troops had such a remarkable reputation that, by the principle of martial momentum, they had to hold and enhance that reputation.

At that time no foreign general could understand how the English had achieved their victory, and this made it all the more impressive. A great part of the victory was due to the training the bowmen had received on their village green since their boyhood. Nearly 500 years later Sir John Moore, founder of the magnificent Light Division which fought in Spain and Portugal, acknowledged that he had made use of the pre-Crécy principle of rigorous training. Apart from this the victory was due to Edward's having hit on a system of dismounted combat, using archers and men-at-arms in combination.

The dictum by which the English and British were to win

hundreds of battles – it could well be expressed as 'shoulder to shoulder and keep the troops steady' – was so well founded at Crécy that in the centuries to come it was rarely shaken.[2] And as this steadiness and discipline were the weapons which won so many fights it might well be claimed that the link in leadership forged at Crécy is one of the strongest.

2 It might also be said that during the Boer War and the First World War slavish adherence to this dictum killed many British soldiers.

NINE

THE AGE OF INNOVATION

The Janissairies; du Guesclin's 'Phantom' Army; Mahomet, Master Gunner; The Magnificent Defence of Constantinople; Isabella, Master Quartermaster; Gustavus, 'Father of Modern War'

A few years before Crécy – in 1338 – the Turks, with the Ottoman Empire just rising, introduced a remarkable type of soldier and called him Yeni Tscheri, meaning new army or new soldier. The words became corrupted into European as 'Janissary'.

The Janissaries were the invention of Ala ed-Din, who could see that a feudal militia of Turkish horsemen, still educated in the tradition of pastoral society, could not hope to conquer and hold an empire for the descendants of Othman, the first Turkish sultan. Turks could not be disciplined to the extremity required, so a new army was formed of sons of Christian, non-Turkish subjects of Othmanli.

The conception was not new, but was a copy of the Mamelukes founded by Saladin and perfected by Es-Salih Ayyub. The plan was to give the Christian boys the best practical education possible, but they would have no parents or country and would swear allegiance only to the House of Othman. Gradually the Janissaries were educated as Moslems, but this was almost coincidental.

The experiment was an outstanding success, for the Janissaries, acquired as children, aged between seven and twelve, and educated or re-educated to an artificial pattern, became the most competent and most feared body of men in the world, as soldiers and administrators. Trained to think militarily and to act with precision, they achieved a degree of cold, inhuman efficiency never equalled. They were as invincible as any military formation in history and they had a more far-flung prestige than Roman legionaries, Swiss mercenaries, Cromwell's Ironsides, English grenadiers, Napoleonic cavalry, Prussian guards, the Anzacs, or Hitler's S.S. Hitler definitely modelled the Hitler Youth Movement on the Janissary system and demanded from his S.S. the same sort of personal renunciation imposed on the Janissaries.

But the Janissaries were little known in Europe in 1364 when a stubborn, sometimes, crude but always brilliant Frenchman, the Constable du Guesclin, began to make his mark on military history as one of the first systematic guerrilla-commando leaders. The disaster of Crécy brought du Guesclin into prominence, and before long he did his country the great service of applying the *coup de grâce* to the chivalry Edward III had so seriously wounded. He also reduced the great English possessions in France to a thin strip between Bordeaux and Bayonne. And he did all this without fighting a battle.

It takes a really great soldier to gain so much without a battle, yet du Guesclin has been decried by some of his own countrymen because, in effect, he suffered too few casualties. But others learned from him – among them the unique Turenne, Saxe, Marlborough, Napoleon, Sherman, several German generals; not that anybody matched du Guesclin in his own field.

His strategy was simply to avoid battle with the main English force while all the time he harrassed and hampered enemy movements and nibbled pieces from the territory they held. His policy was 'No attack without surprise', and in accordance with this principle he swooped on one garrison after another, especially those that he had heard were restless or mutinous or where he could induce local civilians to unbar the gates or let down scaling ropes by night.

He ambushed convoys and reinforcements, waylaid dispatch riders and enemy officers with weak escorts. Every action was carried out with commando-like speed and violence. If something went wrong or a garrison was able to rally in time to make a fight of it du Guescin called off the assault. Why get a bloody nose when he could strike somewhere else and take the place without suffering even a bruise? Yet there was nothing negative about du Guesclin's methods, and the proof of their efficacy is that he achieved his remarkable success within five years.

A new link in warfare was slowly being forged at this time – artillery. The first use of gunpowder to launch objects without thought of penetration may well have been in the Far East. Both Tartars and Arabs made early use of hollow tubes of wood or bamboo, tightly bound with hide, hemp, or wire. They were loaded from the muzzle with alternate charges of powder and an incendiary ball, often of tallow. When the tube was ignited at the muzzle the fire worked around each ball and touched off the powder to discharge the ball ahead. The Mongols had machines which hurled melted fat and tallow-loaded projectiles.

Roger Bacon certainly knew of gunpowder in 1252, and the German monk Berthold Schwartz, who lived in Freiberg until about 1384, made countless drawings of cannons, but he did not invent the cannon; nobody knows who made the first cannon and when. In the fourteenth century both cavalry and infantry had hand cannons – little more than large tubes on the end of a pole. The soldier fired his cannon by igniting powder at the touchhole with a lighted length of rope or stick carried for the purpose.

An Arabic document mentions cannon in 1304; other documents in Ghent refer to cannon in 1313 and 1314, and Oxford has a picture of a *pot de fer* – a dart-throwing vase – in use in 1324. In 1338 there was a cannon at Cambrai, France, which fired masses of darts. In 1339, at the attack on Quesnoy, there were several similar cannon. And from that time onward history refers to them frequently. In 1340 Augsburg, Germany, had a gunpowder mill.

The original cannon was small and fired darts or small lead balls, weighing 3 lb at most. A great variety of early cannons existed, some of them gigantic ones.

In 1368 in France there was the Master of the King's Cannons, and in 1383 the Bishop of Norwich used 'the Great Gun of Canterbury' in the siege of Ypres. In 1391 the Italian city of Bologna had a large supply of iron shot.

Culverins, a type of cannon, are heard of at this time. The Great Culverin fired projectiles weighing 15 lb, the Bastard Culverin 7 lb, and the Middle Culverin 2 lb. By the end of the fourteenth century bombards were in existence, and could throw a ball of stone weighing as much as 200 lb. But they were of little practical use. They were easily crushed by their own action, and they could not knock down a strong wall.

Artillery radically altered the face of war, but the many stories that have been told of the terror inspired by the early cannons are pure fantasy.

While artillery was struggling into life the French chivalry resuscitated itself, despite du Guesclin's exemplary work for his country. Its revival was a tragedy for France; with a four to one advantage at Agincourt in 1415 the French indulged in a ridiculous frontal attack and were beaten bloody, to give Henry V of England a famous victory that he could not have won had du Guesclin been alive and in command.

The siege of Orleans followed as a consequence of the English invasion of France in 1415, but I do not propose to deal with it here. In 1851 Creasy said that 'It may be asserted without exaggeration that the future career of every nation was involved in the result of the struggle by which Joan of Arc rescued her country from becoming a second Ireland under the yoke of the triumphant English.' This might well be true, but, beyond being the first siege in which any important use was made of artillery, the siege and battle of Orleans have nothing to commend them in the martial sense. The hysterical emotionalism which has always surrounded the Maid has somehow led some historians – who should be immune to emotionalism – to conclude that Orleans was a great battle. Without decrying Joan personally, there is something peculiarly shameful and unmilitary in the spectacle of an army being led by a teenage girl, and it is pleasing to reflect that the innovation was not imitated.

In 1430 a year after Orleans, Sultan Mahomet II was born. Cruel and ruthless, but a student and an intellectual, Mahomet became sultan in 1451, and avidly studied the lives and campaigns of Alexander, Julius Caesar, and many other rulers and generals. It is significant how so many of the really great generals of history have not been too proud to admit their debt to the past. Mahomet, who was one of the most outstanding men in Oriental history, certainly admitted his debt.

He lived and breathed war – as a dedicated general must – demanded the strictest discipline, and punished severely the slightest insubordination. He had the great quality of never being discouraged by defeat, and he knew that to remain efficient an army must remain active; he kept his troops continually on the move.

In any study of military development he stands out as the first great gunner; Napoleon, himself a master gunner, learnt from Mahomet. When Mahomet set out to capture Constantinople he had probably 13 great bombards and 14 batteries, each with four guns, of smaller calibre. His largest bombard, cast in Adrianople, fired a stone shot of 1456 lb, and required 60 oxen and 200 men to get it into position. As it took two hours to load its effectiveness was limited. On April 12, 1453, Mahomet opened the first great organized bombardment in history, thus establishing a sinister and enduring link. The Turks concentrated their shot on particular sections of the walls, and the artillery fire went on day and night, to the distress of the defenders and inhabitants of the city, which was defended by a maximum 8,000 troops to Mahomet's 140,000.

Nevertheless, the defenders beat back some large-scale assaults and inflicted thousands of casualties on Mahomet's troops, largely owing to the defensive genius of the brilliant Genoese soldier John Giustiniani, who was ably supported by the veteran German military engineer Johann Grant. On May 18 Mohamet made a further attempt at storming the walls under cover of a *helepolis* or 'city-taker' – a huge wooden tower. The *helepolis* was dragged up to the walls, and from it heavy fire was poured into the defences, but Giustiniani blew up the tower. Mahomet next resorted to mining, copying the methods introduced by Philip of Macedon in 340 BC;[1] that is, his miners dug tunnels and chambers under the walls, propping up the roofs as they proceeded. Then they would set fire to the props in the hope that the walls above would collapse into the cavity. But the defenders, directed by Grant, counter-mined. Grant blew up the Turkish miners, smoked them out, suffocated them by stinkpots, or drowned them. At times both sides met underground and fought bloodily with knife, spear, and axe.

Frustrated, at the point of despair, on May 29 Mahomet launched his greatest assault – a combined one by army and fleet. The main attack was made by three echelons of infantry, the Bashibazouks, the Anatolians, and the Janissaries, in that order, the worst being first and the best last. The defenders, now reduced to fewer than 4,000 fighting men, fought so hard that Mahomet had

1 When he laid siege to Perinthus (Eregli) and Byzantium.

to make five separate assaults, but in the end he triumphed and the great fortress city fell. The attackers lost many more men than the defenders, but this did not perturb Mahomet, for he was an exponent of the theory that the end was worth the means; his enduring influence in this respect was great, and many generals copied him, time and again battering at powerful defensive positions in the expectation that successive attacks would wear down the defenders. This Mahomet mentality often had its successes, but many of them were Pyrrhic. The Mahomet mentality was nothing more than an obsession for conquest regardless of cost, and it was much more of a negative approach to war than the sly tactics of du Guesclin. Extremely insidious, it corrupted even intelligent military leaders, and never more so than during the war of 1914–18, when generals hurled masses of men against fortress-like positions much more formidable than Constantinople ever was. Mahomet had some virtues as a general, but his vices and not his virtues survived in the chain of leadership. The siege and the taking of Constantinople was so politically, religiously, and culturally catastrophic and its effects so profound that for centuries it was regarded as a magnificent military defeat. The view prevails even today. But the praise belongs to the defenders, not to the attackers. Mahomet made his first reconnaissance in force on September 6 1452; despite his vast numerical superiority he did not take the city until May 29 the following year. The clever, spirited defence of Constantinople should be celebrated, not its capture. But evil influences are strong, especially when cloaked in success, and the Mahomet mentality has not yet been eradicated.

While Turkey was emerging as the great power of the East, in Western Europe Spain was becoming powerful, with Queen Isabella proving herself a great general and an even greater quartermaster-general. Isabella, who with her husband Ferdinand assumed joint rule of Aragon and Castile in 1479, has a definite place in the chain of command, and in my view is the only woman in history who can be justly called a great captain. While of lesser stature than Hannibal, Scipio, Gustavus, Frederick, and Napoleon she nevertheless had unique qualities. And she was no mere copyist, but an innovator and initiator.

To conquer Granada – the first step in a series of campaigns which were to establish the Spanish Empire – Isabella developed artillery, engineers, and infantry. Her work with infantry foreshadowed a change as great in its way as the use of gunpowder. She commenced her wars with the customary feudal levies – groups of men provided by the nobles as part of the duty they owed to the Crown. But Isabella soon realized, as many a general had done before her, that the levies lacked discipline and that their sense of independence made them unreliable. So she developed her police force into an army, an early form of national army of professionals, and finally she hired Swiss mercenaries, then the finest infantry in Europe. Intelligent, trustworthy, and fit, the mercenary, however, owed his allegiance to his commander rather than to the ruler who paid the commander. This changeover from levies to professionals was a primary factor in the introduction of modern war.[2]

Isabella's artillery was also formidable. Her bombards threw iron and marble balls and occasionally fire-balls which not only set the defences on fire but terrified the defenders. Pioneers were recruited in thousands to build roads for passage of the bombards. Isabella's supply problems were immense, but she was equal to them. Her supply train consisted of no fewer than 80,000 pack-mules; in all history there is no record of any greater number of animals used in warfare. Isabella herself controlled distribution of rations, managed the billeting of soldiers, and planned the routes to be followed by her convoys.

2 During the feudal era rank and command, as we understand it, did not exist, but the employment of mercenary troops gradually evolved a system. The monarch employed the army commanders and the colonels; the colonels selected the captains who raised the companies; the captains chose their lieutenants, and the men were often permitted to select the non-commissioned officers. This ancient device was substantially the system which applied to the volunteer regiments during the American Civil War. The growth of mercenary organizations made more severe methods of discipline imperative, and in the sixteenth century Ferdinand in Spain, Francis I and Henry II in France, and Charles V in Germany made codes of laws for their respective armies. Punishments were Draconic, and rewards were allotted for courage and outstanding service, but unless a general was able and deeply respected by his men no laws could keep up a discipline such as is taken for granted today.

She also introduced a field hospital – the first recorded instance of one – and a regiment of field messengers. These early signallers proved invaluable in Isabella's campaigns. It should be said that Ferdinand was commander-in-chief of the army and that he was efficient and capable, but he could never have achieved his successes without the magnificent staff work of his wife.[3]

With the surrender of Granada in January 1492 Spain, with the exception of Navarre, was united into one great Christian kingdom. The military consequences were as great as the political ones, for the war had brought forth the finest army in Europe, and foreign observers were greatly impressed by it and its organization, and most European armies adopted Spanish infantry methods.

The outstanding inheritor of Isabella's innovations and of Spanish military inventions was Gustavus Adolphus of Sweden (1611–32), one of the chief figures of the Thirty Years War. Simultaneously with the development of the chain of command there was a chain of inventions, and between 1450 and 1596 many took place in Spain or were developed there. The main ones were:[4]

1450 Matchlock or arquebus, the first infantry firearm.
1463 Bronze explosive shell.
1470 Explosive bombs; wheeled gun-carriage (first recorded use).
1483 Pistol.
1487 Incendiary shell.
1520 Rifling (the grooving in a barrel, which gave greater accuracy, velocity, and range).
1521 Wheel-lock and Spanish musket.
1543 Wheel-lock pistol.
1560 Paper cartridges.
1573 Fragmentation shell (roughly similar to the later shrapnel).

3 Her philosophy of life is best shown by her own admission that she knew only four fine sights in the world: a soldier in the field, a priest at the altar, a beautiful woman in bed, a thief on the gibbet.
4 Some of the dates given are approximate only, as records are both incomplete and contradictory. The word 'lock' refers to the ignition system in firearms.

1575 Hot-shot.
1588 Common shell.
1590 Fixed cartridges (powder and ball in one).
1592 Rifled pistols.
1596 Percussion fuse.

Gustavus, who was only 16 when he became king, profoundly admired Isabella, and her influence on him is as noticeable as Gustavus's influence on later leaders. He enlisted all Swedish males between fifteen and sixty who had no settled dwelling; of the rest all between eighteen and thirty were allowed to draw lots, and only the tenth was taken for the army. Those who worked in vital industries – such as mining or munitions – were exempted, as were food producing peasants who had no sons.

Sweden was the first country in Europe that built up for herself a regular and at the same time national military organization. As early as the sixteenth century the Vasa kings had laid the foundation of a national regular army, and Gustavus perfected it. He also introduced a novel method under which each soldier was supposed to own and be supported and equipped by a certain portion of land, rising in size and importance according to rank and grade. When war thinned his ranks Gustavus was compelled to enlist mercenaries, and regiments came to his army from all parts of Germany, the Netherlands, and Britain, but the Swedes were the kernel of the force.

His artillery and engineers were vastly superior to anything his enemies had to show; they had nothing to compare with his regimental pieces, light iron four-pounders. He took with him to Europe a large force of miners and engineers, both of which Isabella had used in strength.

But Gustavus Adolphus was too progressive a general to make the mistake of fighting his campaigns of 1630–2 with the old Spanish system of weight, by now universal. He wanted mobility. The battles of the Middle Ages had been won by cavalry; for a long time no infantry could withstand the shock of large men on large horses. Then the English archers had found weak places in a mail-clad line, and Swiss pikemen discovered that horses would not charge against a three-deep hedgehog of three-foot spikes on an eighteen-foot shaft. The Spaniards adopted the Swiss pike tactics and supported their pikemen with mustketeers on the flanks. As a result cavalry lost its proper place and horsemen deteriorated into skirmishers and foragers.

Gustavus gave war a new look by altering the equipment and tactics of his cavalry. He used only cuirassiers and dragoons. The main trouble with horse before Gustavus's day was its slowness in charging. Squadrons would ride up to the enemy, and each rank would successively fire and then wheel away to reload. The heavy cavalry lacked dash and never undertook the true role of horse, but the Swedish cuirassiers were taught to ride at a gallop, to fire their pistols at speed, and then push home with the sword. The dragoons carried musket, sword, and axe and were really mounted infantry.

A great infantry reformer, too, Gustavus reduced the length and weight of the musket and replaced the fork firing-rest then in universal use with a thin iron spike – the 'Swedish feather' – which could be used as a palisade stake against cavalry.

The distinction between riflemen, who fired guns, and grenadiers, who threw hand-grenades, dates back to Gustavus; the word 'grenadier' was coined at the defence of Ratisbon by the Swedes in 1632, when the soldiers who took the risk of handling and hurling hand-grenades were given extra pay.

In marches Gustavus dispensed with a rearguard when marching forward and with a vanguard when marching from the enemy – and his men were rapid marchers. In battle he had a keen eye for ground and the ability to make his three arms work together. The discipline of the Swedes was remarkable, religious duties were strictly observed, and crime was very rare. There were regimental schools for soldiers' children, many of whom, as well as their mothers, travelled with the troops. Prostitutes, the bane of German armies, never accompanied Gustavus's armies. As his army was better in organization than any other in Europe, so it was superior in *esprit de corps*, largely because of Gustavus's personal example and because of the 'God is with us' conviction he imparted to his troops.

Again influenced by Isabella, Gustavus introduced field hospitals and regimental medical chests, and is sometimes credited with being the originator of uniforms. In the modern sense this may be true, but Roman military dress had been uniform many centuries before.

The troops were fed from depots – one of the most important of Gustavus's improvements. He established these depots in suitable localities, and saw that his staff of commissaries kept them full with supplies from Sweden or from contributions made by the countries crossed.

His moral and intellectual courage equalled his physical courage; his march into Germany was only a trifle less audacious than that of Hannibal into Italy; his attack-crossing at the Lech river – where he used smoke to cover the crossing[5] was no less dashing than that of Caesar at Zela. Alexander, Hannibal, and Caesar – Gustavus had studied all three, and he possessed their finer qualities. Like all three, he put his brain and soul into his work. In dealing with his half-hearted allies Gustavus showed the patience of Hannibal and the persuasiveness of Caesar.

The wars in the Netherlands in the second half of the sixteenth century had greatly developed engineering. Outworks grew in extent and importance, and inner works were built to enable the besieged to hold the fortress even after the loss of the walls. As an engineer Gustavus had learned all that the Netherlands had to teach and had improved on it. He adopted the system of field fortification brought to perfection in the Netherlands, but altered it in many ways.

The Gustavian method showed its brilliance at the famous battle of Breitenfeld, fought near Leipzig, Germany, on September 17 1631. Here Gustavus proved that mobility was superior to weight. His formations were much more elastic than those of the army of the Catholic League, commanded by Count Tilly. His cavalry was posted strategically at several points, his main artillery was a little left of centre, and the light guns were in front of their respective regiments. Gustavus also had an artillery reserve – the first known instance of such a thing. He ranged his infantry in small oblongs, and the largest unit had only 200 men. Each sub-unit, in which the musketeers were covered by the pike-men, was a small, mobile, hard-hitting human fortress. Actually the battle was not fought as Gustavus had intended, but this only

5 In 1700 Charles XII of Sweden used exactly the same ruse when he crossed the Duna in his war against Poland and Russia.

underlines the effectiveness of the new tactics of mobility, for before their advent it was virtually impossible to change the course of a battle once the two sides were committed to the fight.

Gustavus's tactics gave him more spectacular successes before his death in action towards the end of his climatic victory at Lutzen the following year. The American historian Colonel Dodge, writing in 1890, said that from Alexander to Caesar the art of war rose to a great height; that from Caesar to Gustavus it sank into oblivion, and that Gustavus re-created it. This is far too sweeping a statement, but it does serve to indicate Gustavus's importance as 'the father of modern war', as he is so often labelled. It also hints at the Swede's vital place in the chain of command, for with Gustavus began the third main period of war.[6]

He left valuable lessons for succeeding great captains. They included the benefits of methodical planning; careful accumulation of supplies; energy in marches and manoeuvres; rapidity of fire; the value of taking and holding strong-points; the need for a sure base and efficient communications; the value of sober morale; the immense security that is won by discipline; the fact that the calculated risk was not synonymous with foolhardiness.

At a time when wars and battles were more frequent than they are now, when war was an accepted part of the way of life and touched every man's life, the methods of great leaders were studied more assiduously than they are now, and Gustavus became the prime model for every ambitious soldier in Europe.

Gustavus was not only the founder of modern Continental military organization, but also the founder of modern tactical ideas. One man he profoundly impressed was Oliver Cromwell.

6 The first from remote antiquity down to the decay of Rome; the second during the Middle Ages.

TEN

CROMWELL; THE IRONSIDES; THE BATTLE OF NASEBY

As a man and as a ruler Cromwell was in most respects the equal of Gustavus, so it is no slight to him to say that his military skill was only a reflection of that of the Swede. In any case, everybody else in Europe was imitating Gustavus – or trying to. It says much for Cromwell that he was such a worthy follower of Gustavus.

In 1642, ten years after the death of Gustavus, the Civil War in England broke out. Charles was at Nottingham with a scratch army of 10,000 men, with Prince Rupert – 'Rupert of the Rhine' – in command of the Royalist cavalry. The Parliamentary army had twice the Royalist strength, but was equally ill formed. Little occurred for two years, except that in 1642 Cromwell began to discipline his Ironsides. He began his New Model discipline with a 60-man troop, of which he was captain, but there was nothing new in it. It was merely an imitation of Gustavian methods. Cromwell was deep enough to understand what he and all other Englishmen had watched – the magnificent campaigns of 1630, 1631, and 1632 in Germany – and he was wise enough to apply the lessons they brought out. Cromwell trained himself as he trained his pious yeomen, rising from troop captain to captain-general.

At Edgehill, on October 23 1642, the Royalists had 12,000 men, the Parliament 15,000. Tempestuous Rupert, on the Royal right, charged and routed Essex's left, and then turned to plunder in Kineton. The Royal left had equal success, and the day seemed lost for the Parliamentarians, when thirteen troops of their cavalry came up, among them Cromwell's, and rode down the Royalist infantry. Rupert returned just in time to save the King from capture and to cover the retreat.

But Cromwell knew that it was a near thing. The Parliamentary arm was made up, as he said to Hampden, of 'old decayed serving-men, and tapsters and such kind of fellows'. He wanted 'men of spirit, of a spirit that is likely to go as far as gentlemen will go'. Later he raised these men, 'men such as had the fear of God before them and made some conscience of what they did'. As he saw it, leadership was useless without disciplined followership.

People who ascribe the New Model Army entirely to Cromwell's own invention do his intelligence an injustice. Under his standards were serving many Englishmen and Scots who had fought with the Swedes, and with the Thirty Years War drawing to a close it is inconceivable that Cromwell should not have known what Gustavus had begun twenty years earlier. Cromwell learned the intricacies of drill from John Dalbier, a Dutch veteran, who had seen much service on the Continent, but he made his own rules of discipline, and so well conducted were his men that civilians did not run and hide from them as they usually did when soldiers approached. Following Gustavus, he created in England the beginnings of a regular army.

In May 1643, near Grantham, he won his first independent fight. Outnumbered two to one, his cavalry rode down the Cavaliers without a check. In July he met the Royalists near Gainsborough, and in close-quarter fighting with sword and pistol drove them off and chased them, then astutely covered a retreat when not strong enough to face a larger body of Royalist infantry. In August he became second-in-command to the Earl of Manchester, and in October he again defeated a large force of cavalry near Winceby. A newsletter journalist recorded in May 1643: 'As for Colonel Cromwell, he hath two thousand brave men, well disciplined; and no man swears but pays his twelvepence; if he be drunk he is set in the stocks or worse.'

A letter Cromwell wrote to a friend on September 11 1643, reveals the key to his system of discipline: 'I have a lovely company; you would respect them, did you know them. They are no Anabaptists, they are honest, sober Christians; *they expect to be used as men!*'[1]

In July 1644, at Marston Moor, Cromwell commanded the Parliamentary left wing with 4,000 men. Seizing an opportunity,

1 The author's italics.

he outflanked the Royalist right and utterly routed it. It was no hell-for-leather charge of the kind Rupert made, but a steady methodical trot with an occasional pause to fire and load. Its concentrated, remorseless energy was even more frightening than a wild sabre charge. 'God made them as stubble to our swords', Cromwell said of the Royalists.

Rupert had made a successful charge too, but it had been so impetuous that his squadrons were unsettled and ill ordered; Cromwell's were in perfect order. He struck at the Royalists before they could re-form, and they fled. This battle earned Cromwell and his yeomen the sobriquet of 'Ironsides'.

But the Army was still far from popular with the public. Early in 1645 the Committee of Both Kingdoms – the Parliamentary governing body – wrote to a colonel in the West of England to censure him for 'the very great complaints of the intolerable carriage of the troops'. They were guilty of all kinds of indiscipline and violence – robbery, arson, spoiling, drunkenness, abusive behaviour, and all kinds of debaucheries.

The common people of England suffered almost as much as the inhabitants of any country racked by war – and from both sides. The heavy exactions of the Scots in Cumberland and Westmorland for month after month reduced the inhabitants to despair. In Northumberland and Durham the charges on the farmers were so heavy that the landlord had little or nothing. On each side at this time the soldiers lived mostly by plunder. They carried off cattle and cut down crops, sequestered rents, and assessed fines. They kept up a multitude of small forts and garrisons as a shelter to flying bands who despoiled the country, parts of which were rife with squalor and brutality.

The New Model Army was to change much of this – at least on the Parliamentary side. The New Model Ordinance was accepted by the House of Lords in February 1645, and significantly was of lesser strength numerically than before, for worthless men were weeded out. The Army consisted of 14,400 infantry, 6,600 cavalry, and 1,000 dragoons. The whole body was given thorough drill and discipline at Royal Windsor, and the effect was apparent the moment the Parliament met the enemy, although a Cavalier described them as 'a collection of raw, inexperienced, pressed soldiers'. It has often been assumed that because the New Model

Army came to achieve so much its members must have been volunteers. In fact, Parliament had to compel men to enlist, for it seemed England did not have 20,000 men of militant conscience, willing for the cause to leave shop and farm, wife and home, to submit themselves to iron discipline and face all the perils of very active service.[2]

The artillery, up till now neglected, was reorganized, and the Army was given a powerful train, eventually brought up to 56 guns, some of 6-inch or 7-inch calibre, plus some 12-inch bomb-throwing mortars. At this time, too, the red coat, earlier adopted by Cromwell for some troops, became general, to remain so until 1914.

The Parliamentary soldiers were paid regularly, a clear indication of Gustavian influence, for Gustavus had paid his men regularly, an astounding thing for those times. The New Army soldiers earned about as much as they would have done as ploughmen or carters. They carried knapsacks but no water-bottles, and each man had a portion of a tent. Their staple rations were bread and cheese, considered adequate, honest food. Oddly enough, this new army had no field hospitals, and wounded men had to rely on what help their comrades could give them or on their own help to get them to some sympathetic housewife near the battlefield.

The establishment included a Judge Advocate General and a Provost Marshal General, under whom was a squad of mounted police. Up to sixty lashes could be inflicted, but flogging was rarely necessary in this army of Bible soldiers. Cromwell's successors were not so moderate; in later centuries lashes were inflicted in hundreds and even thousands of strokes.

The average substantive wealth in the Army was not high, and Royalists were fond of taunting the Parliamentarians with their poverty, vowing that the whole pack of them could not muster a thousand pounds a year in land among them. Yet in the New Army, commanded by Sir Thomas Fairfax, thirty of the thirty-seven senior officers were of good family. Pride, a drayman,

---

2 The Wars of the Roses, 1455–87, has resulted in such a deep-rooted dislike for the professional soldier that for 150 years England was left without an army – at a time when military organization on the Continent was becoming a science.

Hewson, a cobbler, and Okey, a ship-chandler, were among the minority who rose from the ranks.

Throughout the war both sides showed remarkable lack of information about each other's movements, and many cavaliers were frankly contemptuous of the Roundheads' New army and were confident of winning the next battle. They amused themselves by carving a wooden image of a man which they called the god of the Roundheads, and carried it in scorn and derision. Some of them even made the mistake of being contemptuous of Cromwell and Fairfax, though they made a powerful team, especially when compared to the Royalists' leaders, Lord Astley, aged sixty-six and too old for effective command, and Prince Rupert, twenty-five and too irresponsible. All four were soon to play their part in the battle of Naseby.

Of all the battles which occurred on English soil only Hastings is more famous than Naseby, an interesting battle on many counts. The Parliamentary Army had abandoned the siege of Oxford, while Charles was stationed at Daventry, thirty-five miles northward, irresolute and hesitant because of the conflicting advice Prince Rupert and Sir John Digby were giving him.

On June 5, 1645 General Fairfax left Oxford and moved his Parliamentary Army north-east to Newport Pagnell. On June 8 Fairfax and his aides decided to attack the Royalist Army, and the following day the Parliament gave Fairfax *carte blanche* in the conduct of the campaign – as a wise step. On June 10 Cromwell was posted to Fairfax as second-in-command.

On June 12 Fairfax drove in Royalist pickets, eight miles east of Daventry, causing the King to retreat hurriedly to Market Harborough, eighteen miles north-east. Fairfax, a student of warfare for a long time, knew that an army retrograde movement should be pushed hard, so the next day he pursued Charles so forcefully that his forward troops captured some Cavalier patrols as they made merry in an inn; according to some sources the Cavaliers were playing a game of quoits. It was typical of them not to have sentries on guard.

When the King heard of this development he called a battle council. Further retreat, with the Roundheads pressing close, would be dangerous, so the Royalists decided to form a defensive position on high ground two miles south of Naseby and covering the road from Naseby. Choice of ground showed sound tactical appreciation. The view was good, but, perhaps because of morning mist, Rupert sent his chief of scouts to reconnoitre and to report on enemy dispositions. This officer returned to say that he had been about three miles forward but had not seen any enemy, a report that Rupert thought absurd – which it was. Rupert took a patrol and rode forward to investigate for himself.

Fairfax had broken camp at 3 a.m. and with Cromwell had ridden forward to seek a position covering Naseby. They crossed East Farndon ridge and descended into the valley, which was boggy and protected by a stream. Cromwell saw that the Royalists, who were strong in cavalry, would not either initiate action or be drawn into it on such ground, so he suggested that the Parliamentarians occupy the ridge. In this he was merely following an age-old maxim to 'take the high ground'.

Rupert arrived at this time near Clipston, from which he saw the Parliamentary force riding back up the hill and reasoned that Fairfax would occupy the ridge. He saw that to the right was better country and a gentle slope up which his cavalry might advance in a flanking movement. He reached a point on the Sibbertoft-Clipston road about a mile south of Sibbertoft.

But in turn Fairfax saw this flanking move and countered it by side-slipping to his left. By nine that morning both armies were marching west on parallel lines about two miles apart. A short march of about a mile brought the armies to an open shallow valley between two slopes – Dust Hill Ridge and Red Hill Ridge – and here they both formed line about half a mile apart.[3]

The senior Parliamentary leader on the spot, Skippon, posted the army forward of a ledge on the southern slope, Red Hill Ridge, but Fairfax when he arrived withdrew the men behind the ledge, the better to make his dispositions in secrécy. Wellington's act in keeping so many infantry lying down just below the crest at Waterloo is strikingly similar.

Rupert had sent for the entire Royalist Army, and it formed up on Dust Hill Ridge, now with no hope of being able to turn the Parliamentary flank. Still, Rupert was satisfied enough with a

3 These ridges are now joined by the Naseby-Sibbertoft Road.

frontal attack, for the terrain was good cavalry ground. Rupert took the right wing cavalry, Sir Marmaduke Langdale the left cavalry, and Lord Astley commanded the infantry in the centre.

Together they formed a mile-long front, too great a distance for 7,500 men in 1645, for it gave the Roundheads a reserve of only 800 under the King himself, who had a commanding view from Dust Hill Farm.

The Parliamentarians had the same frontage and much the same formation, except for one important difference. Cromwell, commanding the cavalry on the right flank, had his horsemen slightly behind the infantry line so as to keep to higher ground. Commissary-General Ireton led the left-flank cavalry, whose left edge was not quite flush with twin rows of strong hedges. Behind these hedges Cromwell posted 1,000 dragoons under Colonel Okey – a remarkable decision, for the dragoons were not only far forward of the Parliamentary line but well in advance of it as well, on the exposed flank. They were supposed to enfilade Rupert's horse when they charged, but were in such a dangerous position that they could easily be themselves enfiladed or attacked from the rear.

The Royalists should have stayed on the defensive; the weaker force usually does. But Rupert was not the type to play safe – his whole knowledge of tactics seemed to be summed up in one word, 'Attack!' – and without reference to Astley he induced the King to order an attack.

By now, with so much obvious military activity in the area, many of the villagers and farmers had fled, but just as many civilians stood at a safe distance from the scene, agog with expectation. They included the human vultures who followed any army in the field, ready to race on to the field after the battle to gather plunder.

As the Royalist infantry line moved Fairfax advanced his infantry just forward of the ledge, where the men waited silently as the Royalists pressed across the field. The moment combat was joined Rupert led his cavalrymen in a charge. Keeping inside the hedges he swept up the slope and smashed into the flank of Ireton's line. Rupert dashed on for another mile until he encountered the Roundheads' baggage-depot, where his Cavaliers wasted time in a fruitless effort to capture it. Had Rupert been as well read as he was courageous he would have ignored the enemy's baggage, especially as he had had a similar experience at the battle of Edgehill. For a full vital hour Rupert and his cavalry were away from the battle. Strangely enough, English and British cavalry made this same mistake many times in many countries.

The Royalist infantry were at first very successful, and forced the Roundheads back over the crest. With Skippon wounded, Fairfax pushed in his reserves to bolster the breaking line, and, setting an example and fighting in the front himself, he succeeded in holding the Royalists. Ireton also showed sound leadership. Part of his cavalry force had crumbled and disappeared under the impetus of Rupert's charge, but as the Cavaliers were now nowhere to be seen Ireton wheeled the remaining part of his force and attacked the Royalist infantry on the flank.

But these were fine, steady troops, and they stopped the cavalry attack and captured the wounded Ireton. At this point Okey, also relieved of pressure from Rupert, and waking up to his opportunity, led his dragoons in a charge against the Royal infantry. The whole centre was now in a confused, massed struggle.

This was the critical moment. Whichever leader could bring a strong force of cavalry to bear on the milling centre would win the battle, or, as the historian Professor S.R. Gardiner put it, 'would have England at his feet'.

Langdale had been leading his Royalist left flank cavalry over fairly difficult country sprinkled with rabbit warrens and furze brush at the bottom of Red Hill Ridge, and eventually they reached the bottom of the rise which was here steeper than elsewhere. Cromwell had been watching their approach, and now, with fine timing, with Whalley he led his cavalry downhill in a charge so relentless that the Royalists – outnumbered two to one – were scattered and pursued. But Cromwell was too much in control to allow all his cavalry to charge off into the blue in wild pursuit. He ordered three regiments to pursue the fleeing Royalists, but kept the bulk of his force on the field, and remained at its head.

He wheeled his cavalry, and in two waves sent them in to attack the exposed flank of Astley's Royalist infantry. Attacked on the three sides, these men were forced back into the valley, where, fighting desperately, they hoped for rescue by the King's reserve. Charles himself was leading the reserve towards the most dangerous spot, the left flank, despite the intervention of at least

one of his officers, when somebody shouted, 'March to the right!'
This unauthorized command was passed down the ranks, and the
whole force turned about and retreated rapidly.

Charles managed to pull them up within a quarter of a mile – a
commendable display of control. It was still possible to make a
charge – the battle raged only 600 yards away – but Charles held
back while the Roundheads surrounded his infantry. Rupert, too,
had now returned from his ridiculous rampage, his horses too
blown and his men too out-of-hand for a further effective charge.
So the Royalist cavalry watched helplessly while their infantry
fought gallantly but hopelessly. Eventually, out of ammunition and
facing annihilation, the survivors surrendered.

Fairfax re-ordered his infantry and prepared to continue the
advance, and Charles, conceding total defeat, retired to Leicester,
with Cromwell in close and continuous pursuit.

The Royalists lost the battle because their cavalry left their
infantry unsupported, a sharp lesson in the need for strict battle
discipline. The Parliamentarians won the battle because their
cavalry supported their infantry and because of Cromwell's
tactical appreciation. A nineteenth-century German military
historian, Hoenig, believes that there was 'scarcely a battle in
history where cavalry was better handled than at Naseby'.[4]

It might be said that Rupert was personally responsible for the
defeat of his own side. One of the most colourful soldiers in
history, he was also one of the most irresponsible. I think it
possible that his deplorable example at Naseby might have led
indirectly to British generals being given restricted commands and
objectives so that no one leader could endanger the safety of all.

In the cold and wind the battlefield of Naseby was a grim scene
that night. Lady Herbert searched over it, with a retainer, for the
body of her husband. They met stragglers laden with loot, and here
and there lay a wounded man pleading for help they had no means

---

4 Major H.G. Eady, a capable analytical historian, considers Gustavus and
Cromwell 'the greatest cavalrymen of history' (*Historical Illustrations to
Field Service Regulations*, Operations, 1929). I do not subscribe to this
interesting viewpoint, but Cromwell was certainly the best cavalry
commander Britain has ever had.

of giving. Practically everybody fit and still active had moved on, leaving the still heaps of dead and the ghastly writhings and gaspings of the still dying. Mangled limbs were scattered about, mixed with the carcasses of horses and the wreckage of gun-carriages and supply carts. Small arms littered the field, and fragments of clothing and feathers fluttered in the wind. The spoilers of the dead had practically finished their work, but a few local women still moved among the dead, some of them trying to find a body not too far gone to try to patch up. Others were gathering spoil.

Lady Herbert went up to one of the women and asked if she could tell where the King's Guards had fought. 'Aye, gossip,' the woman said. 'Be'st thou come a-riffling, too? But i'faith thou'rt of the latest. The swashing gallants were as fine as peacocks, but we've stripped their bravery, I trow. Yonder stood the King's tent, and yonder about do most of them lie; but thou'lt scarce find a landing for thy cattle now.'

Lady Herbert found the fragments of the Royal tent, where the dead lay wedged in heaps, indicating long and desperate fighting, with combatants often fallen clasped together.

Cromwell went from victory to victory, though his successes were marred by the so-called massacres of Drogheda and Wexford. 'I forbade them to spare any that were in arms in the town,'[5] Cromwell explained of Drogheda, but no doubt many non-combatants perished as well. Cromwell was God-drunk, and his conduct was the essence of narrow Puritanism, but it was the way of war in that era.

Cromwell's campaign of 1651, at the end of the Second Civil War, was a supreme example of a general's artistry. On the unprotected rear of an enemy facing hunger and desertion he deliberately left just one door open for his enemy, and they entered it, to be trapped at Worcester by four separate converging forces and destroyed on September 3rd. Three thousand enemy were killed, 10,000 taken; Cromwell lost 200 men.

This was his final personal battle, but he initiated the Dutch War of 1652–4, which ended to England's advantage, and the

5 At the taking of Magdeburg by Tilly in 1631, 40,000 people were massacred in one day.

Spanish War of 1655–9, which, though theoretically a victory for England, ruined her trade to the benefit of the Dutch and caused a serious economic depression. But Cromwell, who had died on September 3, 1658, did not see this disaster.

Few British people appreciate the fact that Cromwell is one of the few great commanders of history who were never beaten; the other notable exceptions are Scipio and Alexander the Great. It is significant that neither Cromwell nor Scipio ever made a direct approach, and their faithful adherence to this principle had much to do with their success. Judged by the success of his nine-year military career, Cromwell emerges as a greater soldier than if measured by the rules of the art of war. His tactics were better than his strategy, and, judged by opposition – a paramount aspect in assessing a soldier's greatness – he does not stand high. His losses in storming strong places, except at Clonmel, were always small and testify rather to poor defence than to brilliant attack. Colonel Dodge, one of many foreign historians and generals who have studied Cromwell's campaigns, has likened him to George Washington as being 'eminent in arms'. This is a fair assessment; he was not a great captain, and he does not quite reach the stature of Turenne, Marlborough, and Eugène, but he certainly holds a secure link in the chain of command.

He proved that the morale of the commander himself and the morale of the troops themselves were vitally important and equally so. At Dunbar in 1650 he appeared to be in an almost hopeless position, but his resolution was astonishing. He was surrounded by Scots and outnumbered nearly two to one, his communications with the sea were interrupted by weather, and his troops were practically starving, yet he indomitably maintained his position until the enemy was led to make a mistake. Cromwell at once took advantage of this, and almost annihilated the Scottish force by battle and pursuit.

His influence in the British military sphere is especially notable, for much of the enduring character of the British Army is even now based on the New Model Army – the organization of regiments, a fixed establishment for artillery and transport and many administrative details, the origin of British military discipline, including the great tradition that an army marching through a country must take nothing without payment.

ELEVEN

TURENNE; MARLBOROUGH;
EUGÈNE; CHARLES XII

The many wars between the end of the Thirty Years War (1618–48) and the beginning of the War of the Spanish Succession in 1702 were indecisive, largely because the development of fortifications had outstripped that of weapons, hence the defensive was dominant. Also, an army was still not formed of self-contained formations but moved and fought as an entity; this cramped manoeuvre and movement, with the consequence that during the wars of the Fronde (1648–55), then the Devolution and Dutch Wars, until the War of the Grand Alliance (1689–97), only one camaign was decisive – that of Turenne during the winter of 1674–5, when France was fighting for her life against a coalition of enemies.

What the later generals of history owe to Turenne is immense but incalculable. He has the distinction of having commanded in more campgians than any other general in history, and he is also unusual in being one of the few great commanders who improved with age – most others deteriorated alarmingly,[1] as other historians also have noted.

His last campaign – he was killed soon after, aged sixty-three – was his finest, if only because he showed that even in

---

1 I refer, of course, to those leaders who actively commanded for a reasonably long period and into their fifties and sixties. Alexander the Great died at the age of thirty-three. Epaminoadas was of the Turenne mould. Almost fifty when he began his military career, he might well have improved still further with age, but he was killed in action twelve years later.

seventeenth-century warfare a decision could be reached by use of intellect and enterprise.

France was in a desperate position, and her allies had all gone over to the hostile coalition. Turenne was forced back across the Rhine as the Elector of Brandenburg moved to unite with a large army under Bournville at Enzheim in October 1674, but was then forced to retire to Dettweiler. The Germans meanwhile occupied Alsace and took up winter quarters in the many towns between Strasbourg and Belfort.

Turenne had always believed in du Guesclin's policy of 'No attack without surprise'. But he improved on this principle, for he realized that 'surprise' did not necessarily mean 'surprise attack'. His first surprise in 1674 was to decide on a midwinter campaign, a remarkable decision in that era when there was an almost written law that gentlemen did not wage war in winter. Turenne lulled his enemy into a false sense of security by placing his fortresses in an obvious state of defence, while he led his entire field army secretly into Lorraine.

Then, with the Vosges to hide his movements, he marched his men quickly south. After a while he split his army into more than twenty smaller units to confuse and distract enemy spies. These groups were ordered to press on through rough country despite the weather – they encountered several snowstorms – and to rendezvous near Belfort. Many a lesser commander would have spent at least a day here consolidating and resting his men. Turenne knew that the slightest delay could be fatal. He launched his army into Southern Alsace – to the utter astonishment of the enemy, who thought he was far away to the south. At Colmar in mid-Alsace the Elector of Brandenburg had enough time to organize a defensive position, and as he had as many men as Turenne he probably felt fairly confident.

But the psychological advantage was with Turenne, his men were winning, the enemy's troops were shaken. Cleverly he made a tactical indirect approach to Turkheim, where the decisive battle was fought. The enemy army melted away completely; in a dispatch to Paris Turenne could say truthfully that not one enemy soldier except prisoners remained in Alsace.

After a comfortable winter Turenne took the field to meet the Austrian general Montecucculi, who had been called to do what others had failed to do. Turenne nearly out-schemed him, too, and clearly would have defeated him on the Sasbach river, when Turenne was killed by a cannon-ball.

I believe that Wellington was consciously influenced by Turenne in that he always chose a position which would provide concealment and free movement for his reserves, as shown by his position at Talavera, 1809, and especially at Waterloo, 1815.

Turenne was a symptom of France's development as an aggressive nation. Louis XIV saw himself as an heroic figure and passionately wanted to make France supreme in Europe. His ambitions were applauded and helped by his brilliant ministers Louvois and Colbert, who between them moulded France into a first-class military nation. Louvois took over the army, centralized its administration, and established an *esprit de corps*. His reforming and innovating hand was everywhere. He improved army equipment and sanctioned much that was new, including the flint-lock musket. Realizing that certain arms of the service were smarting under a sense of injustice and inferiority, he raised their professional status. The infantryman became a man to be admired and the engineer, formerly rarely heard of, a hero. Louvois also improved the artillery and established military magazines at strategic points. While he did all this his colleague Colbert, was building the French Navy into a formidable force.

Both ministers were helped by the military engineering genius, Sébastien Vauban. In his long life of military service Vauban built 33 forts, repaired or improved 300 fortresses and ports, conducted 53 sieges, and was present at 140 actions. He became a marshal in 1703, only a year before Blenheim, and when he died in 1707 he left to the French Army a legacy that endured for the next 200 years. Napoleon, a century later, could be grateful for what Vauban did for France.[2]

Louis, with such men as Colbert, Louvois, and Vauban to aid him, made rapid progress, and by 1678 had added large slices of Europe to France. By 1688 France and Britain had begun their long and bitter duel for colonial territories. France at this time had

---

2 Unfortunately, he also sowed the seeds of the Maginot Line mentality, which helped to defeat France in 1940.

the strongest army in the world. It is interesting to note that on his accession in 1643 Louis found only one regiment of dragoons in the French Army. By 1690 France had 43 such regiments.

Despite Louis's strength the German princes rallied against him, and to help them William III of England formed the Grand Alliance – England, the United Provinces, and the Holy Roman Empire – to meet France. The end of this war was the Treaty of Ryswick in 1697, but it in no way reduced France's armed strength.

After much political manoeuvring and one crisis after another Louis's ambitions again got the better of him, and in 1701 he invaded the Spanish Netherlands and Milan and seized some Dutch forts. He also barred British merchants from the American trade and later stopped English goods from entering France. The Grand Alliance was revived by England, Austria, and the United Provinces, and England prepared for war. It was at this point that William III died of injuries following a fall from a horse and was succeeded by Queen Anne. Louis believed, with some justification, that William's death would cause the collapse of the Grand Alliance. Nevertheless in May 1702 war was declared – and into the spotlight stepped John Churchill, later Duke of Marlborough.

Few generals have faced such a complex task. His soldiers were Dutch, German, and English and they were separated by language, time, and space; one of his allies, Austria, was threatened by enemies on three sides. As Allies, France had Spain and later Bavaria. Marlborough had to stop the French swamping the United Provinces and to stop both the French and the Spaniards from swallowing Austria.

In view of his success in stopping them it is important to remember that Marlborough, in his impressionable early twenties, had seen much service under Turenne, a fact that is not generally appreciated.

Communications remained primitive, armies were still a moderate size, and cavalry remained the decisive arm. Because of this last factor, strategy was largely dictated by the availability of forage – always a tremendous problem.

Because transport was slow and unreliable, generals tended to establish stocks of ammunition in secure places and to fight either at these places or within ready reach of them. This, in turn, led to the acceptance that defence was more important than attack. It was certainly easier; less effort was required and the run-of-the-mill generals never exerted themselves more than absolutely necessary.

But Marlborough was no run-of-the-mill general. He broke away from this type of warfare and returned to the offensive strategy of Gustavus and the attack tactics so successfully practised by Cromwell in England and by the Great Condé of France, who in 1643, during the Thirty Years War, had finally smashed the Spanish military system at the battle of Rocroi. Marlborough was also impressed by Turenne's ability to manoeuvre, he was imbued with Cromwellian respect for system, and he knew personally or had closely studied his opponents.

In most of his battles his platoon or 'divisions' (a division was about a company strong) first fired on the enemy at a range of thirty to fifty paces. Under cover of the smoke made by the discharges his men then bayonet-charged. Repeated infantry attacks held down the enemy and softened them for a shock attack by cavalry. Marlborough issued his cavalry with only three rounds of ammunition, to be used strictly for defence. This was how he forced his horsemen to use the sword.

His system was helped by two great changes which had taken place since 1631 – the universal adoption of the flint-lock musket and the replacement of the pike by the bayonet. The British officially adopted the flint-lock in 1690. This weapon became popular in history and legend as 'Brown Bess'. The bayonet, insignificant though it seemed at the time, was to revolutionize tactics. Some writers claim, extravagantly, that it marked the end of medieval war and the beginning of modern war.

Infantry had become more diverse. Between 1650 and 1700 four kinds existed – pikemen, musketeers, fusiliers, and grenadiers. But by 1703, only a year before Blenheim, the four had been reduced to one main type, armed with flint-lock and socket bayonet. Officers still used a sword.

The lesser number of weapons simplified both tactics and formation. Firing lines were in four and three ranks, replacing the old column and six ranks. Battalions were now subdivided into smaller, more readily controlled groups – such as platoons and sections, Gustavus-style.

After campaigning indecisively in the Lowlands for two seasons Marlborough had more far-reaching plans for 1704. He intended to strike right through from Holland to the Danube, re-conquer Bavaria, and relieve Vienna, capital of the tottering Holy Roman Empire, from the threat of capture by the Franco-Bavarian armies of Louis XIV. For those days he was stretching his lines of communication remarkably.

In the spring he set off along the Rhine. This march was magnificently organized – organization was one of Marlborough's great gifts[3] – and the troops found meals, shoes, bridges, and hospitals waiting wherever they were needed.

The night's stop was always known in advance, and all the men had to do on arrival was pitch their tents, boil their kettles, and lie down to rest. Captain Robert Parker, who took part in the march, wrote: 'Surely never was such a march carried on with more order and regularity, and with less fatigue both to man and horse.' But there had been such a march – that of Claudius Nero's to the Metaurus.

The climax of this great march, which set a standard for other genreals to emulate, was the battle of Blenheim, England's greatest victory since Agincourt. The campaign showed the superiority of concentration and decisive battle over detailed operations and sieges, in which the French had been indulging. Marlborough and Eugène had concentrated forces in an important territory, and the result of the victory was outstanding, although Marlborough's most admired manoeuvre was the forcing of the great French defensive Ne Plus Ultra lines in 1711.

3 With Eugène he was responsible for probably the most interesting example in history of the organization necessary to move and protect a convoy. After the successful action at Oudenarde in 1708 the Allies decided to besiege Lille, and Marlborough collected at Brussels the mass of material needed. The siege-train was 15 miles long, and comprised 80 cannon with 20 horses apiece, 20 mortars with 16 horses apiece, and 3,000 ammunition wagons with 4 horses apiece. By remarkable planning and attention to detail Marlborough and Eugène moved their stores 75 miles through enemy country, from Brussels to Lille, crossing the Dendres and Scheldt rivers in the process, without mishap. Their achievement astonished Europe. 'Posterity will have difficulty in beliving it', the contemporary historian Feuquières wrote.

Allied tactics at Blenheim were certainly not perfect, but the battle was a logical successor to Breitenfeld, and an object-lesson in warfare. The main lesson, probably, was that trenches, heavily garrisoned fortresses, and miscellaneous defensive tactics could not prevail against aggressive spirit and opportunist skill. The subsequent art of war owed a debt to Marlborough and Eugène for their conception of the value of fighting over mere manoeuvring. They opened the way for Frederick the Great and Napoleon.

But before Frederick's birth in 1712 another soldier who was to leave his mark on Frederick and the military chain had risen to his zenith and was within five years of death – Charles XII of Sweden, whom General Fuller calls 'the most extraordinary soldier in the history of war'. Charles's place in military history is unique, for it was his martial character rather than his ability as a general which his successors strove to copy. His men had a faith in his leadership which had not previously been surpassed and which remained unequalled, despite the intense loyalty given to Alexander, Marlborough, Frederick, Wolfe, Napoleon, Moore, Hill, Graham, Buller, Lee, and Montgomery, among senior commanders.

He was young, and his effective military career was relatively short and spiked with disasters, but he is mentioned remarkably frequently in the writings of the great captains and in military histories and treatises. This is partly explicable by Charles's extraordinarily fervent love for war and its hardships; he was probably more interested in fighting than in victory. Nothing perturbed him, and he delighted in dangers and hazards. He was always optimistic, always honest, and though a disciplinarian he was invariably fair. His personal courage was as outstanding as his energy, and he had the tactical eye of a born soldier. When he took the field to prevent Peter the Great of Russia and Frederick Augustus of Poland from stealing his Baltic provinces Charles was only eighteen years of age. After much arduous campaigning, with his soldiers at times suffering indescribable hardships, Charles met the Russians in the great battle of Poltava late in June 1709, and, despite the great bravery of his troops, he was decisively beaten and became a refugee in Turkey. His defeat was due to his blunder in moving deep into enemy country – and Russian country at that – in defiance of communications and supply and in refusing to accept the good counsel of his senior officers.

Whatever Charles did was somehow invested with glory, as at Bender, in Turkey, on February 1 1713, when with no more than 40 men he defended an unfortified house against 12,000 Turks and 12 guns, and not until 200 Turks had been killed – 10 by Charles alone – was he overpowered and taken prisoner.

Throughout November 1715, with quite incredible heroism, he defended Stralsund – on the Baltic coast of what is now East Germany – against a coalition of Hanover, Russia, Prussia, Saxony, and Denmark. With Stralsund reduced to rubble, Charles escaped on December 23 and raised another army. On December 12 1718, while besieging the Norwegian fortress of Fredriksten, he was shot dead in a trench.

Charles was a soldier-leader who would not accept defeat. Wounded, captured, emphatically beaten, he frustrated his enemies by refusing to lie down; he won battles but lost wars. All Europe talked about him; generals were inspired by him, military writers practically deified him. He impressed even Marlborough, who was sent to Leipzig in 1706 to interview him. He brought to military leadership a 'one-sword-against-the-world' attitude which certainly infected Frederick and Napoleon and many of their senior officers as well – such as Seydlitz and Ziethen and Soult and Murat. Many other successful generals have been less consciously influenced by Charles, but owe to him something of what Marshal of the Royal Air Force Sir John Salmond, commander in the field of the RAF in 1918, called 'the virus quality in the blood' and which Salmond had himself.

Charles does not qualify as a great captain – Dodge says he would have done so had he possessed a 'balance wheel' – but he was a great soldier and as personally brave, probably, as Sir Rollo Gillespie (1766–1814), who is often regarded as 'the bravest soldier'.

TWELVE

FREDERICK AND HIS SYSTEM; THE BATTLES OF ROSSBACH AND LEUTHEN

When Frederick succeeded to the Prussian throne in 1740 everybody expected a placid and tractable king, for as a prince he had devoted himself to poetry, literature, art, gardening, and philosophy. But overnight Frederick gave up many of his peaceful interests and became a warrior intent on creating a mighty Prussia. General Fuller, a discerning historian, believes that, 'except for Alexander the Great and possibly Charles XII, Frederick was the most offensively minded of all the Great Captains.' That he was so is partly due to his study of great leaders of the past and to a conscious effort to mould himself in their image and his tactics on theirs, with due improvements of his own.[1]

In particular the battle of Cannae fascinated him, for this was a battle of annihilation, and such battles were to become Frederick's aim and, through him, the aim of every German general ever after.

Frederick wanted the most efficient army in the world, but his methods were vastly different from the crude ones of his father. He gave his soldiers tremendous *esprit de corps* and accommodated them with private citizens and not in barracks, so as to 'keep them human'.

Nevertheless, night marches were avoided, and men detailed to

---

1 Ancient military leaders have always fascinated the Germans. Field-Marshal von der Goltz Pasha wrote: 'We would know what Alexander the Great was like even if the humblest of his infantrymen were to rise from the grave and appear before us. Everything that Alexander was would be found in the walk, the gestures, the glances, the laughter, the anger of that infantryman.'

forage or bathe had to be accompanied by officers so that they could not run away. Even pursuits of the enemy were strictly controlled 'lest in the confusion our own men escape'. Other armies could afford a percentage of deserters; Frederick's supply of men was limited. His recruiting sergeants plied their trade as vigorously as had those of his father. Captured soldiers were nearly always forced to become Prussians and to be prepared to shoot down their fellow-countrymen – though there was nothing new in this system. Some young foreigners were given officers' commissions, but as soon as they had crossed the border into Prussia they were reduced to the ranks.

Before long an English traveller, John Moore, noted that 'the Prussian Army is the best disciplined and the readiest for service at a minute's warning of any now in the world or perhaps that ever was in it'.

Frederick sought his officers far and wide and for their speciality and paid them highly, the amount varying according to an officer's abilities and qualifications; many officers received double that of their British counterparts. The pay of the common soldier was 1s 4d a week, out of which he had to spend threepence in washing and in materials for cleaning his arms.

The training of the Prussian Army was highly advanced, with war situations produced authentically and carried out with a vigorous realism that was much ahead of its time.

History has given too little importance to Frederick's cavalry and artillery. When Frederick became King the cavalry was composed of large men mounted on powerful horses and carefully trained to fire both on foot and on horseback. The force was of the heaviest type and incapable of rapid movement. In fact, the cavalry of all European states had degenerated into unwieldy masses of horsemen who, unable to move at speed, charged at a slow trot and fought only with pistol and carbine.

Frederick, quick to see the error of this system, followed the example of Charles XII and introduced reforms which made his cavalry one of the most efficient bodies of horsemen that ever existed. Frederick paid close attention to the training of the individual cavalry soldier in horsemanship and swordsmanship.

His first change was to prohibit the use of firearms mounted and to rely upon the galloping charge, sword in hand. He taught his horsemen, who were hand-picked, to disregard enemy fire and to charge home. He lightened their equipment and armament and trained them to move rapidly and in good order over every kind of ground. Even so, cavalry serving as flank guards, scouts, or on outpost duty carried firearms and used them efficiently.

Guibert, a French observer, said: 'It is only in Prussia that the horsemen and their officers have that confidence, that boldness in managing their horses, that they seem to be part of them and recall the idea of the centaurs. It is only there that 10,000 horsemen can be seen making general charges for many hundreds of yards and halt in perfect order and at once commence a second movement in another direction.'

The great Marshal Saxe,[2] the real victor of the battle of Fontenoy in 1745, had already laid down that cavalry should be capable of charging at speed for 2,000 yards in good order. The cavalry of most countries could not reach this standard, but Frederick wanted an even higher standard. Frederick's older generals opposed his innovations, but he was capably supported and helped by Seydlitz and Ziethen. Von Seydlitz was one of the most brilliant cavalry officers in history, and in his day he had the reputation of being the best cavalry officer in Europe. He and Ziethen, another dashing cavalry leader, were probably the two officers on whom Frederick most heavily relied.

Out of twenty-two great battles fought by Frederick his cavalry won at least fifteen. At no time in ancient of modern history have more brilliant deeds been performed by cavalry than were achieved by Frederick's horsemen in his later wars.[3]

2 Saxe was a great soldier. He had written, quite seriously, in his *Mes Réveries*: 'I am not in favour of giving battle, especially at the outset of a war. I am even convinced that a clever general can wage war his whole life without being compelled to give battle.' This was du Guesclin's theory.
3 The brilliant Australian and New Zealand Light Horse were mounted infantry more than true cavalry. Mounted infantry did not normally fight on horseback but used their horses merely as a way of reaching a scene of action, where they fought on foot. Cavalrymen, of course, fought while mounted. The unconventional Australian Light Horse regiments fought some actions in cavalry, the most outstanding being their charge at Beersheba, Palestine, in October 1917.

Prohibiting cavalry from firing was to expose them at times to deadly fire from artillery and infantry without a chance to retaliate. To remedy this defect Frederick developed horse artillery, which, by its rapidity, could follow all the movements of the cavalry and camp and fight with it. By keeping the enemy's batteries and infantry at a distance and by its fire it paved the way for the cavalry charge.

For more than thirty years, until 1789, Prussia had the only efficient horse artillery in Europe. Frederick had howitzers for his army, too – large, booming guns with which he lobbed shells on the Austrian reserves sheltering behind hills.

While welding his army Frederick was thinking deeply about strategy and tactics. He concluded that he had only one basic problem – how to take a superior enemy by surprise. It was taken for granted that any army of Prussia would have superior numbers. He evolved this solution: concentrate the inferior strength of my own forces at a particular point with the apparent intention of launching a main attack. This will throw the enemy off balance. Now – how am I to launch my main attack successfully? By finding the answer Frederick achieved immortal fame, but to do so he went back to history, dragging out and dusting off the secrets of Epaminondas, Alexander and Scipio. Also, following Gustavus, by whom he was directly influenced, Frederick planned wars of mobility and rapidity of fire.

The difficulty of Frederick's method, which was always aimed at launching an attack on his enemy's flank, was the skilful development of the column on the march to form the battle-order. The slanting battle formation demanded of the officers and NCOs a high degree of efficiency in giving orders and of the men not only obedience but also an instinctive realization of the situation, the ability to feel what would happen the next minute, and to react with the spontaneity of a *corps de ballet*.

Frederick's drill was intended, as he explained himself, to make the soldier in battle feel conscious of his heart as the result of the harmony between the pace he took and his heart-beat. His marching pace made him calm, and drill had trained him in what he ought to do.

The marching pace allowed officers and NCOs to form up their fighting units and to move them precisely to the inch as they needed them. With the muskets of those days it was impossible to take particular aim. The men merely fired straight in front of them. By directing, moving, and forming his men exactly as he required them the NCO or officer took aim for all. A man acting on his own initiative could throw the whole line into confusion.

The Germans did not invent the idea of marching in step. The idea probably first occurred to the Greeks. The Prussians, in the seventeen-thirties, developed the marching pace from marching in step.

Frederick's system of manoeuvres came to be called Prussian drill, which was simply the method by which Frederick taught his battalions how to respond quickly and decisively to orders. Some writers have called Prussian drill brutal. It was certainly hard, but it was not brutal. It was hard because Frederick, unlike many rulers of his day, did not regard war merely as a rough game. He engaged in a war or battle with the object of winning it quickly; the civilian population suffered during long wars, and the longer a campaign went on the more soldiers tended to lose their will to fight.

Basically Frederick's tactics were extremely simple. He saw that if his army was much more mobile than that of his enemy he had only to wait until the enemy had deployed into line of battle, then attack it violently on the flank. This was the Epaminondas tactic.

For this flank attack he used only part of his force, for he belived – and he proved – that 30,000 men could defeat 70,000 in double-quick time. The remainder of his army he held ready for an emergency or to move in when the rout started.

Probably Frederick was the first great leader since the Byzantine generals, at least seven centuries earlier, to state that many military lessons could be learnt from books and to insist that his officers study their textbooks. In speaking of officers who relied on practical experience alone he said caustically, 'The Prussian commissariat department has two mules which have served through twenty campaigns – but they are mules still.'

His textbook *Military Instructions* is a masterpiece of common sense, for few of his maxims were profound. Here are some of them:

> The first object of the establishment of an army ought to be making provision for the belly, that being the basis and foundation of all operations. [The origin of the famous expression 'An army marches on its stomach'.]

It is an invariable axiom of war to secure your own flanks and rear and endeavour to turn those of your enemy.

The conquering wing of your cavalry must not allow the enemy's cavalry to rally, but pursue them in good order.

To shed the blood of soldiers, when there is no occasion for it, is to lead them inhumanly to slaughter. [A lesson not taken to heart by the generals of the Great War.]

Though our wonded are to be the first objects of our attention, we must not forget our duty to the enemy.

In war the skin of a fox is at times as necessary as that of a lion, for cunning may succeed when force fails. [An echo of Gideon.]

Those battles are best into which we force the enemy, for it is an established maxim to oblige him to do that for which he has no sort of inclination, and, as your interest and his are diametrically opposite, it cannot be supposed that you are both wishing for the same event.

Some of Frederick's maxims might appear cynical, but in the light of the standard of education and of the class distinctions of his era they make good sense. This one, for instance:

All that can be done with the soldier is to give him *esprit de corps* – a higher opinion of his own regiment than of all the other troops in the country – and since his officers sometimes have to lead him into the greatest danger (and he cannot be influenced by a sense of honour) he must be more afraid of his own officers than of the dangers to which he is exposed.

Political intrigue soon absorbed Frederick's attention. Maria Theresa's Chancellor, Prince von Kaunitz, had convinced France that the old rivalry between Austria and France was pointless now that Prussia was so aggressive. He proposed a bargain: If France would help Austria to regain Silesia she could have the Austrian Netherlands. Wooing France carefully, Maria Theresa and Kaunitz pointed out that the French-Austrian coalition of 70,000,000 could crush Prussia's 4,000,000. In January 1756 Prussia and England made an alliance, but in May France and Austria signed the Treat of Versailles, creating a defensive alliance in which they were supported by Russia, Sweden, and Saxony.

Faced with all these enemies, Frederick, in July, posted 11,000 men to watch the Swedes, 26,000 to watch the Russians and 37,000 to garrison Silesia. In August, with 70,000 men he invaded Saxony without declaration of war. The chances of survival, let alone victory, seemed slight. England provided money, but her world-wide conflict with France prevented her from giving effective military support.

Frederick claimed to have irrefutable documentary information that Austria was only waiting until her preparations were complete to launch the whole forces of the coalition against him. His one chance was to strike first and to deal Austria a blow which would cripple her offensive. At the end of August he marched his army into Dresden, Saxony, where he found other documents which he said, proved that he was to be attacked by no fewer than six first-class powers – Austria, France, Russia, Saxony, Sweden and the German States. It was a rare compliment, and, in a way, it delighted Frederick, for it meant that Prussia was now taken seriously. He blockaded Pirna, and in October he defeated the Austrians at Lobositz.

The campaign of 1757 opened at Prague, held by 133,000 Austrians under Prince Charles. Frederick had 120,000 men at this time, his army having been increased by the conquest of Saxony. He took Prague, but at great cost; 180,000 Prussians fell, including Field-Marshal Schwerin, 'who alone was worth 10,000 men'. Frederick then marched on Kolin, held in strength by Field-Marshal von Daun. Frederick devastated his own army by throwing battalion after battalion at the Austrian guns. He did not realize that he had been defeated until an officer, replying to the King's order for yet another charge, said, 'Does your Majesty mean to storm the batteries alone?'

Scenting victory, the Allies now moved to strangle Frederick in a circle of steel, using 400,000 men against him, and by the end of May the ring was tightening. Frederick was undismayed, and, though he suffered losses and Prussia was reeling under the blows, he struck back, sending his cavalry to raid enemy camps and regrouping his scattered troops. Berlin, his capital, was occupied by the Austrian Count of Hadik, who accepted a ransom of 300,000 thalers to depart.

The Russians devastated parts of Prussia, inflicting horrible barbarities on the civilian population. By October Frederick's position was so critical that even he began to believe that the war was lost, but throughout the war the world was amazed at Frederick's capacity to recover.

Training went on continually. Seydlitz exercised his cavalry at full speed over very broken ground, and men were often killed. Frederick once commented on the number of deaths. 'If you make a fuss about a few broken necks, your Majesty,' Seydlitz said, 'you will never have the bold horsemen you require for the field.' It was a significant statement in view of later German training.

Prussian cavalry was taught to rally to the front instead of the rear, in other words to rally after a charge while pursuing, which prevented a reckless, disorderly Rupert-of-the-Rhine pursuit and enabled the commander to follow up victory with greater certainty. The usual task of hussars was to harass a retreating army in detached parties; Frederick's hussars charged in a large body like heavy cavalry.

Seydlitz displayed decision and daring on November 5, when the French and Austrians at Rossbach foolishly offered their flank to the Prussians. Virtually the whole of the Prussian cavalry, in beautiful formation and moving at 'incredible speed', as a French officer described it, charged the enemy. Four times, the Prussians cut their way through the French, under Soubise, and routed them.

Where the Allies were still in column the Prussian artillery destroyed them, and then the systematic Prussian musketry smashed into those Allied infantry who held their ground. The retreat became a rout. The French and their allies lost 3,000 killed and wounded, 5,000 prisoners (including 8 generals and 300 officers), 67 cannon, many colours, and most of their baggage. Those who survived became a rabble on the run.

The Allied leaders showed no generalship at Rossbach. They must have won had they held a line along the Saale river and remained on the defensive, for Frederick had not the strength to attack a static line. Inept at manoeuvre and relying on superiority of numbers, they offered battle – which was exactly what Frederick wanted them to do.

In those days battles were rarely fought in winter. Armies retired to winter quarters, and no military activity more serious than patrolling was carried on until the spring, but Frederick had studied Turenne, and on November 13 he marched from Leipzig on a winter campaign. Frederick himself captured Neumarkt, where he learned that Prince Charles and Field-Marshal Daun had advanced to Lissa. Their right rested on the village of Nippern and their left on that of Sagschutz.

Their army, impressively strong, consisted of about 70,000 men (possibly as many as 80,000), including strong cavalry squadrons and supported by 210 guns. Their 5½-mile front had the right protected by bogs and the left covered by an abattis. The centre was at Leuthen.

Against this strong force in its strong position Frederick had only 36,000 men, made up of 24,000 infantry and 12,000 cavalry. His artillery consisted of 167 guns, including 71 heavy pieces. The battlefield was an open plain, over which Frederick had manoeuvred in times of peace.

On December 5, at five o'clock on a cold morning, Frederick led his army towards Leuthen. A few miles off he assembled his generals and briefed them for battle. 'I should think that I had done nothing if I left the Austrians in possession of Silesia', he said. 'Let me tell you, then, that I shall attack the army of Prince Charles, nearly thrice as strong as our own, wherever I find it. I must take this step, or all is lost. We must beat the enemy or all perish before his batteries. So I think, so will I act. Now go and repeat to the regiments what I have said to you.'

The last instruction is revealing for it was rare in that era for the men in the ranks to be told what the commanding officer had in mind. Frederick believed, rightly, that if he took the men into his confidence they would fight better.

As usual his plan was uncomplicated. He would advance straight up the Breslau (Wroclaw) road, feint at the Austrian right, march across Charles's front, and attack his left to cut his communications. The vanguard moved off, with the men singing a hymn:

> Grant that I do whate'er I ought to do,
>   What for my station is by Thee decreed;
> And cheerfully and promptly do it too,
>   And when I do it, grant that it succeed!

An officer asked Frederick if he should silence the men. The King said, 'No, with such men God will certainly give me victory today.'

All later German generals believed they had the Deity in their ranks, but this applies to most commanders of Christian armies.

The inhabitants of the area had scented trouble days before, with foragers, scouts, messengers, and cavalry patrols continually in movement along the country roads. Everybody knew a battle was brewing, but exactly where? Into which villages would the soldiers move for quarters? Which houses would they fortify? Which fields would be mashed into mud by the thousands of horses and the hundreds of wheels? For many miles around the area farmers had already had their horses, carts, and stores requisitioned – a euphemistic term for stolen – or lived in fear of their being taken. Had the season been summer many families would have evacuated the arena and lived in the open until the hurricane had passed. But this was winter, so most of them stayed where they were until, as fighting broke out and engulfed their hamlets and homes, they were summarily evicted or they fled.

The villagers of Borne were the first to hear or see conflict, for here an Austrian force – a detachment of five regiments under General Nostitz – barred the road. Dawn was just breaking, and the horsemen could be dimly descried through a mist. Frederick ordered a charge and the detachment was scattered and 800 taken prisoner. Nostitz was mortally wounded.

When the mist cleared the whole Austrian army was visible, regiment upon regiment, rank after rank – a formidable and impressive sight.

The taking of Borne gave Frederick a vantage-point, and its height screened from view the advancing Prussian columns. At this point Frederick sent his cavalry against the Austrian right, where they made such a display that Count Lucchesi, commanding the Austrian right, called for support. In haste, Field-Marshal Daun sent the reserve cavalry and even part of his cavalry from the left wing.

While this was happening the four Prussian columns formed into two, and at Borne they wheeled right under cover of high ground and marched south, the whole movement being carried out with the usual Prussian precision, with an advance-guard under General Wedell. Then came, on the right wing, General Ziethen with 43 squadrons and Prince Maurice of Dessau with 6 battalions. The left wing consisted of the major infantry force under General Retzow, flanked by 40 squadrons under General

Driesen. Each body of cavalry was supported by 10 squadrons of hussars, while in the rear was Prince Eugène of Württemberg with another 25 squadrons.

The Prussians seemed to be retreating, and this pleased Prince Charles and Field-Marshal Daun, who observed the movement from the mill at Frobelwitz. Daun said delightedly. 'The Prussians are off! Don't disturb them.'

But just after noon the columns wheeled again, formed line of battle and drove towards the Austrian left near the village of Sagschütz. General Nadasti, the Austrian commander on the spot, saw the overwhelmingly superior force advancing towards him and ordered away rider after rider, asking Charles urgently for help. Help could not come in time. At one o'clock Wedell, supported by infantry and artillery, stormed the defences at Sagschütz.

The Austrians had learned something of the spirit in which cavalry should be handled, for Nadasti dashed out with his cavalry and charged Ziethen's leading squadrons. The Prussian horsemen regrouped behind their six supporting infantry battalions, then followed Ziethen in a counter-charge against Nadasti, over difficult ground. The Prussians were skilled in riding over such terrain while the Austrians were not; they were broken and driven into Rathener Wood. In ninety minutes the entire Austrian wing was scattered, with Prussian hussars pursuing the flying Austrians. Then the Prussians began to roll up the enemy line like a carpet, with their heavy artillery enfilading the Austrian positions farther along.

A fierce fight developed at Leuthen itself, where the Austrians fought gallantly. Unfortunately for them, their generals had not learnt the bitter lesson of the French at the battle of Blenheim – that a village should not be overcrowded with troops. Leuthen was packed as tightly as Blenheim, with the troops in places from 30 to 100 deep. Artillery case-shot played havoc in these rigid lines. With requisitioned farm horses Frederick had brought up many of the heavy guns from the fortress of Glogau. This formidable artillery, as much as the redoubtable infantry and dashing cavalry, won the battle.

The Prussian Guards assaulted the Austrian positions and carried them. Possession of Leuthen did not help Frederick immediately, for the Austrians had formed another line at right angles to their first and had brought up artillery in support.

Frederick's infantry was held off until he sent for his heaviest guns and established them on high ground called the Butterberg, from where they drove the Austrians back. Frederick was master of the battle throughout. He had riders bringing him information constantly, and so was able to move infantry, guns, and cavalry about the large battlefield as necessary. This was unusual for the period; normally once an army was committed the commander could do little to influence events but had to depend on the initiative of his subordinate generals. Frederick gave his trusted leaders plenty of rein, but he rarely allowed overall control to pass from his hands. Adolf Hitler, who professed himself a student of Frederician methods, also kept control in his own hands.

The battle raged with little respite until four o'clock and dusk was approaching. Count Lucchesi, a brave cavalry leader, had assembled a large force of horse and saw his chance to use them when Prussian infantry under General Retzow was held up. Lucchesi made a flank attack, but he had not seen forty squadrons under General Driesen hidden behind the village of Radaxdorf.

Waiting for just such a moment as this, thirty of Driesen's squadrons charged Lucchesi frontally while five drove against his flank and the other five galloped round the Austrian rear. These enterprising tactics overwhelmed Lucchesi, who was killed as his troopers broke and scattered. After losing so much of their cavalry support the Austrian infantry was vulnerable. Driesen charged them in the rear, while General Wedell attacked their flank near Leuthen.

The anecdote about Frederick which the Prussians like best of all tells how Frederick rode frantically about the battlefield after hearing that von Wedell, his favourite, had been killed. Frederick shouted his name continually: 'Wedell! Wedell!'

While the King was shouting a corporal lying among a heap of dead and wounded with great effort said, 'Your Majesty, we are all Weddells here.'

Frederick stopped, gazed at the dying man, and said, 'You have taught me a good lesson and I thank you for it.'

Hopeless confusion followed as darkness fell and the Austrian force disintegrated, many of the troops bolting towards Lissa. Frederick, victorious but tired, also made for Lissa, riding through mobs of broken Austrians.

He rode into the grounds of a château and outside the building met about a dozen Austrian officers. 'Good evening, gentlemen,' Frederick said courteously, 'I dare say you did not expect me here. Can one get a night's lodging along with you?'

The Prussians lost about 6,000 men killed and wounded. The Austrians lost 10,000, plus 21,000 prisoners, 116 guns, 51 colours, and 4,000 wagons. But this was only an instalment. Prussian troops took 2,000 more prisoners on December 9, and on the 19th Breslau surrendered 17,000 men and 81 guns to Frederick.

As a power Austria had lost her reputation, while Prussia emerged as the most dangerous military power in Europe. Frederick had retaken the whole of Silesia except for a single fortress, Schweidnitz.

Few victories have been so enthusiastically acclaimed as Leuthen. Frederick's system and success astonished those who were accustomed to calculate effect by mere quantity. His tactics were to fascinate even Napoleon, who wrote:

> The battle of Leuthen is a masterpiece of movements, manoeuvres, and resolution. Alone it is sufficient to immortalize Frederick and place him in the rank of the greatest generals. All his manoeuvres at this battle are in conformity with the principles of war. He made no flank march in sight of his enemy. . . . He carried out things I never dared to do. He was above all great in the most critical moments. . . . It was not the Prussian Army which for seven years defended Prussia against the three most powerful nations in Europe, but Frederick the Great.

But Frederick had trained that army. Frederick's biographer, General Tempelhoff, wrote:

> Ancient history scarcely furnishes a single instance, and modern times none that can be compared either in execution or consequences with the battle of Leuthen. [This is not true.] It forms an epoch in military science and exhibits not only the theory, but also the practice of a system of which the king was the sole inventor.

The victory at Leuthen was largely due to the perfect co-operation of infantry, artillery, and cavalry, but the confidence of the ordinary soldier in Frederick as a general was the most decisive factor.

Thinking over his victory, Frederick realized how important artillery was. He transferred all the 24-pounders he had captured in Austrian fortresses to his field army, and with these guns defeated the Russians at Zorndorf in 1758. Even when the fortunes of war changed Frederick remained true to his fundamental principle that the battle was won when the heavy artillery dominated the decisive heights and when the light artillery was made so mobile that it could be used on any part of the battlefield. Thus he became the real developer of field artillery. He reduced all the light guns to 3-pounders and attached them to the cavalry. He gave the field artillery medium howitzers so that it could cope not only with moving targets but also with fortified positions. As a result of this reform he was so strong that he was able to support the natural deterioration of his infantry during his long wars. He started with 1,000 guns and finished with 10,000.

Frederick consistently used his central position to concentrate against a part of the enemy's forces, and by employing tactics of indirect approach he won many victories, despite his numbers.

However, at Hochkirch, 1758, and Künersdorf, 1759, superior numbers defeated him. At Hochkirch he opposed 37,000 men to 90,000 and at Künersdorf the Russians had 70,000 to Frederick's 26,000. But with only 30,000 he beat the Austrians at Liegnitz in 1760; they had 90,000.

In this he created a precedent. For the next two hundred years Prussian and German troops were outnumbered almost everywhere they fought – with a few important exceptions.

Memories of many battles fade; those of Rossbach and Leuthen became brighter. Their importance can hardly be overemphasized, for they have dominated German history. They were the rocks on which German pride and sense of superiority were built.

A German historian, writing in 1942 in the middle of Hitler's war, claimed that Leuthen was 'the model and ideal of all future battles of annihilation'.[4] He omitted to say that Frederick was

4 When Hitler planned his last great assault, the Battle of the Bulge, he said to some of his generals, 'History will repeat itself . . . the Ardennes will be my Rossbach and Leuthen.'

inspired by Cannae, but there is much truth in what he says, for all the architects of Prussian and German might who followed Frederick acknowledged that they were building on the foundations he had laid – especially the martial foundations.

Cavalry formations and tactics of most armies were based on those evolved by Seydlitz and Ziethen, and many other armies copied parts of the Prussian military system, but the Prussians, Germans, Bavarians, and Austrians, made most use of Frederician examples.

The near-obsession for a great weight of artillery which infected German generals from the time of Frederick until the war of 1939–45 is directly attributable to Frederick's use of it. So is Moltke's passion, a century later, for mobility. A successful man always has his imitators, and Frederick was *very* successful.

Thirteen

War in Three Continents

*Clive, Wolfe, and Washington; Prussian Influence on the
American Army; The 'New Era' at Valmy*

In the year that Frederick won Leuthen and Rossbach the
English clerk-turned-soldier Robert Clive won the battle of
Plassey, which, though little more than a skirmish in extent,
produced, in Fuller's view, a 'world change in its way unparalleled
since Alexander overthrew Darius at Arbela'.

Fuller was echoing Malleson, who said, in *Lord Clive*, 'There
never was a battle in which the consequences were so vast, so
immediate and so permanent. . . . The work of Clive was, all
things considered, as great as that of Alexander.' Politically this is
true, as Clive himself realized at the time: 'It is scarcely hyperbole
to say that tomorrow the whole Moghul empire is in our power.'

Clive was a capable general. His conceptions were as brilliant as
those of Cromwell, his plans as masterly as those of Marlborough,
his execution was as effective as that of his contemporary
Frederick, and his courage and resolution were as indomitable as
those of Charles XII, all of whom, as a student, he knew much
about. Clive had not been trained as a soldier, which perhaps
explains why, at that time, he was so successful. His mind was
stultified by military conventions, and he was free to act on
inspiration which, I feel, was fired by his military reading.

His compatriot-contemporary James Wolfe was, in contrast, an
ardent and highly educated soldier, aged only thirty-two when
given his momentous independent campaign. His background is
important, too, for his father had fought under Marlborough.
James himself had fought with distinction at Dettingen, 1743,

Lauffeld, 1747, and during the Forty-five Rebellion was present at Falkirk and Culloden.

Wolfe had studied war and battle; he knew that discipline was a weapon. His orders to his battalion, the 20th Foot, which he commanded at Canterbury in 1755, made this obvious:

> The battalion is not to halloo or cry out upon any account whatever . . . till they are ordered to charge with their bayonets. . . . There is no necessity for firing very fast; a cool, well-levelled fire, with pieces carefully loaded is much more destructive and formidable than the quickest fire in confusion. . . . When the enemy's column is within about twenty yards, the men must fire with good aim.

This type of preparation, together with the training of his officers – no British commander in the field ever had finer officers than did Wolfe – made him victorious.

His General Orders issued between May 16 and September 12, 1759 – that is, during the Quebec expedition – show the Cromwellian effort he took to form his small army into as perfect an instrument of war as possible in the time available. There is much of Cromwell in the phrasing of the orders and in their content. The best qualities in the fighting man were 'vigilance and caution'. Plundering was strictly forbidden, as was swearing. He insisted on a high standard of discipline and behaviour and camp cleanliness.

> No churches, houses or buildings of any kind are to be burned or destroyed without orders . . . peasants who yet remain in their habitations, their women and children are to be treated with humanity; if any violence is offered to a woman, the offender shall be punished with death.

But he hated Indians – 'scalping is forbidden except when the enemy are Indians or Canads dressed like Indians'.

Although he was capable of threatening soldiers with death as punishment he disliked flogging and on occasions used ridicule as a punishment, such as making a defaulter stand at the latrine with a woman's cap on his head.

Wolfe had intelligence enough to learn from others. His

unconventional tactics clearly show that he had studied General Braddock's disastrous defeat in ambush in 1755. He had apparently also studied the elastic system devised by Brigadier-General Henry Bouquet, a noted English tactician.

However, this system, which, briefly, enabled a force to move over rough, broken, and forested ground with ability to change direction quickly and fight to front or rear or either flank, was not Bouquet's invention; Eugène had experimented with it in Germany.

After a battle of wits with his adversary Montcalm, Wolfe opened a campaign of 'frightfulness', by bombarding Quebec, cutting off supplies, and laying waste to the country by burning and wrecking. It is so easy to forget, when we complain of 'frightfulness' by our enemies in our own age, that all nations, including our own, have been guilty of it at some time or another. A priest and twenty men who formed the garrison at St Joachim were scalped.

Wolfe's eventual attack, made with the help of the Royal Navy, was as complete in surprise as any in history. His troops scaled the river heights to reach the Plains of Abraham, where they won their famous victory against the French.

Fortescue was to write in *The History of the British Army*: 'With one deafening crash the most perfect volley ever fired on battlefield burst forth as if from a single monstrous weapon, from end to end of the British line.' The British reloaded, stepped forward, and fired again, and did this for about eight minutes, by which time the battle had been decided and was practically over, although it could be said that the mental and moral dislocation of the French had contributed as much to their defeat as had British force of arms.

Wolfe's contribution to the leadership was important, for his training and his tactics reaffirmed the need for steadiness for which British troops were fast becoming noted. About half a century later Sir John Moore adopted Wolfe's system as the basis for training his remarkable Light Division. Also, Wolfe, with his naval colleagues, showed that amphibious and combined operations, intelligently and co-operatively handled, could produce spectacular results.[1]

1 Admiral of the Fleet Lord Keyes wrote in 1943, in his *Amphibious Warfare and Combined Operations*: 'The lessons of history are invaluable and the records of scores of amphibious operations . . . are available from which to gain inspiration and guidance.' Lord Keyes showed that much could be learned from Wolfe's campaign.

George Washington, though he proved himself a competent general and a great leader of men, brought nothing new to war, but he and his Americans did show that tactics had to be adapted to the terrain and vegetation, a lesson the British were tardy to absorb. Again, it was Sir John Moore who benefited most from a study of the American campaigns. The finest light infantry of the day were the 500 riflemen who served under Colonel Daniel Morgan. Mostly Pennsylvanians of Scottish-Irish stock – for some reason they were called 'Morgan's Virginians' – they marched extremely light, refused all wheeled transport, and in one period of three weeks covered 600 miles. Moore had these outstanding light infantrymen in mind when he trained his own light infantry.

The American War of Independence was a combat of irregular rather than of parade movements, and in this it broke away from European tradition. Shooting to kill and deliberate trickery and deception were quite contrary to the rules of eighteenth-century warfare, although they were commonplace facets of Indian warfare. The Americans pretended to surrender and then continued fighting; they swore allegiance one day and attacked the next; to the disgust and exasperation of the Redcoats, they fired from hiding-places and killed British soldiers even in the act of drinking from rivers. Washington himself on one occasion ordered some of his troops who wore red coats to sew on to them the buttons of an English regiment, pass through the lines, and kidnap General Clinton. From this war forward all the so-called rules of war – the moral rules – became absurd, although nations kept on making them.

Actually, despite the initial success of militiamen at Concord and Bunker Hill and the obvious supremacy of initiative over pattern, of irregular warfare over the conventional, Washington was sure, as early as September 1776, that the militia was inadequate and possibly even harmful. He began a struggle with Congress for a semi-regular army enlisted for the duration of the war. However, the American belief in the invincibility of militiamen persisted for many years. Even generals who knew better than this had to be careful how they expressed themselves. 'The Americans possess as much natural bravery as any people on earth,' wrote General Nathanael Greene cautiously in 1776, before daring to add, 'but habit must form a soldier.'

If no general owes anything in particular to Washington,

indirectly Washington owes much to Frederick the Great. Indeed, the United States Army from 1778 was founded on Frederician principles – a fact which American historians seem to ignore. When Washington took his army to Valley Forge for the winter of 1777–8 he was joined by Baron von Steuben, who had served on Frederick's personal staff during the Seven Years War. As he was a remarkably able and perceptive administrator Washington appointed him Inspector-General, and von Steuben went to work with a will to organize, discipline, and train all branches of the fledgling army. Imbued with Prussian thoroughness, trained by Frederick, fired by enthusiasm, von Steuben was largely responsible for turning the Americans into a real army, European leadership had crossed the Atlantic, and Frederick the Great helped to drive the British from America.

Steuben, although commissioned at fourteen, passed through every rank from private, mainly so that he could learn, and learn to teach, the manual of exercise. He demonstrated at Valley Forge the manual of exercise he wanted to introduce into the American Army, and he made the officers undergo the gymnastics of the Prussian cadet so that they could instruct their men. But Steuben was far too intelligent to suppose that Prussian discipline could be transplanted on to these soldiers, and he cut the Frederician maximum to a minimum.

He wrote the first standard set of regulations for the American Army. The prime object of the captain was, he said, to 'gain the love of his men by treating them with every possible kindness and humanity'. This was certainly not Prussian teaching of the seventeen-seventies, but it was nevertheless a typical Prussian approach to get the most out of the men. Some parts of the Prussian military doctrine Steuben forcibly impressed upon the Americans. In the interests of economy of men the Prussian code forbade use of soldiers as officers' servants, a habit which had rapidly developed in the American Army. Steuben wiped it out and had the soldier-servants returned to their military duties.

Oddly enough, the Americans had an overweight of supply organization. Steuben said that at Valley Forge he found more quartermasters and commissaries than in all the armies of Europe together.[2] Indirectly Steuben was helped by many foreigners who had

2 History would repeat itself in the twentieth century!

served in Continental armies. Their influence cannot be calculated, but it must have been significant, despite the proud American assertion that this was a national war.

Neither in America nor in Europe were the chief military lessons learned or heeded. In 1785, when the young Gneisenau returned from America to Prussia, Frederick posted him to one of the worst battalions of infantry, commenting that the people returning from America 'think a great deal of themselves and of their knowledge of war, and they must learn war all over again in Europe.' But Gneisenau, whose link in leadership is for ever secure, had learned a lot in America, and later he had a chance to apply it. The conservatism of European officers is psychologically understandable, but that of the Americans is puzzling. They convinced themselves that the militia had really won the war, that Washington had been misguided in employing Steuben, and that a standing army was unnecessary.

This is not to say that the American military system was Prussianistic; on the contrary, many of its details were in absolute contrast with all Continental and even with the British system. The Americans saw the army as an agency of civil power, to be organized and disciplined with that purpose in view, and not as an end in itself.

From the military, not the political, view-point a much more important battle than any fought in America was the Cannonade of Valmy in September 1792, which distinctly marked the beginning of a new form of warfare. Goethe, who was present on the Prussian side, said to his comrades as he left the field. 'From today and at this spot there begins a new era and you can say you were present.' He meant that Valmy was the symbol of the beginning of unlimited war, of total war.

At Valmy the Prussian war machine was held up for the first time. Germany has always played down this unusual battle and did not accept it as a reverse, but Valmy was a Prussian defeat, and no amount of German juggling with facts can disguise the reverse – though it was a defeat of Prussian leadership rather than of Prussian troops. Yet the Prussians were commanded by the Duke of Brunswick, a nephew of Frederick the Great and regarded everywhere as the greatest soldier in Europe. His rival in the field was General Charles Dumouriez, a political and military leader lifted to high rank by the Revolution – but a capable commander nevertheless.

Brunswick's reputation was founded largely on his successful campaign in Holland in 1787, regarded as an example of perfect generalship. This was true enough, for the Dutch had acted as Brunswick expected them to behave, and, having the typical, methodical Prussian mind, he had been able to counter all their moves. But Brunswick was handicapped by his monarch, Frederick William, who thought of himself as another Frederick the Great – without the slightest justification. There was no unity between Brunswick and the King, except that Brunswick usually dutifully deferred to his monarch.

The Prussian plan was to invade Lorraine with three armies, with a total force made up of Prussians, Hessians, Austrians, and French emigrés, a total number of about 80,000. Brunswick had some initial victories, including the taking of Verdun, after which he planned to take Sedan and go into winter-quarters and so establish himself for the following spring.

But the King, the leading emigrés, and several of Brunswick's own officers opposed the plan. They pointed out that the French men confronting them were not a normal army but an undisciplined, revolutionary rabble' who could not possibly stand up to the superior discipline of the Prussian Army. During the next few days the Prussians moved slowly and Brunswick acted ineptly and missed two chances to destroy large parts of the French Army. Dumouriez was acting with more skill and speed. Finally the Prussian king countermanded an order of Brunswick's that might have saved the day and set in train the inevitable fiasco.

Incredibly the Prussians, without making a reconnaissance, without sending forward a single officer, and without any plan for battle, moved towards the known French positions, where the great French soldier Kellermann was one of the senior commanders. Through no brilliance on the part of the Prussians the French were caught unprepared and forced on the defensive, but Dumouriez had no intention of abandoning the offensive altogether and ordered two audacious attacks on the Prussians – one on their rear and the other on their baggage-train.

For some reason the Prussians expected to find the French in precipitate retreat, but about noon as the morning fog cleared they saw them drawn up in line of battle. Kellermann, posted at a commanding point near a windmill, raised his hat, adorned with a tricolour plume, and his sword and shouted, '*Vive la nation! Vive la France!*' And the men, taking up the cry, replied, '*Vive notre general!*'

The French had 52,000 men in the vicinity that day, but only 36,000 were present at Valmy. The Prussians had 34,000. At this point the 58 guns of the Prussian artillery, commanded by the renowned General Tempelhoff, were in position, or hurriedly getting into position, to face Kellermann's 40 guns, under General d'Aboville, on Valmy Ridge. The distance between them was about 1,350 yards.

French artillery was the best in Europe, largely because of the work of Lieutenant-General de Gribeauval, who had split artillery into four distinct sections – field artillery, siege artillery, fortress artillery, and coastal artillery, every detail being worked out with great skill for each arm of artillery. Gribeauval's system remained in force from 1765 until 1828 and was partly responsible for French successes.

Goethe wrote: 'Now commenced the cannonade of which so much has been spoken, but the violence of which at the time it is impossible to describe. . . . The whole battlefield trembled.' It probably did, for each side fired more than 20,000 shot. But 1,350 yards was a long range for cannon of 1792, and as the ground was sodden clay much of the shot buried itself.

Brunswick ordered an attack on the Valmy position, but the moment the Prussian infantry advanced Kellermann's artillery smashed their lines, and Brunswick stopped the advance before it had gone 200 paces.

At 2 p.m. a Prussian shell blew up three ammunition wagons behind Kellermann and both sides stopped firing. Two French regiments broke, but Kellermann rallied them. The Prussians again considered storming the ridge, but the French artillery came into play again. Brunswick was impressed by the steadiness of the French infantry and noticed that the French cavalrymen stood to their horses. He well knew that once a Prussian infantry attack was under way the French cavalry would charge. He pondered the problem, then called a council of war at which, for the first time in months, he acted as a real commander-in-chief and actually made a decision. He called off the battle.

A Prussian general, Massenbach, wrote, 'You will see how these little cocks will raise themselves on their spurs. We have lost more than a battle. The 20th of September has changed the course of history. It is the most important day of the century.'

The French under Dumouriez and Kellermann had repulsed the most formidable army in Europe and had discredited the most famous commander. Brunswick never admitted it publicly, but the French generals and their men, throughout the campaign, had been superior to him and to his slow-moving, slow-thinking, deliberate troops.

Less than a year after the cannonade the French National Convention passed a law which was, in effect, a declaration of total war.

The young men shall fight . . . the married men shall forge weapons and transport supplies; the women will make tents and clothes and will serve in the hospitals; the children will make old linen into lint. The old men will have themselves carried into the public squares and rouse the courage of the fighting men, to preach hatred against kings and the unity of the republic. . . . The public buildings shall be turned into barracks, the public squares into munition factories. . . . All firearms of suitable calibre shall be turned over to the troops . . . The interior shall be policed with shotguns and cold steel. All saddle-horses shall be seized for the cavalry; all draft-horses not employed in cultivation will draw the artillery and supply-wagons.

On August 29 1793, six days after the publication of this significant document, one of Massenbach's 'little cocks' found himself with the opportunity to raise himself on his spurs. On this day the French besieged Toulon, held by the British, and in command of the artillery was Napoleon Bonaparte.

FOURTEEN

NAPOLEON, PRODUCT OF HISTORY

Twenty-one of twenty-five military writers I regard as being qualified to express an opinion on the subject nominate Napoleon as one of the really great captains. 'One would have to go back to Hannibal or even to Alexander to find his equal [among his precursors]', says Cyril Falls in *The Art of War*. 'Among the world's great autocrats and conquerors Napoleon has but two compeers – Alexander the Great and Augustus[1] . . . as a strategist he has never been excelled . . . as a tactician he possessed a wonderful eye.' – Fuller in *Decisive Battles of the Western World*. The German Colonel-General Ludwig Beck, though not an historian, saw him as 'The most colossal military genius of all time.'

But the other four bypass him. Wavell, for instance, says, in *Soldiers and Soldiering*, 'I cannot rate him as high as Marlborough or certain others . . . an indifferent tactician . . . his handling of cavalry and infantry on the battlefield was often clumsy and wasteful.'

I admire Wavell as a general and as a man, but his estimation of Napoleon shows his defects as an historical military analyst.

However, he admired Napoleon, for elsewhere he wrote:

When you *study* military history get at the flesh and blood of it, not the skeleton. . . . If you can discover how a young unknown man inspired a ragged, mutinous, half-starved army and made it fight, how he gave it the energy and momentum to march and fight as it did, how he dominated and controlled

1 Augustus Caesar Octavian – first Roman Emperor.

generals older and more experienced than himself, then you will have learnt something.

I have myself criticized Napoleon indirectly,[2] but he must be regarded as having no betters and few equals.

Napoleon is the linch-pin in my study of the chain of command, for among generals he was one of the keenest, most intelligent students of military history, making use of everything valuable and practicable that had happened in antiquity and in modern times. And those who came after him benefited from everything that Napoleon modified, amended, or improved upon. He learned too from the mistakes of his precursors, although not all of his successors learned from *his* mistakes.

Napoleon did not initiate the ideas of his own military age; their initiation was the work of Marshal de Saxe, Guibert, Pierre de Bourcet, and others. Saxe, a military genius with wide experience, summed up his philosophy of arms in his *Mes Rêveries* – somewhat misnamed, as it was really an outstanding analysis of war systems and war psychology. Few commanders have acknowledged any debt to Saxe's book, and Napoleon even spoke disparagingly of it – which shows that he had at least read it. But few men are big enough to admit that an idea which they have proved successful might have been another man's brainchild, and this applies as much to soldiers as to fashion-designers.

Saxe's book is important, for it clearly shows the interconnection of old and new ideas and looks ahead to 'revolutionary' innovations. Knowing that the Greeks and Romans had invented military music to make troops march in harmony and not merely to lull them, Saxe wanted to apply music to induce men to forget the hardships of long marches.

He urged the use of light infantry in conjunction with the regular infantry. The light soldiers would be placed about 200 paces in front of the regiments to disturb the enemy, harass him, and conceal the manoeuvres of the regiments. He proposed that

2 'In fact Napoleon brought nothing new to war. What he did was to improve on everything that had gone before . . . with much more skill than his predecessors.' (*The Face of War*, Abelard Schuman.)

every infantryman should carry a breech-loading fusil – although it had not been then invented – and he wanted the men to fire at will as a target presented itself because he felt that firing at command cramped the natural style of aiming and shooting. This was sheer heresy to orthodox officers.

Saxe further urged physical-fitness training, in which jumping and running would be prime activities. And, more heresy, he wanted the soldier's hair cut short, for comfort, cleanliness, and further efficiency. This was a sane idea, but other proposals were not so reasonable. He wanted marriages to last only five years so that more soldiers could be produced; boys of any union would be put into a military school. In this he was resurrecting the Janissary principle and encouraging Nazi eugenic ideas of the future.

In his famous work *Essai General de tactique* Guibert revealed a mind profound enough to analyse the military weaknesses of his time. He wrote:

> Suppose there were to spring up in Europe a vigorous people, possessed of genius, power and a favourable form of government; a people who combined with the virtues of austerity and a national soldiery a fixed plan of aggrandizement who never lost sight of this system; who, knowing how to wage war at small cost and subsist by its victories, could not be reduced by financial considerations to laying down its arms. We should see this people subjugate its neighbours and overthrow our feeble constitutions as the north wind bends the slender reeds.

This concept of a nation in arms – of a return to Spartanism, in effect – which Guibert formulated in 1781, with a total disregard for the rights of individuals, depended for its accomplishment on speed and elasticity, and he evolved details to bring these qualities about. Divisions should practise forced marches, passage of rivers, forming column from line and line from column, with speed and simplicity. Infantry should fight three deep, as that of Frederick had fought against armies which used a six-rank formation.

An assault in column was absurd and ineffective, Guibert said, for depth gave no weight to attack. Horses should not be galloped for the entire distance of a charge; the first 200 yards of a 600-

yard charge should be covered at a slow trot, the second 200 at a fast trot, and the climatic 200 at the gallop. He ranked cavalry as a secondary arm, for exploitation of an infantry victory, for shielding a retreat. All this Napoleon imbibed. And, we may suppose, Hitler, too, lapped up Guibert's philosophy of war even if he was not specially interested in his tactics. *'We should see this people subjugate its neighbours. . . .'*

Guibert was an even more ardent advocate than Saxe of gymnastics. Swimming, running, and climbing should take up much of a soldier's training, while manual exercises and military evolutions should be cut down. Guibert had a twofold purpose in advocating gymnastics: they would show the soldier what sort of accidents and conditions might occur in war, and they would make him more fit and supple and enable him to take a quicker step – 120 paces a minute against the customary 70. Finally introduced into the French Army, this rapid pace ennabled the French to outmarch their enemies.

Guibert, too, demanded individual and independent firing, musketry practice against war targets, concentrating effective fire against a given point. Noise in itself was not deadly, he pointed out, though many officers seemed to think it was. Half a million musket-balls might be fired in a battle and would make a fearsome noise, but perhaps only 2,000 men would be hit.

Guibert reminded his contemporaries that the Romans and others had lived on and at the expense of the country in which they were fighting and quoted Cato – 'War must support war.' Supplies or the need for supplies should not command the general, he said. When, because of the nature of the country, supply-trains were necessary they should all be entirely militarized and should not be planned or controlled by other Government departments or by private contractors, as so many trains were in those days.

Napoleon certainly learned from Guibert. By comparison the baggage-train of a French army in 1806 amounted to only one-eighth or one-tenth of that dragged behind them by an equal body of Prussian infantry.

Napoleon most probably studied the work of Pierre de Bourcet, a staff officer who served during the War of the Austrian Succession and the Seven Years War and later wrote a textbook about mountain warfare. Napoleon's own tactics in mountainous country seem to have been strongly based on de Boucet's principles, while some of his many maxims echo points made by the staff officer.

This is not to say that Napoleon was a mere military plagiarist. He campaigned and fought on new principles, but, as with all the other innovators, he made use of conditions which he himself had not brought about. Napoleon was partly the product of his times; for his early days as an officer were passed in the turmoil of revolution, and he found this atmosphere refreshing. He owed much of his attitude to war to the Baron du Theil, commandant of the Artillery School at Auxonne, at which Napoleon served as a twenty-year-old gunnery officer. Commandant du Theil encouraged Napoleon to study the entire art of war, and among the works he studied was a work on artillery tactics by the commandant's younger brother.

As Napoleon did not initiate the striking changes of his era, so he did not create the army which was to put them into practice. The Revolution had forged this army, and the passions inflamed by the Revolution had inspired the men who filled its ranks. The changes wrought by the Revolution are vividly illustrated by the 'de-generalling' of the Army.

On the eve of the French Revolution the French Army was grossly over-officered. It had no fewer than 1,171 generals against only 80 in the Prussian Army, which was slightly larger than the French. The Austrians had 350 in an army of roughly the same size. By January 1st, 1791, the Revolution's radical cleansing had reduced the number of French generals to 34 among a total of 9,406 officers. The law of February 1780 had put an end to purchasing of commissions; everybody had to start at the bottom.

The Revolutionary armies put to death, generally by order, whatever chivalrous notions still remained alive. Carnot was largely responsible for this, just as he was largely responsible for Napoleon's first major appointment. The spirit which permeated down from above infected the ordinary soldiers with martial ruthlessness, with a truly professional zeal for use of arms, as distinct from pseudo-professional zeal shown by the regular soldiers of other armies. These French soldiers, like the irregulars of the American armies of the War of Independence, shot to kill. To make war loss more permanent French decrees of September

1792 and May 1793 banned the ransoming of prisoners – another nail in the coffin of gentlemanly war. All this was, in a way, a throw-back to barbarism – but it was disciplined, methodical barbarism based on a national political obsession. Under Napoleon the whole system became Caesarian and militaristic.

Inheriting an already dashing army, Napoleon moulded it into a magnificent striking force. The infantry was good, but he bettered it by improving its discipline. The artillery was good, but there was not enough of it, and it was roped to the infantry. Napoleon enlarged this arm and made it independent. The cavalry was good, but tactics up till now had confined its movements and made it, too, closely dependent on the infantry. Napoleon enabled it to reconnoitre, harass, and pursue.

Millions of words have been written in an attempt to explain the 'mystery' of Napoleon and the 'secrets' of his success. The word 'genius' simply is not adequate, no matter whether we give it a practical or a poetic definition. I see neither mystery nor secrets. Napoleon's actions and writings show clearly that he had a passionate sensitiveness for war – as an adventure, as an intellectual exercise, as a vehicle for application of lessons from the past, and as a means to an end. This passion gave him an intense ambition to be the greatest soldier ever, which meant that he had to study other great commanders to find out their 'secrets', to which he was acutely sensitive.

While conceding that Napoleon transformed war it would be difficult to overestimate his debt to the historical literature of arms. Napoleon was more than an avid reader of this literature; he was a firm believer in the value of study of military history. When about to take over command of the French armies in Italy in 1796 he sent for a history of the 1745 campaign of Marshal de Maillebois in the mountains in which he himself was to fight. The parcel of books was lost, but Napoleon obtained others.[3]

3 The first parcel was found aboard a captured ship and was sent to Nelson.

Napoleon, when First Consul, prepared a pamphlet entitled *Parallel between Caesar, Cromwell, Monk[4] and Bonaparte* and flew it as a kite to see which way the wind was blowing. The political significance of this act is immaterial to my analysis, but here is further prrof that he had studied these commanders.

Napoleon certainly studied the great soldiers of antiquity – such as Alexander, Caesar, Hannibal, and Scipio and urged other ambitious commanders[5] to do the same, and though I can find no documentary proof of it I think it extremely likely that he had studied Miltiades, Arminius, and England's Edward III. He was closely conversant with the tactics and methods of Condé, Gustavus, Turenne, Vendôme, Eugène, and Marlborough. His capacious, retentive, and probing mind was pondering stratagems and possible plans long before the immediate need for them arose.

He himself said:

> All great captains have done their great deeds by conforming to the rules and natural principles of their art, and by the soundness of their plans, and the proportioned connection maintained between their means and the results they expect, between their efforts and the obstacles to be overcome. They have only succeeded by conforming to the rules, whatever might have been the boldness of their designs and the extent of their success. It is on this ground alone that they are our models and it is only imitating them that we can hope to rival

4 General George Monk, Duke of Albemarle (1608–70). Napoleon's high opinion of Monk is significant, for Monk used the power of the Army as a means of awing the English Parliament, and the plea of duty owing to Parliament as a means of controlling his army.

5 The Archduke Charles of Austria said, 'A man does not become a great commander . . . without a passion for the study of war.' Also: 'Success is only obtained by simultaneous efforts, energetic resolution and great swiftness of execution.' Charles came very near to defeating Napoleon at the bloody battle of Aspern-Essling in May 1809; Marshal Lannes was killed in this battle. Liddell Hart calls Aspern-Essling 'Napoleon's first serious defeat', but I feel that it was more of a drawn battle, despite the Austrians' numerical superiority.

them. . . . If I always appear ready to meet any emergency it is because I have long meditated on the possibilities. It is no sudden inspiration that tells me what to do; it is study and meditation.

In short, there were times when Napoleon had long-dead commanders at his elbow.

For all of Napoleon's hundreds of maxims there is an actual object-lesson. Take, for instance, the maxim usually numbered 17:

> In a war of marching and manoeuvring, to avoid battle against superior forces, it is necessary to entrench every night and to occupy always a good position of defence. The position which nature usually furnishes cannot shelter an army against superior forces without the help of art.

Napoleon could have pointed to the campaign of the Duke of Berwick against the Portuguese in 1706 – and probably he did. The Duke, with a French and Spanish army, covered almost all of Spain. He commenced the campaign at Badajoz, and after having manoeuvred through the two Castiles, ended it in the kingdom of Valencia and Murcia. Berwick's army made 85 camps and was not once surprised. The entire campaign was fought without a general action, but it cost the enemy 10,000 men.

And Maxim 26:

> It is acting against the truest principles to allow separate action to two divisions which have no communication with each other, in face of an army centralized and with easy internal communication. [Not to be confused with the dictum of 'March separately, strike together', discussed elsewhere.]

The Austrians lost the battle of Hohenlinden in 1800 by neglect of this principle. Their army, under Archduke John, was divided into four columns and marched into an immense forest in order to join on the plain of Danzig, where they were supposed to surprise and attack the French. But these divisions, which had no intercommunication, were compelled to engage singly the French, under Moreau, who had concentrated his forces. He caught the

Austrians in the forest, attacked them on flank and rear, and devastated them, killing 7,000, capturing 11,000, and taking cannons and all the baggage. The whole action was reminiscent of the Teutoburger Wald.

Neglect or ignorance of this maxim was one major reason for the defeat of the German armies on the Russian front in 1941–4. Too many separate actions were fought against an enemy with internal communications.

Napoleon was an attacking general – 'I think, like Frederick, that one must always be the first to attack' – but he fully appreciated the importance of trenches. They were, he said, 'never injurious, always useful, often indispensable'.[6] He had many precepts to guide him. In 52 BC at the siege of Alesia (Mt Auxois), it has been calculated, Caesar's troops dug out 2,000,000 cubic metres of earth from their trenchworks. The Romans of Caesar's day owed as much to their entrenched camps as to their legions, for their camps were practically unattackable. Napoleon must have known, too, that the Emperor Charles V used trenches extensively in the wars of the sixteenth century and that by means of them he successfully opposed an army twice as large as his own. In Marlborough's campaigns both sides regularly dug themselves in. Probably the most notable instance of trench warfare in the eighteenth century was in 1761 when Frederick made his stand at Bunzelwitz in Upper Silesia. With everything going wrong, with not more than 50,000 men under his command, and menaced by 130,000 Austrians and Russians, Frederick from behind his trenches held them off until shortage of supplies forced them to retire.

Some of Napoleon's maxims merely echo his precursors, as, for instance, 'Secure yourself all possible chances of success when you decide to deliver an important engagement.' Fifty years earlier Marshal Saxe had said, 'War should be made so as to leave nothing to chance.'

The quickness of Napoleon's tactical eye, as extolled by Fuller, is well shown in the taking of the Fort of Bard, which stopped the

6 But as early as 1793 he had written, 'It is an axiom in strategy that he who remains behind his entrenchments is beaten; experience and theory are at one on this point.

French Army on May 20 1800, after it had surmounted all the obstacles offered by the St Bernard Pass. Lannes made desperate attempts to carry the fort by assault, but was repulsed with heavy loss. Napoleon climbed a rocky precipice on one of the mountains forming the pass controlled by the fort and instantly saw the possibility of capturing the place. That night he had a road covered with mattresses and manure, and in extreme silence had his guns carried over it in ropes and straps, to a point where they could dominate the enemy fort. In single file cavalry and infantry followed the path marked out by Napoleon and where no horse had ever climbed before. The fort was easily taken.

Frederick had said, 'In war the skin of a fox is sometimes as necessary as that of a lion, for cunning may succeed when force fails.' This principle was hardly profound or new – it was at least as old as Gideon – but Napoleon followed it many times.

In desperate circumstances at Arcola in 1796 Napoleon sent a small cavalry detachment with trumpeters behind the Austrian lines to sound the charge and generlaly make a commotion to deceive the Austrians into thinking that they were surrounded; the ruse worked and the usually steady Austrians fled in panic.

Had he studied the tactics of the ancient Gideon? Did he know that Bahram of Persia had stampeded his opponent's cavalry during a night attack by tying bags full of rattling stones around the necks of his horses? Anyway, I feel reasonably sure that he did indeed know of the two almost bloodless victories – at Carcemish and outside Constantinople – won by Belisarius with a mixture of bluff and daring which persuaded his opponents he was much stronger than he actually was.

Napoleon never advanced towards any 'natural position' held by an enemy, but sought for his own natural position – often across an enemy's rear. This policy greatly influenced Clauswitz.

It was commonplace for a commander to rouse the fervour of his troops by a stirring speech, especially before a battle, and many such speeches have come down to us.[7] But few commanders

---

[7] Condé once inspired his troops before battle without saying a word. Aflame with ardour and unattended, he rode the length of his lines, looking into the eyes of almost every man. It must have been one of the most impressive pre-combat acts by a general.

have had Napoleon's magnetic personality with which to infuse their words with fire. At the age of twenty-seven, when he took over the Army of Italy on March 27 1796, Napoleon supposedly made a famous proclamation:[8]

> Soldiers! You are famished and nearly naked. The Government owes you much but it can do nothing for you. Your patience, your courage have done you honour, but can give you no glory, no advantage. I will lead you into the most fertile plains in the world. There you will find great towns, rich provinces. There you will find glory, honour and riches. Soldiers of Italy, will you be wanting in courage?

Victories followed in rapid succession, among them Montenotte, Mondovi, Millesimo, Dego, Lodi, Arcola, Rivoli, Mantua.

Napoleon carried martial public relations to a height not again reached for another century and a quarter. He made a point of remembering – or seeming to remember – old veterans who had fought in earlier battles; he gave numerous 'pep' talks and issued many proclamations; he displayed interest in the welfare and comfort of his soldiers, and stories of his concern circulated continuously among his troops.

But again, propaganda was not Napoleon's idea. As early as 1792 General Massenbach, who had warned about the Revolution's 'young cocks', complained of this 'new French method of attack, not with sword and cannon, but with far more dangerous weapons, by which they tried to inspire the common soldier with Republican sentiments', Massenbach conveniently ignored Frederick's own blatant propaganda campaigns among communities he had captured.[9]

Some French propaganda tactics were enterprising. Groups of unarmed French soldiers would appear at Prussian or Austrian

8 Supposedly, because I can find no reference to this speech in contemporary accounts of the campaign. It appears that Napoleon first dictated it, from memory, while on St Helena. No doubt he made a proclamation, but the St Helena version could be a polished one.
9 Propaganda had figured in the Civil War in England, when religious and democratic ideas were brought into the service of Cromwell's Army.

outposts, talk in a friendly way about liberty and equality, and leave packages of propaganda leaflets with their 'friends'. These activities completely baffled the Prussians and Austrians, for such passionate belief by common soldiers in political principles was incomprehensible.

Mishaps for which Napoleon was personally responsible he attributed to dead men or others not in a position to defend themselves.

When he took Arcola – and he was in personal danger here – he made sure that paintings showed him on the bridge, tricolour in hand, although in fact he had been in muddy water at the foot of the dyke. His own account of his being first across the bridge was so successfully implanted that it has been perpetuated by practically every historian since the event.

The American historian Alfred Vagts appears to condemn Napoleon for this deception, but I think it justifiable. The personality and popular image of the commander was vital in those days – more so than it is today. It would never have done for Napoleon to be shown up to his waist in dirty water. He needed to create a hero-image to inspire his army further, and this he did. The 'first across the bridge' story was merely good tactics; the tricolour in hand was the Gallic touch.

Napoleon's stern manner, the certainty of his commands, and the rapidity of his movements terrified the older French officers as much as they terrified the enemy. In building a new military system he had first to break down all the old rules and conventions. He promoted men from the ranks to be officers, he gave junior officers more authority and initiative, he insisted on efficiency and on officers being on duty twenty-four hours a day during a campaign.

It was from Frederick that Napoleon saw the necessity for mobility, and in 1804 he based his army on the divisional system. This was not new – French generals had been experimenting with divisions for seventy years – but under Napoleon each division became a self-contained fighting unit, as it is today.

In this year, 1804, the period of constant war started, and in the next nine years Napoleon had 50,000 volunteers and 2,400,000 draftees, in addition to the seamen and *gardes d'honneur.* Up to 1806 French losses, within the boundaries of 1793, amounted to

1,700,000 dead out of 29,000,000 inhabitants – the battle losses were far less than those due to illness – a precedent for the prodigality with which French generals, bewitched by Napoleonic legend, expended men in later wars. Decimation due to illness was everywhere great in this period of mass armies.

However, Napoleon was never deterred by losses, and considered them merely as commensurate with the magnitude of his victories.

FIFTEEN

AUSTERLITZ, A LESSON IN THE ART OF WAR

Napoleon's favourite fight – his own term – was Austerlitz, 1805. In later years he was fond of quoting Austerliz as an example of fine reconnaissance and planning, of firm decision and rapid action. It was, he said, a lesson in the art of war, a reasonable claim seeing that Austerlitz was the most sweeping and final of all his victories.

The approach march to Austerlitz really began at Boulogne, where Napoleon had made his headquarters at a small house while he prepared to invade England.

It was here that he heard that the French fleet, under Villeneuve, had turned back to Ferrol. This was the final reason of many why Napoleon could not proceed with his invasion of England. The news arrived about four in the morning. Napoleon sent for his secretary, Daru, who found him aflame with anger. He paced about the room, abusing Villeneuve for 'ineptitude and cowardice'. Then he ordered Daru to sit down and write.

Daru sat down at a desk littered with papers and maps and took down a remarkable document – the advance against Austria, which was to culminate in the triumph at Austerlitz – the second greatest tactical victory in military history. (The first was Cannae, 216 BC) Without reference to notes or to maps Napoleon gave Daru the complex details of the march and its halts, the various routes for separate corps, numbers and quantities, times and dates. In the end the entire campaign was on paper. Later Daru was to marvel at the incredible way in which everything fell into place exactly as Napoleon said it would. This is why the preliminaries to Austerlitz are as interesting as the battle itself.

In an incredibly short time he gathered his scattered army and marched to meet his foe. Carnot initiated and Napoleon developed the idea that divisions while operating separately should co-operate towards a common goal. The ability to travel light accelerated the mobility of Napoleon's armies and enabled them to move freely in forested or mountainous country. Being unable to depend on supply-trains for food and equipment gave thrust to hungry and ill-clad troops in striking at the rear of an enemy who had great supply-trains on which he depended.

Napoleonic armies marched rapidly, too. 'The strength of an army, like the quantity of motion in mechanics', Napoleon said, 'is estimated by the mass multiplied by the velocity. A swift march enhances the *moral* of the army and increases its power for victory.' On one occasion a corps under Marshal Lannes covered 65 miles in 50 hours; Bernadotte marched his men 75 miles in 69 hours.

Napoleon also said:

> The first quality of a soldier is fortitude in enduring fatigue and hardship; bravery but the second. Poverty, hardship and misery are the school of the good soldier. . . . Tents are not healthy. It is better for the soldier to sleep out, for he sleeps with his feet to the fire, which soon dries the ground on which he lies; some planks and a little straw protect him from the wind. . . . Tents give an enemy information as to your number and position.

Poverty, misery, and hardship Napoleon's soldiers got. Other armies of those days had long supply and baggage columns. Napoleon's were much shorter because his soldiers had to live off the land – which meant that they robbed the peasants whose farms they passed. Whenever it was known that an army was coming the farmers would hide everything they could and drive their stock some distance away. But Napoleon's troops were expert foragers, and they could sniff out hidden bags of apples or flour as easily as they could a pig. A large Napoleonic force passing through the country left a swathe of poverty in its wake as it seized everything eatable. Only once in a while was a farmer paid for what the Army took. In enemy countries it stole everything it could carry, eatable or not. Tents were not provided, so the men slept under whatever cover they could find – in a barn or a haystack, under a cart. If no cover was available they simply slept in the open, around a fire if the weather was cold. Often they slept through heavy rain.

Battles followed in quick succession as Napoleon marched into the heart of Europe . . . Gunzberg, Hallach, Albeck, Elchingen, Memmingen. Then, before the Austrians knew what was happening, 30,000 of them under Field-Marshal Mack were surrounded at Ulm and had to lay down their arms.

These first defeats were followed up with typical Napoleonic drive. Those corps which had escaped the disaster at Ulm were pursued and, one after the other, destroyed. The Tyrol was over-run and its strong positions were occupied by Marshal Ney. From Italy Napoleon heard of Masséna's successes against the renowned Archduke Charles, while at Dirnstein, Marshal Mortier had defeated the Russian First Army under Kutusov.

In the midst of all these victories Napoleon heard of the French defeat at Trafalgar. 'I cannot be everywhere,' he said simply. He could not altar the course of the war at sea, but he could make history on land. He marched on.

Napoleon had seven corps, under Bernadotte, Marmont, Davout, Soult, Lannes, Ney, and Augereau, with cavalry led by Murat and the Imperial Guard as a reserve. It was a magnificent force brilliantly led, well deserving its new title – the Grand Army.

The men who formed Napoleon's 'brotherhood of marshals' were an inspiring group: Murat, the dashing, brilliant cavalry leader who had led French horsemen on all the battlefields of Italy and Egypt; Lannes, glorious at the battle of Montebello; the veteran Soult, hero of Altenkirchen and of Zurich, experienced in years of war in Germany; Bernadotte, a statesman as well as a noted leader; Davout, stern and strict, his gallantry and determination unsurpassed; Ney, *le brave des braves*, who had risen from simple hussar to general of division in eleven years; Augereau, veteran of the Pyrenees, the East, Italy, the Rhine, and the Netherlands, another man who had risen from the ranks; Marmont, long a comrade of Napoleon and a brilliant artillery-man. At the time of Austerlitz, however, Marmont was still not a marshal; he received his baton in 1809. There was also Marshal Berthier, Napoleon's brilliant Chief of Staff, a wonderful administrative soldier and tactician, whose duty it was to transmit

Napoleon's orders. And we must not forget Masséna, the money-loving smuggler and military genius.

In all Napoleon had twenty-six marshals, although at the time of Austerlitz there were only eighteen, and many were on duty elsewhere. They were young, too, with an average age of about thirty-nine. Napoleon himself was only thirty-six. Berthier, aged fifty-two, was an old man in comparison with the rest. The youth of Napoleon's marshals had a lot to do with the spirit with which they conducted their campaigns and battles.

On November 13 1805, Napoleon entered Vienna, without resistance, for the enemy had gone. He then began to spread out his corps. But before any army could push northward out of Vienna the Danube had to be crossed. Napoleon's only route was across the Spitz bridge, which the Austrians held in strength. Also, the bridge was mined and would certainly be blown up at the first sign of attack.

Napoleon wanted the bridge intact, and he told Murat and Lannes so; these two swaggering Gascons promised to capture it singlehanded. How they achieved their boast makes one of the finest stories of the Napoleonic period.

They put on their most magnificent uniforms – ostrich feathers, gold-embroidered tunics, blue trousers, red morocco boots. On their breasts were their shining decorations, on their belts their diamond-hilted swords. Then together, but without escort, they cantered calmly towards the bridge.

The Austrians could not help but be aware that the strangers were men of importance, and the word soon went round that two of Napoleon's famous marshals were approaching. They crossed the bridge and asked for the commander, who happened to be Prince Auersberg, a rather old and indecisive commander.

The Prince asked why they had come.

'Haven't you heard of the armistice?' Murat asked.

'It has just been signed, and by its terms the bridge has been handed over to us,' Lannes said.

Prince Auersberg was surprised and suspicious, and an argument occurred. While Lannes and Murat kept the Austrian commander busy another adventurous French commander, Oudinot, was bringing up a party of his noted grenadiers. They were creeping towards the French end of the bridge, where they shielded sappers who uncoupled fuses from demolitions charges.

But the charges remained at the Austrian end of the bridge – and they were covered by guns. At this point Prince Auersberg decided to retire from the bridgehead. Not all his men were so gullible. A sergeant saw Oudinot's grenadiers, and, putting two and two together, he ordered his men to fire on the marshals. Lannes and Murat pretended to be amused. Murat, casually, said to Auersberg, 'Is this your famous Austrian discipline, where sergeants countermand the orders of generals?'

The Prince was stung by this and had the sergeant arrested. But an Austrian gunner, who could also see that the whole thing was a French trick, laid his gun on the marshals. Lannes promptly sat on the barrel. Oudinot ordered his grenadiers on to the bridge, an act suspicious enough to arouse even Prince Auersberg's doubts. 'Why are those men advancing?' he demanded.

'They are not advancing at all,' one of the marshals said disarmingly, 'but the weather is so cold that they are marking time to keep their feet warm.'

Auersberg had no more time to wonder about the proceedings. Oudinot ordered his men to double, and within minutes they had secured the bridgehead. It was a brilliant and audacious feat, typical of Napoleon's marshals.

Nevertheless, it was about this time that Murat, and Soult too, began to lose their nerve. Napoleon's position was certainly dangerous, for his corps were spread out along hundreds of miles. Marshal Masséna was coming up from Italy, but he was a long way off, and it was very doubtful if he could arrive before battle ensued. In fact, Masséna was finding Venetian territory too profitable in loot to want to reach the barren lands between him and Napoleon.

Napoleon pushed on towards Brunn, which he reached on November 9. At this point he had 65,000 men, and much of his army was still dispersed, for he had been forced to post some troops to keep check on Hungary and Bohemia and to garrison the captured Vienna. But only 40 miles away was a force of at least 83,000 Russians and Austrians, under the Emperor Alexander and the Emperor Francis II. Within three weeks these forces would be doubled by armies moving towards them. In addition, another 200,000 Prussians might also soon take the field. So rapid had French movements been that many soldiers had fallen out of sheer exhaustion; one battalion of the Guard had temporarily lost 400 men from this cause. A saying current in the Army was, 'The Emperor makes more use of our legs than our arms!'

But morale and the will to fight were so high that the stragglers were doing their best to catch up before the battle they knew was inevitable. At Brunn, Napoleon gave his army a week to recover its strength, recover its strays, and to repair its boots and weapons.

But Napoleon himself took no rest, and on November 21 he reconnoitred the wide, high plateau of Pratzen. It must have been a striking scene, and in its way this scouting expedition was even more important than the battle which was to follow.

First came watchful vedettes – the scouts whose duty it was to protect Napoleon and his party in front and on the flanks. Then, on a grey horse, came the short, sallow-faced Napoleon himself, dressed in a grey overcoat and wearing long riding-boots. On his head was a low, weather-stained cocked hat.

He was followed by a large group of officers, their senior rank proclaimed by the heavy lace on their plumed hats, uniforms, and saddle-cloths. Behind these officers was a strong squadron of carefully picked cavalry in dark-green dolmans with furred pelisses slung over their shoulders and huge fur caps surmounted by tall red plumes.

Napoleon rode in silence over the plateau, his alert, intense eyes missing nothing. He studied carefully the little village of Pratzen and the steep slope down to the muddy stream below, the Goldbach river.

None of his staff spoke to Napoleon, for they knew better than to interrupt him in the midst of one of his famous reconnaissances. Finally he drew rein and turned to face his staff. 'Gentlemen', he said, 'examine this ground carefully. It will be a field of battle upon which you will all have a part to play.'

So discerning was Napoleon that he had seen at once that here the battle must be fought. Every day after that he scouted the country, drew maps, and studied them closely all the time insisting that his generals also examine the terrain. Before the battle of Austerlitz commenced Napoleon accurately predicted the exact order of events, and even forecast the time of day for each incident in the series that would make up the fight.

Napoleon had lived with the theory of Austerlitz long before he ever saw the place. It could be described as a 'pivot battle'; Napoleon may well have used this term himself.

Basically it depended on the swinging of a line from some impregnable hinge at one end, while the other end, either fallen back under pressure or voluntarily retired, would progressively weaken the enemy centre. Napoleon's idea was that when the situation had developed to the point where his own line was in danger of being outflanked he would attack the enemy with an unexpected reserve. This extra weight, delivered at the critical point and time, would decide the issue. Just where he had especially hoped for success the enemy would find himself hopelessly entangled. Inevitably his strength would be further drawn towards the threatened point, his centre would be still further weakened and might even be pierced. Once broken into two sections the enemy army would be lost beyond redemption.

It was now certain that the united army of two mighty empires was close by, and that both the Russian and Austrian monarchs were prepared to trust their fortunes to trial by battle. With their generals and their soldiery they were eager to retrieve their previous misfortunes and disgraces at Napoleon's hands.

They had already beaten back the French advanced guards at Wischau, and this gave them confidence. It is fairly safe to assume that Napoleon had ordered his Guard to give ground in order to lead the enemy on. This was a favourite ruse of his. Murat fell back from Posoritz and Soult from near Austerlitz. The Russian Emperor, Alexander, convinced Francis of Austria that they should attack Napoleon before he could collect more troops.

This was precisely why Napoleon needed a little more time. Bernadotte had not come up with his corps, and Davout's corps could only be present if action was postponed.

Napoleon halted the retreating French troops on his chosen battlefield. The outlying corps of Bernadotte and Davout were recalled. By discipline and training Davout raced his corps 70 miles in 48 hours to take part in the attack on the right of the line.

Munitions, food, and ambulances were placed at chosen points, Napoleon then confidently announced that the battle would take place on December 1 or 2. He had only to wait for the enemy to come to him.

Napoleon sent Savary to present his compliments to the Emperor Alexander – and also to see as much as he could of the enemy preparations and morale. On his return Savary told Napoleon that the Russian leader was surrounded by 'a set of young coxcombs' whose every look and gesture expressed overweening confidence in themselves and contempt for their opponents.

All the reverses of the previous campaign against the French were the result, the Russians said, of unpardonable cowardice among their allies, the Austrians. The first battle would show the French how well the Russians could fight.

Later the Tsar sent a young aide-de-camp to return the compliment carried by Savary. Napoleon then stage-managed a scene of desperate haste in the French lines, so that the young officer could return to Alexander with the news that the French were in near-panic. This added even further the Russians' confidence – which was what Napoleon wanted. His one fear was that the Russians might decide against battle.

The Goldbach marked the front of the French army. This river rose across the Ormutz road, flowed through a steep-sided dell and then into Menitz Lake. At the top of its high bank was the wide Pratzen plateau, which Napoleon did not occupy. It seemed to Napoleon's staff that he had erred in giving up such useful ground to his enemy.

'I have granted the plateau to the enemy deliberately,' he told them. 'By holding it I could here check the Russians, but then I should have only an ordinary victory. By giving it up to them and refusing my right, if they dare to descend from the heights to outflank me, they will be lost. I will devour them.'

Napoleon rested his left on a rugged height which some of his veterans called 'the Santon', after a similar height in Egypt. On the crest was a little chapel whose roof had the appearance of a minaret – and the French veterans remembered minarets from Egypt.

Napoleon strengthened this height with field-works, which he armed and provisioned like a fortress. He specially chose the defenders and put the Santon under command of the able General Claparede. 'Fight till your last cartridge and, if necessary, die here to a man,' he told Claparede.

He meant exactly what he said – and he never doubted that his troops would fight to the death. No troops specially selected for such a task ever betrayed his trust.

His centre was on the right bank of the Goldbach. Here double lines of troops under Soult and Murat, Duroc and Oudinot, were concealed by the windings of the stream, by scattered clumps of wood, and by undulations of the ground.

His right was entrusted to Davout's corps, but only one division of infantry and one of dragoons had been able to come into line in time. Posted at Menitz, they held the defiles passing Menitz Lake and the two other lakes of Telnitz and Satschan. Napoleon had need of a determined general here, and Davout was that man.

In general, Napoleon's line of battle was an oblique one, with its right thrown back. Napoleon had deliberately given it the appearance of being defensive, even timed. He wanted the enemy to commit themselves to an attack on the right in an effort to cut his lines of communication and the line of retreat to Vienna. If they could be led into this trap the difficulties of the ground would check them long enough for Napoleon to send help to Davout.

At the same time, with his left impregnable and his centre ready to punch hard, Napoleon expected to be able to attack the Russo-Austrian flank and rear.

The Russians and Austrians were not stupid. They knew their centre would be weaker than elsewhere along the line, but they believed that they could cover the weakness by advancing on to the plateau and holding it. They fully believed – and this was their big mistake – that Napoleon intended to remain on the defensive. He was only pretending to be on the defensive. The Allies believed that Napoleon was worried about his communications. In fact, he hardly gave them a thought, for he knew he would not be retreating.

The right of the Russo-Austrian army, under Princes Bagration and Lichtenstein, rested on a hill near Posoritz. Their centre, under Kollowrath, occupied the village of Pratzen and the large plateau, while their left, under Doctorof and Kienmayer, stretched towards Satschan Lake and the marshes.

The village of Austerlitz was to the rear of the Russo-Austrian position. The Emperors of Russia and Austria slept here the night before the battle – and this was why Napoleon gave his victory the name of the village. It was a vanity typical of the man.

Napoleon might have been pleased with his choice of battlefield, but the people who lived in the villages through which the fight would rage were desperately unhappy. By now nearly all had abandoned their homes and shops and farms, taking whatever they could carry. They had little hope of finding their buildings intact after the armies had fought and moved away. Some would be destroyed during the battle; the soldiers would burn others in the frustration of defeat or the exuberance of victory, or perhaps simply to keep themselves warm. They would take away anything portable, useful, or valuable and probably smash anything they could not carry. 'Glorious victories' were never glorious for the people who owned the battlefield.

Napoleon's actions so puzzled the enemy's headquarters that they thought he might even be planning a retreat before action. He withdrew the mass of his forces still farther, till they were along the Goldbach river. He no longer held the plateau at all, which seemed extraordinary. It was such a natural defensive position that the Austrians and Russians actually wondered if Napoleon was losing his nerve.

Then, at a distance of about a mile, the two armies waited in bivouac, with piled arms, eating and resting around their fires – the Allies covered by clouds of Cossacks, the French by a thin line of vedettes.

The weather was cold but clear, and Napoleon, established in an old hut, could see the entire field. From here he could move brigades, battalions, and squadrons about the field like so many chess-pieces. In the afternoon he saw through his telescope Russian columns on Pratzen plateau moving from their centre to their left, concentrating opposite the front of the French position at Telnitz.

Their intentions were obvious even to a subaltern in his first action. They had convinced themselves that the French intended to act on the defensive and that they would not attack in front. Therefore, the Russians and Austrians reasoned, they had only to mass troops on the right, cut off the French from Vienna, and then destroy them.

They forgot that by moving major forces to the left they weakened their centre, and that on their right they were leaving their own line of retreat unprotected.

Napoleon was so pleased that he trembled in anticipation.

'What a shameful manoeuvre!' he said. 'They are running into the trap. They are giving themselves up! Before tomorrow evening that army will be mine.'

Napoleon had more of a sense of humour than history gives him credit for. He ordered Murat to take some cavalry towards the enemy, to move about uncertainly and hesitantly, and then to retire as if alarmed. The ruse was successful, and Napoleon, when he heard of it, chuckled.

The Emperor now issued a proclamation to his troops, offering them certain glory in the coming battle, assuring them of his personal leadership, and promising them cantonments and peace after the victory.

Napoleon did more than give orders to his subordinate commanders. He decided on a novel way of encouraging his men. He gave orders that each battalion was to be paraded and that its commanding officer was to read out to the men the plan for beating the Russians and Austrians. He did not much care if the enemy heard the plans. He assumed that if they did hear, then they would think the whole thing a trick. It certainly was a new idea, for at that time and for many years to come private soldiers were told nothing about the plans for battles in which they fought. Much later General Montgomery was to emulate Napoleon in this way.

The men settled down to their evening meal – some biscuits and stale bread and some pieces of half-cooked meat. Lucky ones had a few potatoes or the luxury of an apple. They drank wine, tea,[1] or plain water. Then the veterans went to sleep – lying in that bitterly cold weather with their feet to the fire. The younger, newer soldiers lay down as ordered, but they did not sleep.

As always, Napoleon went quickly to sleep. Before midnight he was awakened to be told of a sharp enemy attack on the right. It had been repulsed, but Napoleon mounted and rode out between the two armies to check dispositions. He rode right into a Cossack outpost and had one of the narrowest escapes of his life.

The Cossacks attacked him at once, and he would have been killed or captured only for the courage of his escort, who held off the Cossacks while the Emperor rode for safety. His horse became

1 A popular drink in French armies of the period.

bogged in the marshes, and Napoleon had to make his way by foot through his lines.

An extraordinary incident now took place. A soldier made a torch of straw to light Napoleon's way, and in the flame he appeared to the soldiers near by almost as a vision. As this night was the anniversary of the coronation, they were prepared to believe that his appearance among them was a supernatural omen.

Seldom has an army shown such spectacular devotion to its general as the French did to Napoleon that night. Napoleon, at first annoyed and then a little embarrassed, was really deeply proud of the men's spontaneous affection. 'This is the happiest night of my life,' he told his staff.

Exploiting the moment, he moved from camp-fire to camp-fire, cheering the men, thanking them for their loyalty, assuring them of victory, explaining that medical aid would come to them as quickly as possible if they were wounded.

'Promise us,' shouted a veteran grenadier, 'that you will keep yourself out of the fire.'

'I will do so,' Napoleon answered; 'I shall be with the reserve until you need me.'

The thousands of enemy who saw the blaze of light along the French front were first of all startled and then pleased and heartened, for they thought that the French were burning their shelters as a preliminary to retreat.

For the men in the ranks the coming battle might have been an exciting prospect, but it was also a grim one. That night, on the field of Austerlitz, the battle-hardened men were under no illusion about their chances of survival.

The battle would be fought at close quarters. Muskets had an accurate range of less than 100 yards, and there was no point in firing at a greater range. Many times infantry advanced to within 20 yards before firing, and as reloading took about a minute every shot had to count.

Napoleon relied heavily on individual initiative, though his troops were capable of a shoulder-to-shoulder British-style movement when necessary. Soldiers stood steady in their ranks, perhaps for hours, while enemy cannon-balls tore through the ranks. This was a stern test of discipline, both imposed and personal. On the restricted front of battle, from a few hundred yards to, rarely, three or five miles, bodies would lie in heaps about the troops still standing.

There was a good reason for these rigid tactics, for if infantry were caught out of formation the hovering cavalry would pounce and cut them to ribbons. The only real infantry defence against cavalry was steadiness. As men fell, so the survivors closed their ranks, always presenting that shoulder-to-shoulder wall of resistance, for after the cannon fire and the musket volleys there would be baynet fighting.

Often a soldier's sufferings began only when he was carried or when he staggered into the barn, house, or tent being used as a hospital. Here surgeons wielded saw and knife and probe with more enthusiasm than skill, amid a foul mess of blood, rags, and dirt.

Less than 50 per cent of wounded could expect to survive gangrene, loss of blood, or tetanus. Operations were performed without anaesthetic, hence surgical shock was severe and often fatal. The wonder of it is that any wounded man survived. Vinegar was the only antiseptic, disinfectant, and dressing for wounds. Typhus, caused by lice, killed many soldiers who had survived wounds, while dysentery and ague were common.

Soon after dawn on December 2 Napoleon had a meagre breakfast, buckled on his sword, and said cheerfully to his staff, 'Now, gentlemen, let us commence a great day.' His marshals gathered for detailed instructions. First of all, however, Napoleon outlined his basic plan. Briefly, it amounted to this:

He would wait and check the enemy's attacks on his flanks, while he made a violent attack on the Allied centre to cut their forces in two. Then he would turn an overwhelming force on their extended left and crush them into pockets among the lakes.

The Allies had a numerical superiority of 22,000, and probably they thought they had other advantages. But, in fact, Napoleon had two overriding advantages: the Allied line was completely exposed to view, while Napoleon's was hidden; the French line was more compact and uninterrupted.

In thick, cold mist the Allied attack began about eight o'clock. Napoleon listened to the thunder of artillery and the rattle of musketry and permitted the enemy to become fully committed. It was one of his maxims never to frighten off the enemy before they could engage their troops to the point of no recall. Just before the fighting began the mist broke over the field and the sun shone brilliantly through. Napoleon took the 'Sun of Austerlitz' – as he afterwards called it – as an omen of success.

As the guns opened Soult mounted to ride off to his command waiting in the ravine, where they were quite out of sight. 'Soult,' Napoleon said, 'how long will it take your men to reach the summit of the plateau?'

'Twenty minutes, sire,' Soult said.

About this time, in the centre of the line, the two enemy emperors – Alexander and Francis – were climbing the eastern side of the plateau, which was deserted and apparently open for their occupation.

'Ah! Then we can give them another quarter of an hour,' said Napoleon, looking at his watch. For another fifteen minutes the French right held while the French centre stood silent, waiting. Then Napoleon waved his arm. . . .

To the blaring music of regimental bands, divisions led by Vandamme and St Hilaire, spearheading the corps of Soult and Bernadotte, went up the Pratzen height at the double and attacked the Russians, right, centre, and left.

The Russians, still busy in their general movement to the left, were taken completely by surprise. They managed to scramble into some sort of formation, but French bayonet charges broke every line they formed, and as early as nine o'clock Napoleon commanded the plateau.

Meanwhile, Prince Lichenstein had paraded 82 squadrons of cavalry, and Bagration supported them with many infantry divisions and a strong artillery force opposite the Santon. Here Lannes and Murat fought an independent battle to Napoleon's pre-arranged plan.

Facing the Allied might, Lannes had General Caffarelli's division on his right and Suchet's division on his left. They were supported by the guns of the Santon. Two massive columns of cavalry – comprising the divisions of Kellermann (son of the victor of Valmy), Nansouty, Walther, and d'Hautpoul – were on Cafferelli's right, while some light cavalry was pushed forward to observe.

Murat gave the Allies no chance to take the initiative. To open the fight he sent in Kellermann with his light cavalry, and this brilliant general charged and put to flight the enemy vanguard.

Uhlans under the Grand Duke Constantine attacked Kellermann, who retired his weaker force through Caffarelli's infantry, whose musket fire stopped the Uhlans. Kellermann reformed and charged again. Then the battle really boiled. Murat led several charges, taking with him Kellermann, Walther, and Sébastiani, all of whom were wounded, the first two seriously.

The French 5th Chasseurs broke a Russian battalion and captured its standard, a tremendous and encouraging feat of battle in those days. To capture a standard was virtually to destroy a unit. Seeing this, a regiment of Russian dragoons dashed to the rescue. Mistaking them in the smoke for French troops, Murat ordered other French infantry to cease firing.

The Russians were able to break through the French ranks and to surround Murat himself. Splendid horseman and swordsman, Murat fought his way out of the trap to safety. At this point the Allies went on the offensive, but Murat and Lannes were not really worried. Murat ordered Nansouty to attack with his cuirassiers – big men on big horses and armed with long, heavy swords. Nansouty led his men in three deliberate charges, crushing the Russian cavalry back on their infantry, scattering the infantry itself, and taking eight guns.

These charges enabled Caffarelli's division, backed by a division sent by Bernadotte, to cut the centre of Bagration's infantry. The Frenchmen drove the larger part of the enemy towards Pratzen, while the smaller part fought on at the end of the line.

The Allied cavalry, rallying, rode in to support Bagration, who now found himself facing the bayonets of Suchet's infantry. The Austrians and Russians might have had a chance, but they were out-generalled. A brilliantly combined French movement of dragoons, cuirassiers, and infantry was too much for the enemy. A bayonet charge by Suchet's men put the finishing touch to the battle, while a series of rapid light-cavalry attacks completed the rout and drove the enemy survivors towards Austerlitz. On this part of the field alone the Russians and Austrians lost about 1,500 men killed, 8,000 prisoners, 27 cannons, and 2 standards. Gallopers took the news to Napoleon.

Napoleon's right was having a hectic time. Davout's 10,000 men – tired after a hard march to get into position – were holding 30,000 enemy led by Buxhöwden, who had assumed command of corps led by Doctorof and Kienmayer. That they did hold them was due to their own courage and to the enemy inability to deploy in the narrow passes – which was nothing more than Napoleon had foreseen.

Despite this advantage the pressure on the French troops was immense. Soldiers of lesser calibre could not have held the enemy. Napoleon, as always, was fully aware of the position, and he ordered the Imperial Guard and some grenadiers to threaten the flanks of the massive column attacking Davout. To weaken the enemy thrust further he sent two divisions of Soult's troops marching to the rear of Buxhöwden's columns.[2]

In every battle there is a crisis. Now, at one o'clock in the afternoon, Napoleon faced his crisis for Austerlitz. Near Pratzen, Russian infantry, supported by the Russian Imperial Guard, made a desperately fierce assault on the divisions led by Vandamme and St Hilaire.

Napoleon, from his position of vantage, saw the enemy masses sweep on to his own lines. The odds against the French were great. He knew his troops would hold for a time, but for how long before being swamped?

On his right he saw that the Russians were pressing Davout hard and threatening his rear. The artillery roared into such a crescendo that it seemed the Allied flanking movement on the French right must succeed. Then, heartened, he saw troops under Duroc moving to support Soult and Davout. The right flank would be safe, after all.

Back at the centre repeated attacks by the Russian Chevalier Guards and cuirassiers of the Russian guard, brilliantly led and vigorously pushed home, broke and scattered two of Vandamme's battalions. Napoleon saw one of these battalions lose its eagle standard and was bitterly disappointed. These were the men who had earlier gained such spectacular success. Now they were terrified.

In vain senior and junior officers tried to stop the panic. The mob knocked down and trampled over at least one young officer when he stood in their path. Some of the men, seeing Napoleon close by, shouted hoarsely, 'Vive l'Empereur!', but they kept on going.

2 Just as Claudius Nero had done at the Metaurus.

When his single remaining aide moved forward to try to stop them Napoleon said contemptuously, 'Let them go.' They were the only Frenchmen that day to break ranks, and later their general, Vandamme, was inconsolable at the disgrace.

Now Napoleon acted decisively. He sent General Rapp to bring up the cavalry of the Imperial Guard. Rapp brought up the Mamelukes, of which he was Colonel, the *Grenadiers-a-Cheval* under General Morland and the Chasseurs of the Guard – all picked horsemen. Then he led them against the flower of the Russian cavalry and drove them back with heavy loss. Russian horsemen fell or were captured in droves. It was one of the most bitterly contested cavalry fights in history.

Napoleon's confidence in his Guard cavalry was not misplaced, and eventually General Rapp, a strong, aggressive leader, returned to his emperor and saluted him with bloodstained sword. 'Sire,' he said, 'we have overthrown and destroyed the Russian Guard and taken their artillery.'

'I saw it,' Napoleon said. 'Gallantly done. But you are wounded.' He frowned at the deep sabre cut on Rapp's forehead.

'A scratch, sire,' the cavalryman said, and returned to his duty.

But General Morland, disdaining death as Napoleon demanded that his cavalry generals should, had found it on the field. He died under Russian sabres at the head of his grenadiers, one of the few senior French leaders to lose his life, through many were wounded.

Count Apraxin, a young artillery officer captured by the chasseurs, was brought before Napoleon. 'I wish I could die,' Apraxin cried. 'I am dishonoured! I have lost my battery!'

Napoleon had a horse brought for the count. 'Be calm, young man,' he said. 'It is no disgrace to be conquered by a Frenchman.'

The French were now successful on their centre and left. Many of the enemy, including all the reserves, were fleeing towards Austerlitz, harried and hurried on their way by artillery of the Imperial Guard. The French artillery was used intelligently and effectively throughout the battle, as well it might be seeing that Napoleon himself was a master gunner.

Murat and Lannes had the left completely in hand, and Napoleon trusted them to bring the battle here to an end. He sent Bernadotte, with a large part of the Guard, to finish off the enemy who had been driven off Pratzen plateau.

With the climax of the battle approaching, Napoleon left the heights to take part in the fight. He led Soult's corps, plus a force of cavalry, reserve artillery, and infantry remnants in an attack on the rear of the Russo-Austrian force near Telnitz and the lakes.

This hapless force of 30,000 men, still entangled in the defiles, found itself attacked on three sides. Though tired out from incessant, day-long fighting, the men fought on bravely, but their position was hopeless and their suffering great. Their only way of escape was across frozen Menitz Lake. Thousands of men rushed on to the ice with horses, artillery, and wagons.

The French gave them no respite. Artillery kept up a fire, and much shot fell on the ice and cracked it. With the weight of men, horses, and equipment, the ice soon broke and split into fragments. Thousands of Austrian and Russian soldiers fell into the cold water, there to drown, though the French pulled many others to safety. It was an appalling spectacle, and it put an end to the battle.

Of the 30,000 men who had gone into action with Buxhöwden in the morning only 2,000 escaped. The rest were either dead or prisoners.

By four o'clock the battle was over and the guns were quiet. The only disappointment from the French point of view was that Bernadotte had allowed the whole of the enemy right, which had been defeated by Lannes and Murat, to escape past his front and make towards Hungary. Napoleon was furious about this, for it confounded his maxim that a beaten enemy must be followed up and destroyed to prevent his rallying.

As always after a great fight, the battlefield was a ghastly sight, and wounded soldiers suffered dreadfully on the frozen ground. Napoleon stayed on the field, personally helping some of the wounded. Surgeons and their orderlies were busy, but they could not hope to cope with the vast numbers of casualties. Working parties were bringing in the dead and wounded and piling their gear.

As darkness fell on that winter night icy rain and mist drove over the field, making it impossible to find all the wounded men. Napoleon ordered that strict silence was to be observed, so that calls for help could be heard. He himself was on the field until ten o'clock, by which time he had reached a small post-house at Posoritz, where he stayed the night.

Despite their suffering and hunger, the French troops were elated. It was different for the Russians and Austrians. Their rout was complete. The Russo-Austrian army lost 12,000 killed and wounded, 30,000 prisoners including 20 generals, 46 standards, 186 cannon, 40,000 artillery limbers, and all their wagons and baggage. About 25,000 demoralized men survived the catastrophe. The French lost 6,800 men.

Napoleon's order of the day to his army was brief but sufficient. 'Soldiers, I am content with you.'

Legend has it that when William Pitt, Prime Minister of England, heard the news of Austerlitz he had the map of Europe on his wall rolled up so that he could not see it. The gesture meant that Napoleon now controlled Europe. Pitt's death, soon after, is believed to have been hastened by the shock of Austerlitz.

But if politicians hated Napoleon, generals strove to emulate him. In one way or another he left an indelible stamp that impressed itself deeply on commanders who followed him. Perhaps the most significant aspect of the battle of Austerlitz is that Wellington used Napoleon's own defensive-offensive tactics to defeat him at Waterloo.

SIXTEEN

PRUSSIAN COLLAPSE AND PRUSSIAN REFORM

A brilliant military writer who died two years after Austerlitz, Dietrich von Bülow, said that battles of the future would be decided by tirailleur-fighting. Discipline and courage were merely contributing factors; the mass and quantity of the combatants decided the issue. 'A general must praise the men in order to make them worthy of praise,' he said, echoing Napoleon, of whom he was an admirer.

Some leaders did praise their men, but leaders and Governments forgot them once they were too old or unfit for fighting. For instance, the only pension granted to the discharged German veteran was a licence to beg publicly.

Another great reformer was Georg von Behrenhorst (1733–1814), a former aide of Frederick. Behrenhorst wrote, in 1797:

> The art of war calls for a vaster amount of knowledge and more inborn talents than any of the other arts, in order to reform a system of mechanics which does not rest upon immutable laws, but upon the unknown.

Von Behrenhorst saw further than his contemporaries.

> New inventions allow passing advantages, then they become general, and then the whole thing reduces itself to mere bare manslaughter, just as it was in the beginning. The art of fighting *en masse*, because it necessarily frustrates itself by its own development, cannot possibly belong to those steps of progress which mankind is destined to make.

But the Prussians were slavishly content to follow Frederick's system, and were flattered, too, that the British had tended to copy it. Reide, in his *Military Discipline* of 1795, noted:

A very great change has taken place within the last four or five years in the discipline of the British Army which is now entirely modelled on that of the Prussian, as established by Frederick the Great. The utility of that monarch's tactics has long been known and in part adapted into our service.

Principles might remain constant, but practice does not, and in 1806 Prussia, saturated with militarism, but now only lightly veneered with modern military skill, was presumptuous enough to challenge Napoleon and the French, although their recent victory at Austerlitz had resounded throughout Europe as one of the most brilliant battles in history. History would have wept at the result.

Napoleon expected King Frederick William to retire behind the Elbe and dispute its passage until his Russian allies could join him. He was surprised when he heard that the Prussians were concentrating west of the Elbe; this forward movement defeated the Prussians from the beginning, and so completely that the Prussian army disintegrated.

The French advanced in three great columns into the rocky valleys that led from Franconia into Saxony – an army, when the cavalry and artillery of the Guard joined it, of 186,000 men, led by martial masters – men like Davout, Murat, Ney, Lannes, Augereau, Bernadotte, and Lefebvre.

The Prussians changed plans repeatedly, exposed their magazines, left their flanks invitingly open, and made many marches by crossroads and byways in country for which the Prussian staff had not a single map. After many skirmishes came the historic clash at Jena.

Napoleon, who never made the mistake of underrating an enemy – even the Prussians of 1806 – addressed Lannes' corps. 'Soldiers,' he said, 'the Prussian Army is turned as the Austrian was a year ago at Ulm. . . . Fear not its renowned cavalry; oppose to their charges firm squares and the bayonet.'

In a terrible charge Murat and his cavalry arrived and swept through the Prussians in a whirlwind of slaughter. No battle can show carnage more merciless and horrible than that surge of the heavy horsemen among the flying Prussians after Jena. They spared nothing in their path, and every one of those 15,000 long swords was red with blood from point to hilt. And all the while the French bandsmen played, while Prussians in their many colourful uniforms scrambled for brief safety.

Jena is the classical pursuit of military history, and was strongly reminiscent of Alexander's pursuit of Darius after the battle of Arbela in 331 BC The only other pursuits which approach Jena in effectiveness are Waterloo; Tel-el-Kebir, 1882; the final offensive in Palestine, 1918; the British pursuit of the Italians in North Africa, 1940.

But Jena, sanguinary though it was, was not the major battle of the campaign, even it is the best remembered. Another action, fought near Auerstadt at the same time, broke up the main body of Prussians and covered Marshal Davout with glory.

With 28,750 men to face at least 66,000 Prussians, Davout set about his task with such characteristic attention to detail that he inflicted 10,000 casualties on the Prussians, captured 3,000 men and 115 guns, but without numerical superiority could not bring about the chaos Murat had inflicted at Jena. The Prussian war machine was systematically broken.

But mistakes can drive home a lesson, and the long-term result of the disaster was that Prussia and Germany were never again unprepared for war. Their soldiers were never caught unready for command nor their soldiers unfitted for combat. The German Armies of 1813, of 1870, 1914, and 1939, and of today were the offspring of the remaking of Prussia after the disasters of Jena and Auerstadt.

Frederick William III, more mortified than any of his subjects, called on Gerhard Johann David von Scharnhorst to reorganize the Prussian Army. The creator of the new German military idea was the pupil of an exceptional man, Count William, Prince of Schaumburg-Lippe. As a British mercenary he had been made Field-Marshal of Portugal, but the role of a British mercenary did not suit him, so he returned to his own country. There he had an artificial island built in the Steinhuder Lake and constructed a fortress on it, which he called Wilhelmstein. In this fortress he drilled his subjects and thought so much about the art of war that he formed a small military school there. This first military academy of modern times never took more than twelve pupils, who were admitted without regard to birth or means. The Prince himself examined every candidate as to his suitability. In contrast to ther military schools, the boys there were not only initiated into the secrets of one kind of fighting, but into military matters and theory in general. Scharnhorst was accepted as a pupil in 1773 and became the prince's favourite student. After the death of his prince, Scharnhorst went into Hanoverian service as an ensign and became a remarkable artillery captain. On returning from his first war he made the admission: 'I have learnt nothing in this war. As a matter of fact no-one who has systematically studied military science can learn much in war.'

Scharnhorst, Gneisenau, and others – including Scharnhorst's favourite pupil, Clausewitz – were men in the mould of Frederick the Great. They realized that Prussia had to be reforged, and to do this they had to militarize the Prussian people. They first of all inspired the school-teachers of the country; the school-teachers, from primary school to university, went to work with a will on the minds and emotions of the children and young people. They were infected with nationalism, filled with militaristic fervour and a belief in 'Prussia's destiny'.

Scharnhorst pleaded for an increase of the army and a regular militia. He wanted a special propaganda war newspaper to stimulate and arouse the nation and its soldiers.[1] He objected to the prevalent idea that the talent of the general was the sole deciding factor. A resolute nation could win even under mediocre leaders – if the nation had strength of will and high character.

'When the necessity of a war is once recognized by a nation, nothing further is needed than the resolution of the leader to conquer or die,' he wrote, echoing the Spartans, the Athenians, and the Romans.

After Jena, with so many officers failing and falling, Gneisenau so stood out as steady and competent that he was given greater

1 In later times propaganda war newspapers and magazines were common-place in Prussia and Germany. In 1939–45 one of the most successful was *Signal*, published in many foreign languages – including English – for circulation in the Channel Islands

responsibility. In the following spring he was sent to take over one of the few points still held out behind Napoleon's lines – the little fortress of Kolberg on the sea-coast of Pomerania. His brilliant defence of the place until the armistice won him unique popularity throughout the country.

Scharnhorst himself, Gneisenau, Clausewitz, Grolman, and Boyen – both majors – were the inner circle of the reformers, and like that of all reformers their way was hard.

Scharnhorst believed that the French had survived from and triumphed against the attacks launched against them because 'They were able to conduct the war with the resources of the whole nation and in the last resort to sacrifice literally everything to the continuation of the struggle.'

But in France the reform had come from below. In Prussia it had to come from above, and the reformers' task was much more formidable and complex. One cardinal principle of the new Prussian system was localization. Each army corps was a little army complete in infantry, cavalry, and artillery, recruited and permanently stationed in a particular province. Each regiment was raised in and permanently connected with a town or group of villages. Not that this adaptation of the old tribal system to modern war was anything new, but the Prussians intensified it. It made mobilization a simple business in the case of reservists.

Beyond doubt, the most drastic, far-reaching, controversial, and unpopular edict was that comfort in war had to end. This policy, copied from the French, foreshadowed the German Army of the future – indeed of all future armies – but it furiously angered Prussian officers at the time.

The reformers performed another major service to military efficiency. They restored the artillery and engineers to their rightful place of honour, for Scharnhorst and his colleagues were not interested in inter-service rivalries. They wanted to win any war in which Prussia might engage.

Scharnhorst also cleared out the scientific part of the secrécy in artillery. 'With the single exception of theology,' he said, 'there is no study which is so full of prejudices as artillery.' He founded schools for training artillery NCOs and ensigns and created the first artillery testing board. Every technical innovation had to be submitted to this board so that no general could disregard it merely because it was new or inconvenient to him.

In 1942 a German writer (in *Signal*) said that Frederick's and Scharnhorst's ideas have continued to live until our own day, and that no fundamental change has taken place in the sphere of artillery tactics since Frederick the Great. Only, the principles have been developed down to the last detail.

One of Scharnhorst's greatest deeds was that he relieved subordinate commanders of their fear of assuming the responsibility of taking action. Another was to build up behind Napoleon's back a new secret army. Also, he had created an institution which, enormously enlarged, carried on the military school of Steinhuder Lake in the Prussian Army. His creation was called the Great General Staff. The name was to be found elsewhere, but the thing itself was not. In most other countries the 'general staff' was merely the association of individual army leaders plus some additional senior officers too old for field commands. In contrast to this the Prussian creation was an independent organization with two great tasks – the pre-preparation for war and the training of a suitable younger generation of officers for the future General Staff.

In the academy and in the General Staff the officers once more learned Hannibal's and Frederick's idea of destruction. Officers were told – as Hitler was to tell them much later – that the history of the art of war proved that only those army leaders who had trained and intelligent troops at their disposal (troops, that is, whose training and good sense enabled them to distrust instinct on the field of battle) had been able to apply the idea of destruction. Instinct drove people together on a battlefield into one great mass, but logic kept them apart and made them obey the commands of the leaders.

Scharnhorst died from wounds received in the battle of Lützen, 1813, but Gneisenau lived on to become the chief director of Prussian field strategy during these campaigns and during that of Waterloo, even though Blücher was the Prussian commander in the field. Clausewitz served on the staff of an army corps during this campaign.

Gneisenau carried on and perpetuated Scharnhorst's work of reorganization, while Clausewitz – an experienced practical soldier and a voracious reader of military history – gave the Prussian Army, in his writings, a practical theory of war on which it acted for the next century. No military writer has been so deified as has Clausewitz – and far beyond the borders of his own country, for he has been translated into at least thirty languages.

SEVENTEEN

CLAUSEWITZ, HIGH PRIEST OF WAR; WELLINGTON

Prussian officers swore by Clausewitz's work. It was a point of honour among them to insist that he was the best and most knowledgeable writer on war; no officer would have dared to differ from an opinion expressed by Clausewitz.

Clausewitz ranked the military profession supreme over all. It was, he said, an intellectually determined activity of men. His description of an army imbued with soldierly spirit is especially illuminating, for in it we see the German Army of the future.

An army which retains its accustomed order under the most devastating fire, which is never overcome by fear and fights for every foot of the ground, which even in the chaos of defeat does not lose its discipline or the respect for and confidence in its leaders, an army which regards every effort as a means towards victory and not as a curse on its banners, which is reminded of all these duties and virtues by the short catechism of one single conception, the honour of its weapons – such an army is imbued with the soldierly spirit.

Clausewitz's notes – for that is all they were – were published in 1832 in book form, the year after his death.[1] Some of these notes had been delivered as lectures or had been separately published before this, but the publication of them in book form – a 1,000-page

1 About the same time the Archduke Charles of Austria wrote a series of military essays which were greatly admired and closely read by military students of the last century.

tome under the title *On War* – crystallized his whole martial philosophy, and as a philosophy on war it remains unrivalled.

Thousands of German officers of all ranks appear almost to have made decisions, paramount and petty, with a copy of Clausewitz's book in their hands. It was largely his teaching which led Prussia and Germany, as a unity, into preparation for unconditional and absolute war and the determination to put this preparation into effect.

Whole generations of Prussian, German, and Austrian soldiers were brought up on his book, and there were times when Clausewitz's ideas were used by other nations against the Germans, and times when these nations, by over-rigid adherence to Clausewitz's teachings, defeated themselves.

'War belongs to the province of social life,' Clausewitz said.

State policy is the womb in which war is developed, in which its outlines lie hidden in a rudimentary state, like the qualities of living creatures in their germs. . . .

War is the province of physical exertion and suffering. A certain strength of body and mind is required, which produces indifference to them. With these qualifications, under the guidance of simply a sound understanding, a man is a proper instrument of war. If we go further in the demands which war makes on its votaries, then we find the powers of the understanding predominating. War is the province of uncertainty; three-fourths of those things upon which action in war must be calculated are hidden more or less in the clouds of acute uncertainty. Here above all a fine and penetrating mind is necessary. An average intellect may, at one time, perhaps hit upon this truth by accident; an extraordinary courage, at another, may compensate for the lack of this tact; but in the majority of cases the average result will always bring to light the deficient understanding. . . .

As long as his men, full of high courage, fight with zeal and spirit, it is seldom necessary for the Chief to show great energy or purpose in the pursuit of his object. But as soon as difficulties arise – and that must always be when great results are at stake – then things no longer move on by themselves like a well-oiled machine. The machine itself begins to offer resistance, and to overcome this the commander must have great force of will. . . .

The military virtue of an army is one of the most important moral powers in war, and where it is wanting we either see its place supplied by one of the others, such as the great superiority of generalship or popular enthusiasm, or we find the results not commensurate with the efforts made . . . the astonishing successes of generals and their greatness in situations of extreme difficulty were only possible from only two sources and only by these two conjointly. The first is a succession of campaigns and great victories; the other is an activity of the Army carried sometimes to its highest pitch. Only by these does the soldier learn to know his powers. The more a general is in the habit of demanding from his troops, the surer he will be that his demands will be answered.[2] The soldier is as proud of overcoming toil as he is of surmounting danger. . . .

We do not ask, how much does the resistance which the whole nation in arms is capable of making, cost that nation? But we ask, what is the effect which such a resistance can produce?

War is nothing but a continuation of political intercourse, with a mixture of other means. . . . Is not war merely another kind of writing and language for political thoughts? – It has certainly a grammar of its own, but its logic is not peculiar to itself. . . . In one word, the Art of War in its highest point of view is policy, but, no doubt, a policy which fights battles instead of writing notes. According to this view, to leave a great military enterprise, or the plan for one, to a purely military judgement and decision is a distinction which cannot be allowed, and is even prejudicial. . . .

There is no human affair which stands so constantly and so generally in close connection with chance as War. But together with chance, the accidental, and along with it good luck, occupies a great place in war. If we take a look at the subjective nature of war . . . it will appear to us still more like a game.

---

2 History bears this out time and time again, for nearly all great generals have been 'great demanders'.

Primarily the element in which the operations of war are carried on is danger. But which of all the moral qualities is first in danger? Courage. Now certainly courage is quite compatible with prudent calculation, but still they are things of quite a different kind, essentially different qualities of the mind. . . . From the outset there is a play of possibilities, probabilities, good and bad luck, which spreads about with all the coarse and fine threads of its web, and makes War of all branches of human activity the most like a gambling game.

While Clausewitz was evolving his philosophy, while Prussian militarism had been undergoing a rethinking and Europe was bending the knee to Napoleon, British arms were becoming active in Iberia. Two commanders stood out here – John Moore and Wellington. Moore, a dedicated soldier, would have achieved great deeds had he lived. Carola Oman, one of his biographers, says that Moore had practically no fiction in his library. Most of his books were connected with arms, and most were by foreigners – von Ehwald, Tielke, Sontag, de Rottenburg. He complained of the lack of good books by British military men. Caesar was the 'prime object of his admiration as a soldier'.

Late in 1808 Napoleon, in Spain to plan the country's subjugation, heard that the commander now pitted against him was Moore. 'Moore is now the only general worthy to contend with me,' he said. 'I shall move against him in person.'

This was a remarkable compliment, for though Napoleon rarely made the mistake of underestimating an opponent he equally rarely praised them and sometimes derided them, as he did Wellington. It is interesting that Napoleon and Moore were such keen students of history. In appalling winter conditions Moore was forced to retreat to Corunna, where he died of wounds.

From the British point of view the Peninsula War was an outstanding example of enterprising, patient strategy – a policy aimed at wearing out the enemy rather than knocking him out. Like Turenne in 1675, Wellington in his first campaign broke up the opposition before it had chance to form. But Wellington was capable of a knock-out punch when the opportunity occurred. He showed great audacity in the Vimiero and Talavera campaign and in the storming of Ciudad Rodrigo and Badajoz.

Wellington was a fine tactician and an accurate judge of the materials he had to work with. He realized that his predecessors had given him a steady, solid army. Turenne-like, to protect his men and mystify his enemy he usually made full use of cover by ground – in fact, in his time, he was outstanding for this. He developed defensive-offensive tactics – that is, he induced his enemy to attack and then attacked him in return. His tactics demanded artillery dispersion, whereas Napoleon favoured concentration.[3]

His greatest strength was that as far as humanly possible his command was all-embracing and supreme. He once said, 'The real reason why I succeed . . . is because I was always on the spot – I saw everything, and did everything myself.' In essence Wellington's command was Napoleonic.

His campaigns in Iberia cannot concern us here, for they added little to leadership though they added much to the reputation of the British soldier. Wellington's victories in Spain did not, in any case, cause the French collapse. The continuous strain of the relentless guerrilla warfare was more wearing on the French, more damaging to their morale, and caused more casualties and losses of equipment, weapons, and stores than their intermittent defeat in battles. Wellington's forces were really only a strategic detachment from the forces in Europe.

Wellington's emotional impact on the British people was enormous, and his place in history is safe. Significantly, his Iberian campaigns are still a set subject for British Staff College students.

In 1814 Wellington brought his Peninsula campaigns to a close where he won Toulouse, and while not seeking to detract from the many merits which sustained him through so much arduous campaigning I think it is fair to say that the British Army won the many battles which had brought Wellington from Madrid across the Pyrenees into France.

It is equally true to say, conversely, that Napoleon rather than his Army won the astonishing series of French victories in the campaign of 1814. Vastly outnumbered by his enemies now

---

3 Napoleon showed that at times sheer offensive power could succeed where surprise or mobility might fail. At Friedland, in 1807, he used new artillery tactics – massed gunfire at a selected point, a sort of break-through policy later favoured by the Germans.

converging on France, Napoleon realized that he could not expect to gain a military decision, so he aimed to dislocate the co-operation between the Allied armies, and he exploited mobility more remarkably than ever. He inflicted a series of defeats against them, and on five occasions attacked the enemy in the rear.

His strategy and tactical handling of his army were never more brilliant. With small, poorly equipped forces he defeated Blücher, Yorck, and Sacken in turn. His victories at La Fothière, Montmirail, Champaubert, Étoges, and Craonne were remarkable. But while he fought at one point the Allies continued to march and in the end their 300,000 men were too much for his 30,000, and finally Blücher defeated Napoleon at Laon.

Waterloo cannot find a place in this book, for, though Napoleon, Wellington, Blücher, Ney, Grouchy, Soult, Vandamme, d'Erlon, Kellermann, and others were present, the battle was not distinguished by any brilliance of manoeuvre. Napoleon left too much to fortune, and Fate caught up with him, but he nearly mastered it, despite more setbacks – largely caused by subordinates – than most commanders have ever faced in a battle.

Of the several reasons for Napoleon's failure at Waterloo one of the most important was the incompetence of Ney and Grouchy – but then he himself had selected them for high command. I think it very likely that the lesson to be deduced – choose carefully those sub-commanders who are to have independence of action – was not lost on succeeding great captains. Napoleon also confounded one of his own maxims concerning concentration of forces in that he could have collected as many as 36,000 additional soldiers from secondary theatres; such added strength could easily have decided the issue in his favour, especially on June 14, four days before Waterloo.

Waterloo was a particularly bloody combat, and it marked the end of an epoch. Wellington's main triumph was that his defensive-offensive method was proved sound. Later Wellington himself put the battle in true military perspective. Napoleon, he said, 'just moved off in the old style' – that is, in columns – and was 'driven off in the old style' – by men in line. Wellington had made his men into a precise firing body, and his tactics were typically English, his inheritance from the great commanders who had gone before him.

On the night of the battle Wellington said to Lord Fitzroy, 'I have never fought such a battle and I trust I shall never fight such another.' To his brother he wrote, 'In all my life I have not experienced such anxiety for I must confess I have never before been so close to defeat.'[4]

With Napoleon fading from the scene as a great commander it is particularly apposite at this point to quote from the eleventh edition of the Encyclopaedia Britannica, 1920, which states unequivocally that

> Among all the great captains of history Cromwell alone can be compared to Napoleon. Both in their powers of organization and the mastery of the tactical potentialities of the weapons of their day were immeasurably ahead of their times, and both also understood to the full the strategic art of binding and restraining the independent will power of their opponents, an art of which Marlborough and Frederick, Wellington, Lee and Moltke do not seem ever even to have grasped the fringe.

And, remember, Napoleon himself urged students of arms to study Cromwell and actually likened himself to Cromwell. How much of Cromwell's methods did he himself adapt for his own?

After 1815 the rest of the first half of the nineteenth century was more important for military and quasi-military inventions than for great battles or great generalship. In many countries British soldiers fought fierce, poorly publicized minor battles and endured the rigours of long campaigns in terrible climates. True to their history, nearly always unruffled, they won most of their battles – sometimes in spite of their generals, who in this age were among the most wooden-headed commanders in all history.

It is always possible to recognize a potential aggressor and to foretell a war if one looks far enough ahead. But in 1833 when Prussians became the first to grasp the supreme potential importance of the railway in war nobody in Europe took any

---

4 It is ironical to reflect that in 1799 Napoleon disbanded the French Balloon Corps, despite the valuable service it had rendered in its brief life of five years. In 1815 it could well have saved him with its observation of Allied movements.

notice. In 1833 F.W. Hakort wrote that a railway between Cologne and Minden and another between Mainz and Wesef would be of great importance in defence of the Rhineland. C.E. Ponitz urged general railway construction to protect Prussia against France, Austria, and Russia. Friedrich List pointed out that railways could raise Prussia into a very powerful state, and in that year, 1833, before a single rail had been laid, he planned a network of railways for Germany which is substantially that of today. 'Prussia', List wrote,

> could be made into a defensive bastion in the heart of Europe. Speed of mobilization, the rapidity with which troops could be moved from the centre of the country to the borders and the other obvious advantages of interior lines of transport would be of greater relative advantage to Germany than to any other European country.

While Germany planned, Britain and other countries plodded along towards the spectacularly stupid debacle of the Crimean War – a display of soldierly courage at its best and of leadership at its worst. The armies of Europe were rigidly professional at this time, and most of them – the French Army was the only notable exception – were wedded to a pathetic directness which was considered soldierly. The charge of the Light Brigade was a symptom of this directness. Fortunately for the Allies, the Russians were also extremely direct and had no more intelligent tactics than to march masses of men straight into cannon- and musket-fire.

The war proved once again that the British line – the 'thin red line' in this case – could still beat the column formation of its enemies and that British fire discipline was examplary. About the only tribute that can be paid to anybody's leadership is to say that the French attack on the Malakoff was better conceived and better executed than the British one on the Redan. I do not intend to be a party to any attempt to immortalize the names of any of the inept generals who commanded during the war.

EIGHTEEN

THE BATTLE OF SOLFERINO, 1859

Alfred Vagts in his *A History of Militarism* says: 'On the whole the time following the Restoration of 1815 and closing only with the Great War in 1914 was one of relative quiet. Between Waterloo and Marne stretched a dull period of tranquillity.'

That is one of the most extraordinary statements ever made by an historian. This 'dull period of tranquillity' saw these major wars – the Crimean, American Civil, Franco-Austrian, Prusso-Austrian, Franco-Prussian, Russo-Turkish, Spanish-American, Boer, Russo-Japanese Wars. The host of minor-wars – and not everybody would agree that all these *were* minor wars – include: the Kaffir Wars; the Maori Wars; the Kandyan (Ceylon) war; the Burmese Wars; the Afghan Wars; three Chinese Wars; the Sikh Wars; the Austro-Sardinian War; the Indian Mutiny; the Ashanti Wars; the Egyptian and Sudan Wars; the Servo-Bulgarian War; the Prusso-Danish War; the Sino-Japanese War; the Greco-Turkish War; the Chilean War; the Boxer Rebellion; the Turco-Italian War; the Balkan War. I could list hundreds of actions which could be classed as battles. *A time of relative quiet, a period of tranquillity!* How could this possibly be so in the great century of empire-consolidating and of intense nationalism?

One of the greatest, most significant, and most interesting battles of the century was that of Solferino in 1859, fought between the French and the Austrians. Sanguinary, tragic, distressing, violent, Solferino has been strangely neglected in military studies, perhaps because it is lost in time between the Crimean War and the American Civil War, both of which have tended to push it out of sight.

Napoleon Bonaparte had been dead thirty-seven years when Solferino was fought, but he won the battle as assuredly as if he and not his nephew – Louis Napoleon – had been in command. This requires some explanation and modification, and we will find it in an account of the battle.

Since the fall of the Roman Empire there had never been a time when Italy could be called a nation any more than a stack of timber could be called a ship. This was true even in the days of the medieval magnificence of the city-states of Venice, Genoa, Milan, Florence, Pisa, and Rome. But after that period Italy became a field for intriguing dynasties and the wars of jealous nations.

Napoleon – 'the Corsican tyrant' many Italians called him – turned out to be a counter-irritant and paradoxically a cleansing one. For a while at least Italy was rid of the Hapsburgs and the Bourbons, had the political divisions of the country reduced to three, and saw justice administered fairly and taxation apportioned equitably. More than this, the Napoleonic occupation gave the Italians a new consciousness of themselves as a race.

After 1815 the cruel, corrupt, and crazy princes climbed back on to their thrones, and the map was remade into the same old patchwork – with the difference that the spirit of freedom was in the air. After 1848 the Austrians came back to Italy and were guilty of atrocities against the independent-minded Italians. A man found even with a rusty nail – 'A potential weapon' – was shot.

The Italians hoped for help from France, but Napoleon refused it until the attempt on his life by the Italian Orsini in Paris in January 1858. The Emperor and Empress were virtually untouched, but 8 people were killed and 156 wounded by Orsini's bombs. Napoleon, often the target of would-be assassins, now decided to unite with Italy against Austria, at least strongly enough to annul the hate of every assassin in Italy.

On New Year's Day 1859 Napoleon told the Austrian ambassador, 'I regret that our relations with your Government are not so good as they have been hitherto.' In the diplomatic language of the day this was tantamount to a declaration of war, but by tortuous diplomacy the Italian statesman Cavour induced Austria to make the formal declaration of war – in April 1859.

Napoleon arrived in Genoa on May 12th to take command of his own army, the Sardinian Army, and that of Piedmont, the kingdom of his ally, King Victor Emmanuel. Napoleon Bonaparte himself had never had such a rapturous welcome; Genoa was wild with delight and colour as decoratively uniformed French troops poured into the city, their élan high and lusting for action, proud of the world's acknowledgement of them as the finest troops in existence. Most of them professionals, they welcomed a return to the first of Napoleon's battlegrounds. The stately grenadiers of the Imperial Guard, the infantry élite of France, fresh from their luxurious quarters in Paris, roughed it on the dry bed of a river – and exalted in it. Napoleon had revived for them the uniform of the Old Guard of his uncle – huge bearskins, dark blue coatees, white breeches, and gaiters.

From Algeria were hussars in light-blue tunics and baggy red trousers strapped over the foot. Algerian sharpshooters – or Turcos, as they were called – were present in their fantastic uniform of jacket and baggy knickerbockers of light blue, yellow leggings, red sashes, and turbans. Indifferent to minor punishments, death was the only sentence the Turcos respected, and even a firing-party had little terror for them. Slouching, irresponsible, but equally colourful Zouaves brought with them many hundreds of pets – monkeys, parrots, and dogs – a menagerie for each battalion. Most of the Zouaves were French, not African as generally believed.

The Bersaglieri were the most picturesque men in the Piedmontese Army – and some of the toughest soldiers of their time. Short men, selected for their strength, depth of chest, and agility, they were trained commando-style to make forced marches, to swim rivers in full equipment, and to scale mountains impassable to ordinary infantry. The idols of Italy in 1859, they wore a green uniform with a large round hat, pulled down over the right ear and with a plume of cock's feathers down the back.

No secret was made about the troop assemblies, but the hundreds of guns landed in Genoa were closely guarded, for these were new rifled guns, and the French were sensitive about secrecry. As fast as possible the troops were pushed up to Piedmont, which had already been invaded by the Austrians. At one time there was panic in case the Austrians reached Turin before the French could arrive, but rapid marching by the French over the Alpine passes and the procrastination of the Austrians combined to save Victor Emanuel's capital.

Eight days after Napoleon landed in Italy the first of a series of battles was fought. At Montebello and at Palestro the Allied armies beat the Austrians, who made a gallant but also unsuccessful stand at Magenta. Then they retreated slowly to a strong position east of the Mincio river, their front covered by the river and their flanks guarded by forts at Mantua and Peschiera on Lake Garda.

The Allied armies, hampered by lack of transport – the Austrians had commandeered most of it – followed the Austrains, and on June 23 camped on both banks of the Chiese river, fifteen miles west of the Mincio. At two that morning they resumed their march, for Napoleon had been told that the Austrians were in positions east of the Mincio. In fact, they had recrossed the river and by nightfall on the 23 the leading Austrian columns were occupying ground on which the French had been ordered to camp on the evening of the 24th. The Austrian Emperor, Francis Joseph, had planned to attack the Allies while they were crossing the Chiese, but his information was as faulty as that of Napoleon.

The two armies were marching towards each other, their commanders expecting battle in three of four days' time. In fact, they were within hours of contact. The situation was grimly piquant. The Allies had 150,000 men and 400 guns; the Austrians 175,000 men and 500 guns. These two massive forces were moving in the dark along every road of a 12½-mile front.

The first touch of the encounter occurred when a detachment of French cavalry saw, but were not alarmed by, a large hussar watching by the roadside. The horseman disappeared momentarily, jumped a ditch into the road, and charged the French officer in command, sabre-slashing him twice. A volley from the French detachment brought the hussar down, and echoing into the hills was the signal that the two armies had met. It was an electric moment.

This, then, was to be an encounter battle – a battle fought without a premeditated plan, without efficient reconnaissance, without proper dispositions. The French had cavalry forward, they had pushed out scouts, they even made balloon ascents on the 23rd, but nobody reported anything that might indicate a counter-offensive or an attack. This would never have happened to Bonaparte: he would have had his cavalry screen ranging forty, fifty, even a hundred miles ahead and on his flanks.

There is an odd notion that an encounter battle, because it nearly always devolves into a 'soldiers' battle', cannot illustrate generalship. On the contrary, an encounter battle by its very nature challenges the training, discipline, and control of every man involved, as well as command and response to command. Such a battle shows up an army in its true colours, for it then must fall back on its moral reserves. The moral reserves of the French Army of 1859 were Napoleonic, and though Napoleon III was no great captain – he was, for instance, a dislodger of enemies rather than a destroyer – that day he showed signs of Napoleonic skill and method.

Though neither the Allies nor the Austrians had known a battle was so imminent, many civilian inhabitants sensed it. Solferino, a natural battleground, had been the scene of many earlier fights, and the ground-drum of hundreds of thousands of boots and hooves and the rolling of guns and wagons spread ominously over the still countryside. Experienced civilians packed a few essentials and quickly headed south; others packed more than they could carry and ran in any direction – often into trouble. The elderly, the disabled, and many others stayed in their homes – and some died there.

Many villagers hid in cellars, vaults, wells, and even in trees, staying there for twenty hours or more, without light or food, until they could struggle out to gape at the death and devastation.

Austrian staff organization at this time was inferior to that of the French. The whole force was under the Emperor with his own staff, while the First Army, under Field-Marshal Count Wimpffen, and the Second Army, under General Count Schlick, a cavalry general seventy years old, also had their own separate staffs.

The arrangement produced nothing but chaos. Imperial headquarters still issued voluminous detailed orders for each corps, and the intervening army staffs, far from simplifying orders or showing any initiative, succeeded only in inflicting further delays. The direction of several armies is only feasible when general directives take the place of orders; the French had long realized this, just as the Prussians were realizing it.

But all the necessary conditions for working such a system – uniformity of training, methods, and doctrine, abstention from interference in details by the supreme command – were lacking in the Austrian Army of 1859.

Nevertheless, Francis Joseph had made some salutary changes in administration, notably an order to the infantry to send their heavy equipment and parade full-dress to the fortresses; this greatly lightened the overburdened infantryman.

Despite the French superiority in organization the Austrians were the first to react to the battle contact – largely because they had more favourable terrain – and early on the morning of the 24th they occupied every vantage-point between Pozzolengo, Solferino, Cavriana, and Guidizzolo. Their formidable artillery spiked a line of low hills to form the centre of a front more than twelve miles long. From their vantage-points on the hills the Austrians swept the French with shells, case-shot, and grape-shot. Dirt and dust mingled with the fumes of smoking guns and shells.

The hill of Solferino, the key to the position, was a formidable stronghold. It stood then – as it does now – at the head of a valley network, so steep that the roads along them are locally known as the Steps of Solferino. On the dividing spurs were strong stone buildings, a church, a convent, a high-walled cemetery, an old feudal tower – all commanding the approaches to the hamlet. The houses, built on terraced gardens, rose tier above tier on the slope. Early in the day war arrived in Solferino, with the Austrians occupying the place in force. It became a nest of miniature fortresses which would have to be breached by cannon or taken by escalade. But, strong though it was, it had a grave tactical disadvantage – the reverse side of the hill was so steep that it could be descended by only one winding path.

If General Schlick, commanding at this point, had studied Napoleon's tactics at Austerlitz he would have allowed the French to occupy Solferino and other heights and would then have shelled them mercilessly from even higher flanking hills. As things turned out, this is what the French did to the Austrians.

Away from the hills spread the plain of Medole, with long lines of poplars marking the roads and with solid farmhouses standing like islands in a sea of vines, mulberry-trees, and standing corn. The plain was wonderful cavalry country, and in this arm the Austrians excelled, but during the day they made no grand charges, for one cavalry leader, Lauingen, panicked and withdrew his splendid division from the field before the battle began.

The day was warm even before sunrise, giving promise of great heat later. The Austrians had been marching all night; the French had been on the move since before daybreak and had had nothing but coffee. Every man involved must have known as the sun came up that some real soldiering would be done that day.

Because of the length of the front we shall need to describe the battle sectionally.

Quite early the vanguard of Niel's corps, the Fourth met a strong force of Austrian cavalry in front of Medole, but after a skirmish Niel drove them off and stormed Medole. He received a message that MacMahon intended to move left to aid d'Hilliers, who was in trouble to the north, and that the Austrians were dominating every height. Would Niel also turn left to avoid causing a gap? Niel agreed, provided Canrobert, commanding the Third Corps on the extreme right, guaranteed his flank. But Canrobert was unable to assist Niel until late in the afternoon, for Napoleon had ordered him to watch for 25,000 Austrians who were said to be threatening the French right from Mantua. The Austrians did not appear, but Canrobert was paralysed until 3 p.m., and until then took no part in the battle. It was a major historical lesson in the evils of faulty reconnaissance.

Niel found out that Wimpffen had brigades on all roads leading to Guidizzolo, and a whole division was making for the large farmhouse on Casa Nuova, about a mile out of Guidizzolo. This farm was surrounded by ditches, walls, hedges, and trees, its outbuildings gave flanking fire, and Austrian engineers had improved these natural advantages into a major strong-point.

Niel concentrated his 42 guns on the farm, but could make no impression, and by noon, with fresh Austrians advancing, he knew that only determined assault could take the place. After heavy shelling he unleashed his infantry, and in fierce hand-to-hand fighting they took the farm, smashing down barricades and doors and hunting Austrians from room to room. A detachment of engineers was put to work to loophole the walls facing the Austrians, and the 6th Chasseurs were ordered in as a garrison to hold or die.

Wimpffen's First Army made several counter-attacks on the farm and on Robecco – a hamlet captured by Niel south of the farmhouse – but despite great gallantry the Austrians could not retake the positions. Still, the French suffered severely. One battalion, surrounded by Austrians, was retiring when the ensign carrying the eagle was mortally wounded; an elderly sergeant picked up the standard, but a shell took off his head; a captain grabbed the pole, but a shot smashed both him and the standard. Other men died to save the eagle, which after the battle was found under a mound of dead.

By modern standards the very carrying of a provocative target during battle is suicidal enough, let alone certain-death attempts to save it, but the days of close-quarter fighting, though fading, were still alive, and the eagle served as a rallying point. More than this, the French Army of 1859 was still imbued with Napoleonic fervour about regimental eagles.

When the action started field hospitals were set up in farms, houses, convents, and churches, and sometimes even under trees. A prominent black flag in those days marked the location of first-aid posts or field ambulances, and both sides generally respected them. Officers were always treated first, then non-commissioned officers, and finally privates. The doctors had no rest. Two French surgeons had so many amputations and dressings to attend to that they fainted. Another became so exhausted that two soldiers had to steady his arms while he operated.

The canteen women moved about the field under enemy fire, and were often wounded as they went among the wounded men to give them water.

Early in the afternoon Niel's position was critical; his men were worn out with exertion, hunger, and heat, and his formations were broken and confused. Napoleon had filled the gap between his left and MacMahon's right with the cavalry of the Guard and two hussar regiments, which were ordered to charge so as to give Niel breathing-space. The charge was so spectacular and successful that Niel restored order and even moved seven battalions against Guidizzolo. But this was too ambitious, and his men were beaten back by withering fire.

MacMahon, meanwhile, had been forced to remain on the defensive facing Cassiano, and for several hours the fighting on his sector was confined to an artillery duel. To do Napoleon justice, he had firmly grasped his uncle's idea that artillery fire to be effective must be overwhelming and concentrated under the direction of one commander. The French grouped their artillery in masses; the Austrians fought their batteries independently, with the result that a single Austrian battery was in action against 24 of the new French rifled guns. To distract the French gunners and to enable the battery to withdraw, some Austrian horse-artillery batteries, supported by cavalry, made a demonstration.

But their batteries came into action singly, and at 1,700 yards the French opened fire on the first battery and wrecked five out of its six guns. As the second battery galloped up the French guns wiped it out. Then the French guns turned on the cavalry. They hit 500 of the cavalry and artillery horses in the action, which lasted only a few minutes.

Baraguey d'Hilliers' First Corps was hotly engaged around Solferino. Napoleon told d'Hilliers early in the day to take the village, and slowly and painfully this tough general had by noon won the lower slopes of Solferino's cone-like hill, but the Austrians clung to the spurs and commanded the valleys. They broke up a major French attack on the old tower, but French artillery smashed breaches through the convent and cemetery walls, and French infantry poured through them, to take the positions with the bayonet.

Napoleon now ordered the Chasseurs of the Guard to reinforce the First Corps. They were formed up in the dense columns that had survived in the French Army since the days of Bonaparte and, with their colonel at their head, awaited the signal. The bugles sounded the charge, and the colonel shouted, '*Bataillon en avant – pas de gymnastique! En avant, en avant!*'

'*Vive l'Empereur!*' shouted the Chasseurs. They were cheering Bonaparte had they only known it.

The whole mass pounded up the hill, the sun bright on their sword bayonets. Shells, musket fire, yells, and shrieks made a frightful din, and the Chasseurs dropped fast, but the survivors reached the first houses, wavered under volley-fire, then in a wild rush swept the white-coated Austrian infantry and the Tyrolese jagers before them. The attack was indirectly assisted by the Austrians themselves, for, in accordance with an often fatal practice of those days, one corps was being replaced by another up that narrow track at the height of the battle.

Every house, every garden, and every vineyard was a fortress, and the French had to take each by force.

'I saw several small enclosures covered with bodies,' a newspaper correspondent wrote. 'I counted more than 200 in a small field.'

By two o'clock, after repeated assaults, the French had mastered Solferino and threatened the Austrian centre.

All around Solferino and especially in the cemetery the ground was littered with broken weapons, helmets, shakos, mess-tins, cartridge-boxes, belts, remnants of blood-stained clothing.

Meanwhile some Voltigeurs of the Guard and other troops were slowly forcing their way along the heights towards Cavriana – French élan and intelligence against Austrian doggedness and skill at arms. On Monte Fontana the Turcos were put in to winkle out the Austrians. Lovers of bayonet-fighting, the Africans crawled, ran, and jumped from rock to rock and cover to cover, and, yelling like fiends, took the hill. But the Austrians, reinforced, retook it. The Turcos came back for more, captured the hill, and were again dislodged. The sweating, battle-grimed Austrians, who had received no rations other than a double round of brandy, lay panting on the hill.

The hand-to-hand struggles were nightmares of frightfulness, with Austrians and Allies trampling one another under foot, killing one another on piles of bloody corpses with butt, bayonet, and sabre. Many a man, wounded or without weapon, used rocks, his fists, and even his teeth on an opponent. Some picked up enemy soldiers and threw them into ravines.

By mid-morning the heat had been torrid; soon after noon it was fierce, and whole regiments, oppressed by fatigue, threw off their knapsacks so as to be able to move and fight more freely. Every mound, crag, and height was the scene of a fight to the death. Very little chivalry showed itself that day. The Croats of the Austrian Army clubbed to death every wounded man they encountered; the Algerian sharpshooters gave no quarter to wounded Austrians.

The French gunners now started to drag their guns up the heights, and when the horses could not move them they man-handled the weapons. Even then there were too few artillerymen, so the Grenadiers of the Guard, normally so dignified, hauled the guns to the crest and formed a chain to pass up cartridges and shells. From these heights the French shelled the Austrians off Monte Fontana.

Napoleon himself came up to inspire the men attacking Cavriana, and he and his brilliantly uniformed escort instantly became a prime target. A colonel urged the Emperor to retire – 'It is at you they are aiming.'

'Very well,' Napoleon said – with a smile, according to legend – 'silence them and they will fire no longer.'

A French officer is supposed to have written, 'The expression gave us fresh vigour, and I know not how it was, but at a bound we gained a hundred metres, and twenty minutes later we had taken Cavriana.'

I think it very likely that Napoleon III had learned a lot about personal publicity from his uncle.

At times French troops showed enterprise worthy of their Revolutionary history. An Austrian cavalry regiment charged French mounted skirmishers, but in doing so passed a battalion of Chasseurs who were lying down in the standing corn. As the Austrians rode by the Chasseurs stood and raked them, while two French batteries took the regiment in flank.

Artillery constantly changed position throughout the day, with horses, guns, and limbers pounding over dead and wounded, pulverizing, pulping, and mutilating the already damaged bodies. The French grape-shot, effective at distances hitherto unknown, inflicted casualties even on distant Austrian reserves.

The Austrian right was as busily engaged with the Sardinians and Piedmontese as the left and centre were with the French. The Sardinians were roughly handled. Some of their columns came under practically point-blank grape-shot fire, and the men were so shocked that they panicked; some ran two miles before they could be stopped. Finally, strongly reinforced, they made several more exhausting assaults, but General Benedek, a commander in the Blücher mould, fought them successfully all day. This battle is often separately known as the battle of San Martino.

The proud Bersaglieri were badly battered here, and many a feathered hat lay on the battlefield. Though they were to fight again, the Bersaglieri never did fully recover from their mauling at San Martino, and by the time of World War II, though still the élite of the Italian Army, they were much inferior to the Bersaglieri of 1859.

Of the 25,000 Sardinians and Piedmontese engaged around San Martino and at Pozzolengo 179 officers and 4,428 men were killed or wounded – evidence both of a hard fight and of inept leadership.

The Austrian Emperor had had his centre broken, but his left flank held its own against the French Fourth Corps, and his right flank on Lake Garda was still secure. He correctly saw that the best move was an all-out attack against Niel's tired men at Casa Nuova, and ordered Wimpffen to use three corps to 'crash through' the French line and then roll it up. The Austrians fought well, and in line wave after wave of them beat against the walls of the farm, still held by the 6th Chasseurs. Then a French lancer regiment exploded from cover behind a belt of trees and speared the Austrian assault to destruction.

In other assaults the Austrian infantry had time to form square, and the cavalry attacks were easily beaten off, but the necessity for halting and forming square had wasted too much time, and the Casa Nuova defenders had strengthened their positions. Wimpffen believed the assault was hopeless, but Francis Joseph made several furious and desperate attempts to bring his exhausted and beaten troops into action, and in the centre the Austrian rearguard held out for two hours in several successive positions against the attacks of MacMahon and the Guard.

Fighting was still continuing when a violent storm, soupy with dust, broke up the battle and gave the Austrians cover while they retreated east of the Mincio. The battle had raged for fifteen hours.

The losses were: Allies, 14,415 killed and wounded and 2,776 missing (a total of 17,191); Austrians: 13,317 killed and wounded, 9,220 missing (total 22,537). The Sardinians' share of the Allied losses amounted to 5,521. Two months later the total figure was practically doubled by dead or those in hospitals from sickness, fever, sunstroke, or excessive exhaustion.

Napoleonic spirit and training, Napoleonic artillery, theory, Napoleonic trust in well-chosen marshals and generals – these won Solferino. But what was the maximum time a nation could live on a legend? In France's case just another eleven years.

It has been said that the American Civil War marked the

beginning of truly modern warfare. In the sense that more military inventions were used in this war than in previous wars this may be true, but then the same applies to every great war. Solferino was the prime punctuation mark in warfare between 1815 and 1914. It showed that set-piece chessboard battles were over, that the era of great-area battles had begun. But the war was short, and few foreign countries had been quick enough to send skilled observers to Northern Italy to study military developments. Significantly, Prussia was one of the few; she had observers with both sides. Their intelligent detailed reports to the General Staff were closely studied and acted upon. It was no coincidence that seven years later Prussia decisively and completely defeated Austria in a mere seven weeks' war.

Solferino was fought at the height of the tourist season, and though most visitors fled from the area some remained. One of these at the little town of Castiglione della Pieve, near which the battle started, was Henri Dunant, a Swiss. Dunant was so appalled by the sights and sounds and smells of Solferino that he became the founder of the Red Cross.

Dunant and the other civilians who exhausted themselves by their efforts to help the wounded had reason to be appalled. All that first night injured men were brought in or struggled in by themselves, but not until sunrise on the 25th did anybody discover the full horror of the battlefield, littered by dead, dying, and wounded men and animals and the battered and ghastly debris of war.

It took three days and nights to bury the dead on the battlefield, but in such a wide area many bodies lay hidden in ditches or trenches or under bushes or mounds of earth and were found only much later. Burials were perfunctory and not always efficient, so that limbs often protruded from the earth. Some badly wounded men, inevitably, were buried alive.

Castiglione was the most important rescue centre, and overcrowding in the place became 'unspeakable', as Dunant was to write. Mule carts came in at a jolting trot, so that the wounded men in the carts cried out continually in pain.

The number of convoys increased so much that the authorities, the townspeople, and the able-bodied troops could not cope with the situation. There was food and water, but men died of hunger and thirst; there was plenty of lint, but not enough hands to dress wounds. Wounds were infected by flies, heat, and dust. On the floors of churches lay Frenchmen and Slavs, Germans and Arabs, Rumanians and Croats, Sardinians and Algerians. 'Oaths, curses, and cries such as no words can describe resounded from the vaulting,' Dunant wrote.[1]

With faces black with flies that swarmed about their wounds men gazed around them, wild-eyed and helpless. Others were no more than a worm-ridden inextricable compound of coat and shirt and flesh and blood. . . . A wretched man . . . had had his nose, lips, and chin taken off by a sabre cut . . . a third, with his skull gaping open, was dying, spitting out his brains on the stone floor . . . at the entrance to the church was a Hungarian who never ceased to cry out . . . a burst of grapeshot had ploughed into his back, which looked as if it had been furrowed with steel claws, laying bare a great area of red, quivering flesh. The rest of his swollen body was all black and green. . . . Over against the wall, about 100 French non-commissioned officers and soldiers were stretched in two lines, almost touching. . . . They were calm and peaceful. . . . They suffered without complaint. They died humbly and quietly.

But many died in desperate agony from untreatable wounds or while having a limb amputated without anaesthetic. 'In these Lombardy hospitals,' Dunant wrote, 'it could be seen and realized how dearly bought and how abundantly paid for is that commodity which men pompously call Glory!'

Dunant, a civilian, forged a new link in military command – recognition of the necessity for skilled and adequate medical services. He did not initiate Army medical services; doctors, of a kind, had accompanied armies for centuries, and Florence Nightingale had already set a splendid example at Scutari in the Crimean War, but Dunant by the publicity he gave to the aftermath of Solferino created a universal awareness of the need for proper medical services.

1 In his famous book *A Memory of Solferino*.

NINETEEN

TEN TEMPESTUOUS YEARS

*The American Civil War; Moltke introduces Technical War; The
Battle of Königgrätz; The French Collapse*

Historians of general history – and even many military
historians – have written that the American Civil War
introduced the conception of total war and of
psychological warfare, and they cite General Sherman's semi-
punitive march from Atlanta to Savannah to prove the point.

True, Sherman was a ruthless, totalitarian general. 'It is useless
to occupy Georgia,' he reported,

> but the utter destruction of its roads, houses and people
> will cripple their military resources. I can . . . make Georgia
> howl. . . . We are not only fighting hostile armies, but hostile
> people, and must make old and young, rich and poor, feel the
> hard hand of war.

And the hard hand of war the South did feel. Sherman
marched 300 miles with an army of 62,000 men, all of them
living off the country. They cut a swath of destruction 50 miles
wide, destroying railroads, arsenals, and other military objectives,
putting communications and industrial centres out of action, and
seriously damaging Southern morale.

But there was nothing new about this. Sherman could point to
hundreds of earler genreals who had been more ruthless than he,
to dozens of campaigns in which civilians suffered more acutely
and for longer than the Southerns – during the Thirty Years War,
for example – to the British, who at that very time had made a

practice of burning down the villages of their enemies in India and elsewhere. Sherman's march was less devastating than many made by Napoleon and various of his marshals, far less barbarous than those made by the Russians and Turks. To allege that Sherman 'invented' totalitarian war is irresponsible and betrays a lamentable lack of knowledge.

Still, Sherman proved that the indirect approach to the enemy's economic and moral rear was decisive and far-reaching. General Edmonds, the official historian of the First World War, said, 'It was the operations of Sherman's grand army of the west which led to the collapse of the Confederacy.' These operations had a profound effect on the generals who studied it.

It is wrong to believe – as many people do – that the generals of the Civil War were inferior. Historians who have studied the Civil War rate high the standard of generalship. In fact, the war brought forth more really able commanders than any war in history other than the Second World War – Sherman, McClellan, Lee, Johnston, Meade, Jackson, Grant, to mention a few.

General Grant had something of Napoleon's make-up, as is seen by his indirect approach, using several thrusting columns, in the Vicksburg campaign – although he adopted this approach only after more direct approaches had failed. Unfortunately, he did not learn as rapidly as Napoleon, and he suffered subsequent defeats because of direct approaches.

The war also introduced an astonishing range of martial innovations or improvements. There was the repeating rifle – the Spencer initially – wire entanglements, land-mines and booby-traps, grenades and mortars, explosive bullets and flame-throwers, submarines, naval mines and torpedoes, railroad artillery, revolving gun-turrets, telescopic sights, trench periscopes. Requa's machine-gun – one of the very first – was introduced, and in 1864 the South contemplated using 'stink-shells', although there is no record that they were actually used.

Amphibious attacks and aerial observation came into use, while sabotage was used so extensively that its techniques were not equalled until the Second World War. The Military Telegraph Service made a big difference to the war, and was in fact a major weapon, particularly for Union forces. During the last year of the fighting the Service laid an average of 200 miles of wire a day.

General Grant, when Commander-in-Chief, kept day-by-day control over half a million men spread over an area of 800,000 square miles.

Railways offered tremendous opportunities to enterprising generals. Time after time both sides moved troops to the scene of battle by train. At one crucial period the Federals rushed 16,000 men a distance of 1,200 miles in a week, an astonishing achievement for its time – and one that was carefully noted by the hand-picked Prussian observers at the front.

The rifle made the defensive the stronger form of warfare; the offensive became more difficult and more costly. And this, in turn, led to armies of greater size, for more men were needed to tackle a job. In 1864 the total Union forces were 683,000 – an immense army by any standards. The Confederates had only 195,000.

Tactical changes were much slower than technical ones because tactics were the responsibility of senior officers, most of whom were old and violently opposed to change. They did not much like technical improvements for that matter, but these were inevitable.

Change was most rapid in Prussia. In 1864, while the American Civil War was still in progress, the Prussian capture of the Danish redoubts of Duppel hinted at Prussia's frightening military efficiency. In 1866 the great battle of Königgrätz – or Sadowa as it is sometimes called – showed it off completely. Bismarck, the Minister-President, wanted a war with Austria and consulted von Moltke, possibly the greatest military brain Prussia or Germany has produced, and as keen a student of military history as Napoleon.

Moltke promised him victory – but only in a short war. Moltke had his short war; technically it lasted seven weeks, but hostilities were limited to three weeks, fighting to seven days and to one decisive battle.

A rare combination of realist-visionary, Moltke saw that the new inventions would allow a war to be opened quickly and concluded quickly. He founded a Railway Department in the General Staff. In 1866 he had a Railway Corps, the first in Europe. 'Railway troops' had been successful in the American Civil War, just finished. Moltke also ordered ready-made mobilization plans, kept up to date day by day, so that the Army could go into action within hours.

He showed how it was now possible for a commander-in-chief to remain many miles behind the lines yet intimately control complex troop movements by telegraph. At any moment a divisional general could contact the C-in-C because the C-in-C was always in the one spot. No longer was there a frantic search by gallopers to find the man in charge. Moltke was one of the first generals to organize battles from a large map. At the same time Moltke gave his subordinate commanders a lot of individual initiative.

The great battle-thinker, 'the silent one in seven languages', as the Prussian General Staff called him, had many maxims, but perhaps the most important was 'March separately, strike together.'

Late in June 1886 he sent three main armies into Bohemia on the upper Elbe, where the Austrians were concentrating. Totalling 220,000, they were led respectively, by the Red Prince, the Crown Prince, who was Queen Victoria's son-in-law, and General von Bittenfeld. These three armies left from seperate points and marched towards different points. Moltke sat among his maps in the offices of the General Staff, with his hand on the telegraph wire.

When the troops were marching towards the battlefield the King of Prussia began to doubt whether a victory could really be won if an army were divided into so many parts, and these parts were transported along many routes to the battlefield. How could he be certain that this disjointed and complicated machinery would join itself up again when it got there? The King sent Bismarck to Moltke to ask about the state of the operations. Bismarck came back and merely said, 'It is all right.'

The Austrians tried hard to block all three armies, but the destructive needle-gun, the long lance of the plunging Uhlans, and the slashing sabre of the cuirassiers cleared the way through a series of preliminary triumphs. The Austrians, though strong in cavalry, still had muzzle-loading firearms.

By June 29th all the Austrians with their Saxon allies and Hungarians – about 215,000 of them – had retired under the shelter of the guns of the fortress town of Königgrätz, on the left bank of the Upper Elbe. This united force was commanded by General Benedek, who had chosen his position very well and had transformed the whole field into a natural fortress.

The battle took place on July 3 along a front of five miles. In the centre the Prussians pushed battery after battery into action and kept up heavy fire, but the Austrians had ranged the ground better, and their fire was more effective.

Columns of Prussian infantry moved forward to storm the villages of Sadowa, Dohalitz, Dohalicka, and Benetek, where desperate hand-to-hand fighting occurred for the first time. But the mêlée here was nothing to the furious fight in Sadowa Wood. The Austrians clung to their positions under shells and bullets, but by eleven o'clock they had been bayoneted out.

King William wanted to storm frontally some entrenched Austrian batteries on Lissa Heights, but Moltke abruptly countermanded the royal order. A frontal charge against guns was not heroism to Moltke, but military stupidity.

After hideous bloodshed and frightful scenes the Crown Prince turned the Austrian right flank according to Moltke's plan. By four in the afternoon the Prussian line of attack resembled a huge Cannae-like semicircle hemming in the masses of battered and broken Austrian troops. The nature of the ground had prevented much use of cavalry, but on the line of retreat to Königgrätz several lance and sabre conflicts occurred. The Austrians were forced into full flight, pursued by cavalry, volleyed at by infantry, showered with shells. By superior arms, superior numbers, and superior strategy Prussia, at the cost of 10,000 casualties, had won a resounding victory. Austria lost 40,000 men, including 18,000 prisoners, and 174 guns.

Frederick the Great had taken seven years to humble Austria; Moltke had needed only seven days to achieve the same result.

While Bismarck schemed Moltke and von Roon carried on the work of perfecting the military machine. With the help of the railway and the telegraph Moltke managed armies of a size hitherto unknown. Not for Moltke any more than for Napoleon the conceit that one soldier of his own race was worth three of any other race. One man equalled one man, who merely cancelled each other out. Therefore to win a battle a general needed a majority, and the bigger the majority the better. This was at a time when the French believed that quality outweighed quantity; one Frenchman was at least as good as one and a half Germans; ergo a small French army could defeat a big German army.

Moltke became the great representative of the German school. In him was united the will of Napoleon with the mind of

Scharnhorst and Clausewitz. He combined vast knowledge with great willpower. His pupil Count Schlieffen said in his memory:

> This man of action, when he was called to do immortal deeds, was sixty-five years old. He was a man of the map and the compasses and the pen. . . . He could not boast, as Napoleon had, of having for nineteen years made a military promenade through Europe, but within six weeks he succeeded in encircling three proud armies. . . . He did not conquer, he destroyed!

Without being so well acquainted with the battle of Cannae as Schlieffen, Moltke, through his critical study of the Napoleonic campaigns, had arrived at Hannibalistic or, to be accurate, Greek ideas.

The Germans aimed at the annihilation or total dispersement of the enemy's army. This was possible, however, as the examples of Epamimondas and Hannibal, Frederick the Great, Napoleon, and Moltke proved, only when the attacker initiated a mobile battle with the object of falling upon the enemy's flank or of encircling and destroying piecemeal.

Moltke calculated the distance that a marching army corps took up on a road, and he arrived at the surprising figure of four and a half or five miles. If he wanted to march a second army corps along the same road and from the same place, the second corps could not start till the next day. It needed the rest of the time to let the first corps pass and then to get started itself. Moltke drew the conclusion that every army corps needed its own road. That is to say, the armies would march separately and only join forces on the battlefield to strike the great blow. Translated into Hannibal's way of thinking: 'It is important to know in advance how am I going to place my army. If I know that, I can arrange the march. All my available forces must be on the scene of action in time, the rest is determined by courage and luck!'

To translate such a seemingly simple idea into deeds he needed an exact knowledge of every detail of troop movement and every apparently unessential thing. The troops had to know every movement necessary for the manoeuvre, and Moltke needed to know to the second how much time the individual needed. An enormous amount of calculation was necessary to collate and work out all these thousands of small facts. Everything that can be done by intelligence in the case of war should, according to Moltke's doctrine, be done before the battle. With Moltke begins the modern era, the era of gigantic armies, the age of 'technical' warfare. Napoleon III still believed that it was not necessary to make any dispositions before the commencement of the fighting. Moltke, on the other hand, once the fighting had begun, merely played the part of an observer on the battlefield. During the Franco-Prussian War, at the battle of Sedan, Moltke did not issue one single order to the troops engaged in the fighting. This is probably the greatest staff triumph ever celebrated on the battlefield. He considered that the task of the commander-in-chief of an army had been carried out when the plan for the disposition of the troops had been decided, even down to what might seem to be the most trivial details.

When France declared war on July 19, 1870 every Frenchman was wild with confidence. The French certainly had many advantages. They had the revolutionary Chassepot breech-loading rifle with twice the range of the Prussian Dreyse needle-rifle. They had the mitrailleuse, a machine-gun of 25 barrels, axis-grouped, which was sighted to 1,200 metres and could fire 125 rounds a minute. France had a greater population, more money, and greater industrial output. Her army was one of veterans, who had fought in the Crimea, Italy, and Algeria. Napoleon III was to command in person the armies in the field and would win back the old Rhine frontier, and his marshals were men like MacMahon, Bazaine, and Canrobert.

But Prussia won because she intended to win, because the Prussian General Staff planned to win. Never had there been an army staff like this. War had become the national industry of Prussia, and its officers were war-businessmen. They brought to their trade a unique degree of efficiency. They used railways for war in a way the French had never dreamed of.

The old way of warfare was gone. The hallowed old combination of 'brilliant', usually intuitive leadership, high morale, and 'magnificent' cavalry charges was no match against a finely organized mass army, superior in number and directed not by instinct but with cold-blooded competence.

Moltke reckoned correctly that the French would not be able to bring more than 250,000 men against his 381,000 and that, because of their railway communications, they would be compelled to assemble their forces about Metz and Strasbourg – which meant that they were separated by the Vosges mountains. He assembled his three armies behind the fortress of the middle Rhine and planned to split the French Army.

The two main French armies remained separate in Alsace and Lorraine and allowed themselves to be beaten separately. Moltke practised great enveloping manoeuvres because of his numerical strength, and he succeeded in bottling up the larger parts of the French armies in Metz and Sedan.

With the coming of the breech-loading rifle the French doctrine had changed; it decreed that the way to win battles was to sit tight on a good position, preferably on high ground, and destroy the enemy by rapid fire. French military schools traught that the defensive was now the superior, though a cavalry charge was occasionally permissible. The last great cavalry charge of history – that of General Galliffet's Chasseurs d'Afrique – took place at Sedan, and a single heavy volley was enough to shatter it.[1]

The German doctrine was that only attack could give real results. It might be more costly, but the cost had to be paid. To attack was to assert from the outset the sense of power and the determination to win. This was reaffirming the doctrine of Miltiades, Hannibal, Scipio, and others right up to Napoleon.

A few historians have said that Moltke's strategy was essentially that of a direct approach. Liddell Hart says that Moltke relied on the sheer smashing power of a superior concentration of force. Theoretically his approach was indeed direct, but his objective was disguised. To say he had no guile is misleading and tends to malign the man, but his guile was that of method rather than of animal cunning.

Throughout the many battles of the Franco-Prussian War German artillery played a great part. Efficient breech-loaders served by competent crews, they played havoc with French defences. The guns were never short of ammunition; Moltke's

---

1 The British charges at Omdurman and elsewhere after 1870 were heroic and spectacular, but not great in the sense of being on a grand scale.

plans had seen to that. And every shell burst, unlike many of the French ones, which simply buried themselves. When German staff officers rode through areas and towns and fortifications devastated by artillery the lesson was not lost on them. 'If the artillery preparation is heavy enough the infantry can simply take over after the bombardment.'

The Franco-Prussian War should have shown the trend of future wars to leaders of armies and leaders of nations. It was inevitable that the French should copy the Prussian prototype,[2] because the vanquished usually reform themselves on the pattern of the victorious.

2 Before 1871 was over a French parliamentarian demanded that the French Army model itself on the Prussian. 'The victory of Germany has been the victory of science and reason. Prussia is our best model. We need a military law closely copying the Prussian system.'

TWENTY

THE NOT-SO-GREAT WAR

The German Spartan System; The French Roman System;
1900–18; Decline in the Art of War

Following the Franco-Prussian War there was a rapid improvement in armaments. Most significant was the adoption of small-bore magazine rifle and smokeless powder, first used on an extensive scale in the Boer War. The attackers now no longer necessarily had the initiative.

A paramount lesson learned in many campaigns was that discipline was often more important than leadership, overwhelming numbers, or the development of arms. As usual, discipline was best exemplified by the British infantry. Standing fast under every attack, they calmly and deliberately did what they were told, and in the end they triumphed – until the Boer War. For much the same reasons the Americans won their Indian wars and their Cuban, Philippine, Nicaraguan, and other campaigns.

Now and then the cavalry had a chance to shine, as did the British horsemen in some of the battles against the dervishes in the Sudan and in parts of India and Persia. But if anybody noticed that cavalry units spent most of their time in scouting, manoeuvring, and ceremonial parades nothing was said.

Cavalry was fading, but the highly irregular tactics of the Boer horsemen gave British arms a rude shock during the war of 1899–1902. These ragged, ununiformed farmers, outnumbered and outgunned, consistently defeated the best generals and regiments of the British Army, the army which was so proud of its martial record. Some of the defeats were disastrous in their magnitude.

213

The secret of the Boers' success was twofold – mobility and magnificent shooting. 'The Boers slink like curs behind rocks and fire cover,' Louis Creswicke, a leading English war historian complained.

The Boers fought as had the Eastern horsemen of the Middle Ages. They used their horses merely as a means of transport; they did not fight on horseback, and they were always under cover in action. The British, brave in old tradition, fought in the open. Horse and foot, loyal to their past, they charged valiantly and vainly and died in their thousands. The infantry often flouted a cardinal rule of war and charged up rocky hillsides.

A small number of defenders could lie well concealed along a wide front. For instance, at Colenso 4,500 Boers were spread along a front of 13,500 yards. These thin, long fronts could not be pierced, and rifle frontal attacks could no longer succeed.

The German Official History crystallized the lessons of the Boer War:

> In South Africa the contest was not merely one between the bullet and the bayonet, it was also between the soldier drilled to machine-like movements and the man with the rifle working on his own initiative. Fortunate indeed is that army whose ranks . . . are controlled by natural, untrammelled, quickening common sense.

Machine-guns had been developing steadily, reaching a deadly peak of efficiency. Among them were the Gatling, the Gardner, Nordenfelt, Hotchkiss, Colt, Maxim, Lewis, Vickers.[1]

As early as 1902 the *Swiss Military Review* published an article by an unconventional French officer, Emile Mayer, in which he said:

---

1 In 1881 a London Volunteer Unit, the Rangers, somehow unofficially acquired two early-pattern machine-guns for trial and practice. An official rebuke was not long in coming: 'Report why you are in possession of unauthorised weapons, which are entirely unsuitable for infantry use.' This was more than thirty years before the machine-gun became the master of the battlefield.

The next war will put face to face two human walls, almost in contact, only separated by the depth of danger, and this double wall will remain almost inert, in spite of the will of either party to advance. Unable to succeed in front, one of these lines will try to outswing the other. The latter, in turn, will prolong its front, and it will be a competition to see who will be able to reach farthest. There will be no reason for the war to stop. Exterior circumstances will bring the end of the purely defensive war of the future.

Some years earlier M. Bloch, a Warsaw banker, had foretold the same thing and the Bloch-Mayer theory was proved by the pushing, mauling struggle in Manchuria between Japan and Russia in 1904.

France and Germany had studied this war through observers on the spot, and while the Germans learned more than the French both sides missed the main conclusion – that the preponderance of projectiles in defence must lead to trenches.

After 1871 the French had discovered Clausewitz, and, as they thought, they made his doctrines work for them. In 1908 Foch preached Clausewitz at the French Staff College, where senior officers were prepared for high command. But to teach Clausewitz without qualifications was misguided because his thoughts, many of them more idealistic and intellectual than practical, had been conditioned by the age in which he lived. His ideals could be re-established in another age, but not his methods. In any case, Clausewitz was obviously working for the Germans, not the French. The Germans understood his *philosophy*, but the French stifled their own independent thought by lavish devotion to his *theories*.

Foch and his colleagues, accepting new weapons – mainly artillery – without being aware of the limitations they imposed, believed that they would add considerable momentum to attack. The Germans already knew, from their skilled observers in foreign wars, that heavy guns aided defence rather than attack.

Liddell Hart cites the French staff officer. Colonel de Grandmaison as saying that 'the French Army knows no other law but the offensive. All attacks are to be pushed to the extreme. . . to charge the enemy with the bayonet to destroy him. . . . This result can only be obtained at the price of bloody sacrifice.'

The French generals of the period preceding the Great War – and they included Foch – childishly believed that the infallible answer to the bullet was high morale. This was why, they said, the French Army was unbeatable.

Led by de Grandmaison, the French advocates of the direct-approach offensive formulated in 1912 what was known as Plan XVII – an infamous piece of work. This plan called for an all-out attack against the German centre – a frontal and almost whole-front push. Yet the French strength was only barely equal to the German strength, and the Germans would be fighting from their own fortified frontier zone. Such arrant imbecility is difficult to comprehend.

Defenders of the direct approach even quoted Napoleon in support of their foolishness, although Napoleon would have agreed with Churchill that the enemy alliance should be viewed as a whole and that an attack in some other theatre of war would be equivalent to an attack on an enemy's strategic flank. The Gallipoli campaign of 1915 was just such an attack.

Plan XVII played right into the Germans' hands, for they too had a plan – the Schlieffen Plan, prepared by Graf von Schlieffen in 1905. Schlieffen, Moltke's pupil and successor, was definitely inspired by both Cannae and Leuthen – Cannae by virtue of its grand envelopment tactics and Leuthen in regard to the movements within this grand design.

At that time Schlieffen had 72 divisions available; he put 53 on the right, 10 on the Verdun pivot, and only 9 on the left. As the French attacked in Lorraine and pressed back the German left wing the massive German right wing would slam through Belgium, hit the French in the back and knock them on their face.

Basically, by 1914 the German system was Spartan in type and amounted to a wall of advancing men without any specific reserve. The French system was Roman-type, a lighter front leading a heavy rear. The Germans, methodical as ever, based all on an elaborate plan backed by sheer force; the French, carrying their individualism to extremes, pinned their faith to skill and to intuitive ability to use ground and opportunity to best advantage. They thought they could easily outwit the 'stodgy Germans'.

Foch's appreciation of history was acutely limited. He saw little importance in the vital possibilities of the defensive-offensive – that is, to induce the enemy to exhaust themselves in a vain assault and then to launch a violent counterstroke – although these tactics have paid greater dividends than any other in history. Foch proclaimed Napoleon as the grand master of war, but did not analyse his idol's masterpiece, Austerlitz, and did not make use of the lesson it taught. This in itself proves Foch's intellectual limitations.

France had produced more truly brilliant generals and military thinkers than any other country in history, so it is all the more surprising that between 1904 and 1918 she should have produced generals so stodgy that they discounted the possible use of motor vehicles in war.[2] They said that cars were too big and therefore made vulnerable targets, that they were slow and would break down and were therefore not so reliable as horses; that they could only travel along a road, unlike cavalry which could travel anywhere; that they made a noise and would therefore give away positions to the enemy. The generals said much more in this vein. Developments had come too fast for them.

Another prime architect of French near-defeat was General Bonnal, a deep but dim-witted devotee of Napoloenic strategy. He had imbibed so much military history that he won the reputation as the leading strategist of his day. But Bonnal was a copyist, incapable of applying Napoleonic theory to changed practical conditions, and his plan – likened by General Fuller to 'the Jena plan is elephantiasis' – to counter any stroke by the Germans was unworkable.

Had Schlieffen's plan been acted upon the French must have been defeated early in the war, but Moltke 'the younger' (the great Moltke's nephew) botched it by adding more and more divisions to the left, and by making it safe he destroyed the great plan, with the indirect result of the battle of the Marne, September 1914, a decisive conflict and turning-point, for with the German loss of the battle the war developed into a siege, as Bloch and Mayer had foreseen.

As early as January 7th, 1915, Lord Kitchener wrote to Sir John French: 'The German lines in France may be looked upon as a fortress that cannot be carried by assault . . . with the result that . . . operations [may] proceed elsewhere.'

---

2 Although General Galliéni was astute enough to commandeer 1,200 Paris taxis in September 1914 and used them to rush reinforcements to the battlefront of the Marne.

But Kitchener's warning was unheeded. From the beginning the conflict of 1914–18 was a fearful war, the bloodiest in history. It was the war of the machine-gun, and the Germans excelled in its use. Over and over again the British and French charged the German lines, nearly always to be repulsed. The Germans, who should have known better, charged the British and French machine-guns with the same result. There was a little give and take, but year after year the position was virtually one of stalemate. And all the time the big guns thundered, blowing many thousands of men to pieces. Many might have survived had they not been so grossly overweighted with equipment. In the end about one man in every three had no known grave. Many were simply lost in the bottomless mud which the artillery and the rain had created. The predictions of the prophets had come true. In the trenches men fought with bombs, bayonets, boots, shovels, pickaxes, and even bottles. Many trenches became graves.

The casualties were stupendous, greater than ever before experienced. On the first day of the first battle of Ypres the British lost 40,000 men. Statistics beggared the imagination, but the generals knew nothing else other than bombardment and frontal attacks.

Great masses and heavy artillery led to no proportionately decisive results – and never will do so. It is incomprehensible why most leaders of the Great War could not understand that the dominance acquired by artillery and machine-guns would clog warfare to the point of bloody stalemate.

The Germans, eager for a break-through, used poison gas. Some gas was designed to suffocate, some to blister. The first men caught in it died dreadful deaths.

Scharnhorst had once advised officers 'not to be caught by their own enterprise', and had German tacticians heeded this they would not have used gas, for the prevailing winds on the Western Front were westerlies, making the use of gas much more favourable for the Allies than for the Germans. They were hoist with their own petard.

Wellington's line of Torres Vedras in 1810 pointed the way to the trench warfare of 1915–18. But the German invaders had an advantage Wellington had not enjoyed – that of living in the most fertile lands of France and Belgium. Also, Wellington always remained strictly on the defensive; to win all he had to do was to hold his own. But the Allies in 1915–18 ran the risk of losing it if they could not drive the Germans from France and Belgium. So did the invaders unless they could pierce the defenders' lines. Therefore the deadlock was involuntary and continuous as each side struggled to drive the other out. Neither side won more than local and temporary success on the Western Front until 1918.

On the Eastern Front in 1914 Ludendorff showed that he had learned from Frederick about the 'interior lines' form of indirect approach. As Hindenburg's Chief of Staff he made the daring move of withdrawing nearly all his troops from one front and rushing them into action against the flanks of General Samsonov's army, practically destroying it – a manoeuvre Turenne would have applauded.

Ludendorff was responsible, too, for one of the more capable pieces of generalship when he competently withdrew part of the German forces to the Hindenburg Line in the spring of 1917. He anticipated a renewed Franco-British attack on the Somme and had a new trench line prepared from Lens to Reims via Noyen. He devastated the area behind his original positions and then withdrew to the newer, shorter line. This manoeuvre, though defensive, threw out of gear the Allied spring offensive and gained Germany a year's respite. This operation was so much like Wellington's at Torres Vedras that it is difficult to resist the conclusion that Ludendorff – an intellectual and educated soldier – was influenced by it.

Study of the war from the standpoint of my analysis would be fruitless. Generalship was obstinate, criminally stupid, ridiculously rigid, almost totally unenterprising, pathetically feeble, and absolutely inhuman. It is only charitable to concede that the generals had to do their best in a type of warfare into which they were forced and of which they had no personal experience. The lessons of 1914–18 were sharp ones, and later leaders profited by them and, indeed, are still profiting.

After much study the only leaders to whom I can attribute any comprehension, enterprise, or evidence of profound military thinking were Fuller, who was so outspoken that he made enemies; Elles, victor of the tank battle of Cambrai, November 1917; Salmond, commander of the RAF in the field in 1918; Monash, the brilliant Australian Jew, who probably would have succeeded Haig; Currie, the enterprising Canadian; Allenby and

Chauvel, whose work in Palestine was classical in its planning and execution; Liman von Sanders, Commander-in-Chief of the Turkish forces in the Gallipoli peninsula; Mustafa Kemal, who on three separate occasions proved his genius during the Gallipoli campaign; von Hutier, victor against the Russians in the battle of Riga, 1917; and Ludendorff, occasionally.

Perhaps the greatest – and least known – of them all was Colonel (later General) von Lettow-Vorbeck, the German military commander in East Africa, who was the only German Commander to remain undefeated throughout the war. No fewer than 120 Allied generals were sent against him; he mastered all.

Throughout the war no senior French commander showed any outstanding ability. Foch was no more than mediocre. Gallieni, given the opportunity, could have shown brilliance.

It is no coincidence that all these commanders were ardent disciples of the doctrine of suprise and mobility. What Field-Marshal Wavell said of Allenby in a biographical study applies to all of them. 'The soft modern doctrine of safety first, which so often marks the decline of business, of Governments, of armies, of nations, found no place in Allenby's creed.' The term 'surprise' comprises general and tactical surprise, and 'mobility' includes, of course, boldness, and rapidity of decision and action. These modern leaders were the moral successors of Cyrus, the founder of the Persian Empire and victor at Thymbra, 546 BC; of Miltiades at Marathon; of Epaminondas – the victor of Leuctra, 371 BC; Gustavus, Frederick, Napoleon, and Lord Roberts, whose advance against the Boer leader Cronje in 1900 was an almost classic example of the complete strategic surprise of an enemy.

Apart from the few senior commanders mentioned, the leading generals of the Great War seemed bent on breaking every link in the chain of command, for they ignored or flouted every principle propounded throughout the centuries. For instance, it is axiomatic – as Liddell Hart has pointed out – that a commander should never renew an attack along the same line or in the same form once it has been repulsed. The Great War commanders did just this – many times. Many great captains, historians, philosophers, and observers have called the waging of war an 'art' or 'science'. In the Great War this art or science degenerated into a trade – butchery. From a scientific point of view the whole unholy shambles was disgraceful.

Towards the end the German offensive of March 1918 was a splendid conception that deserved to succeed, but Ludendorff spread his strength according to the enemy's strength and did not concentrate it against the weakest resistance – thereby confounding one of his own principles. He further violated it when, after breaking the Allied line south of the Somme, he persisted in attacking a powerfully resistant section of the line at Arras. When it was too late he sent reinforcements to the place of least resistance. He had made a fracture at the point where the British and French armies joined, and the French had told Haig that if German progress continued here they would have to pull back French reserves to cover Paris. Ludendorff could have wrenched that fracture wide open, but he gave no weight to his effort here. In the end he had driven three solid wedges into the Allied lines, but achieved no great damage and left the Germans themselves wide open to counter-attacks.

A few farsighted people, including Winston Churchill, saw early in the war that some new development was needed. Churchill, then First Lord of the Admiralty, wrote an historic letter to the Prime Minister, Herbert Asquith, which read in part:

The present war has revolutionised theories about the field of fire. The power of the rifle is so great that 100 yards is held sufficient to stop any rush and in order to lessen the severity of artillery fire trenches are often dug on the reverse slope of positions, or a short distance in the rear of villages, woods or other obstacles. The consequence is that the war has become a short-range instead of a long-range war as was expected, and opposing trenches get ever closer together, for mutual safety from each other's fire.

The question to be solved is not, therefore, the long attack over a carefully prepared glacis of former times, but the actual getting across 100 or 200 yards of open space and wire entanglements. All this was apparent more than two months ago, but no steps have been taken and no preparations made.

It would be quite easy in a short time to fit up a number of steam tractors, with small armoured shelters, in which men and machine guns could be placed. Used at night, they would not be affected by artillery fire to any extent. The caterpillar system would enable trenches to be crossed quite easily and the weight of the machine would destroy all wire entanglements.

Forty or fifty of these engines, prepared secretly and brought into positions at nightfall, could advance quite certainly into the enemy's trenches with their machine-gun fire, and with grenades thrown out of the top. They would make so many *points d'appui* for the British supporting infantry to rush forward and rally on them. They can then move forward to attack the second line of trenches.

In *The World Crisis* Churchill wrote:

Accusing as I do without exception all the great Allied offensives of 1915, 1916 and 1917 as needless and wrongly conceived operations of infinite costs, I am bound to reply to the question, 'What else could be done?'

And I answer it, pointing to the Battle of Cambrai [in which tanks were successfully used] '*This* could have been done.' This in many variants in better and larger forms, ought to have been done, and would have been done if only the generals had not been content to fight machine-guns with the breasts of gallant men and think that was waging war.

Paradoxically, the nation to make the most use of tanks and mechanization generally in later years and to achieve the most *with* them was that which had suffered most *from* them – Germany. In the next Great War German tanks and armoured cars of the highly efficient Panzer Corps overran country after country, often without being forced to fight, so great was the intimidation-power and surprise of the tank. It was now no cumbersome, creeping caterpillar, but a surging, speeding battleship on land.

The only surprising thing about the tank is that anybody should have been surprised that it had arrived and that it was so effective. The tank was nothing more than a compact, mechanized, modernized version of the ancient phalanx. Both had the same characteristics – they were armoured, relentless, practically irresistible, frightening, mobile.

The Not-so-Great War

I can imagine that Miltiades, Hannibal, Alexander, Caesar, Scipio, and the others must at times have thought, 'I wish I had armour on wheels and some way of making it go forward continuously.' *Continuously*. This is the key word. Every great commander of every age has longed and striven for *continuous* attack, for while ever he mainains movement he is winning.

TWENTY-ONE

THE GERMANS APPLY HISTORY; THE PRELUDE TO ALAMEIN.

The moment the Great War ended the world started to prepare for another war – not consciously, perhaps, but inevitably. And when the Treaty of Versailles – that monumental misbegotten masterpiece – was signed preparation became more definite, at least with the Germans.

Clausewitz had written:

> The military power must be destroyed, that is, reduced to such a state as not to be able to prosecute the war. . . . The country must be conquered, for out of the country a new military force may be formed. But even when these things are done, the war, that is, the hostile feeling and action of hostile agencies, cannot be considered as ended as long as the will of the enemy is not subdued also.

No Allied statesman who took part in the treaty negotiations understood Clausewitz; nor did they appreciate the profound influence he had on German military thought. The Allies did *not* destroy Germany's military power; they did *not* conquer Germany; they had *not* subdued the enemy's will. The conclusion drawn by the Germans who then commanded and who later were to command was obvious: *We were not beaten.*

Clausewitz even had a principle for them to fall back on: 'The final decision of a whole war is not always regarded as absolute. The conquered state sees in it only a passing evil, which may be repaired in after times by means of political combinations.'

The lengths to which Germany went in her preparations for war have been discussed in detail elsewhere[1] and do not need elaboration here. It is enough to know that all her preparations were based on Clausewitz's theory, Moltke's organization, and Frederick's intention, a meaty compound further thickened by ingredients supplied by Statesmen, strategists, and tacticians from Arminius to Hindenburg.

From the point of view of leadership one of the few notable wars between 1918 and 1939 was the Kurdistan campaign of Air Vice-Marshal Sir John Salmond. Salmond, who showed great enterprise during the great battles of 1918, was the first British air officer to command a joint Army-RAF expedition. Coming after the stagnant military thinking of 1914–18, his campaign was remarkable for its initiative and sense of adventure, but did not receive the publicity it deserved.

The Kurdistan campaign was a small war, but it was a jewel of a campaign. Cutting loose from his bases, as Grant had done in his 1863 Vicksburg campaign, Salmond sent his infantry columns deep into the fastnesses of Kurdistan to stop Turkish infiltration into the territory of Mosul and to squash the Turkish-inspired Kurd rebellion.

It had become increasingly difficult for a commander in the field to commit himself and his forces to an action purely on his own initiative, but this is precisely what Salmond did. It was a decision Napoleonic in its arbitrariness, and his execution was in keeping with all the best tenets of the great captains. For the first time in history Salmond used aircraft to transport troops to the battle area, and he used them, too, to drop great amounts of supplies and to evacuate wounded.

His most important contribution to command was to show that even in modern war audacity paid dividends and that surprise could be achieved. Right from the beginning he had a moral supremacy over his enemy.

In 1918 Salmond had not wanted to make peace with the Germans; he felt that not enough of them had been killed. That is, he was in accord with Clausewitz. Even while Salmond was conducting his remarkable campaign in Iraq the Germans were recovering.

1 Not least in the present author's *Jackboot, the Story of the German Soldier.*

One of the prime architects of Germany's military recovery was von Seeckt, the Scharnhorst of the twentieth century. Scharnhorst had built up a secret army without Napoleon's knowing about it. Using Scharnhorst's methods, von Seeckt built up such an army without the Allies knowing about it, a classic example of bequeathed skill.

It fell to Adolf Hitler to use this army. Now it is a common mistake to regard Hitler as a mere megalomaniac, an insane-politician. Hitler was a military commander, the supreme leader of the largest armies in history. Despite his many vices and failings, Hitler was a student of history, an enterprising commander, and at times an astute one. More importantly, he was entirely Frederician in military outlook. Probably he knew as much about Frederick's campaigns as any German university professor specializing in Prussian history.

According to Hitler, technical inventions did not change strategy. 'Has anything changed since the battle of Cannae?' he asked.

Did the invention of gunpowder in the Middle Ages change the laws of strategy? I am sceptical as to the value of technical inventions. No technical novelty has ever permanently revolutionized warfare. Each technical advance is followed by another which cancels out its effects. Certainly the technique of warfare advances and it will create many more novelties until the maximum of destruction is reached. But all this can produce only a temporary superiority.[2]

He also said:

I do not play at war. . . . There is only one most favourable moment. . . . I shall not miss it. Let us not play at being heroes, but let us destroy the enemy. . . . My motto is: Destroy him by all and any means.

2 Quoted by Hermann Rauschning in *The Voice of Destruction*.

In 1935 Hitler was reported to have said:

> If I were going to attack an opponent I should act quite differently from Mussolini. I should not negotiate for months beforehand and make lengthy preparations, but . . . I should suddenly . . . hurl myself upon the enemy.

This is perfectly logical, if we accept the premise that a nation fights a war to win. If the aim of war is more permanent peace, then the sooner it is over the better. The idea of declaring war and giving the potential enemy even an hour to prepare himself for the blow is ridiculous.

Germany had the great advantage of a realistic testing-ground: during the two and a half years of the Spanish Civil War she sent about 50,000 specialist officers and men to try out new German equipment under war conditions.

Very few British officers after the First World War bothered to read German military books, but German officers certainly read British military books, and to good effect. One outstanding German commander not too proud to learn from the British was General Heinz Guderian. He became deeply interested in armour through reading English books and articles on tanks and their tactics – by Liddell Hart and Fuller, among others. He also read de Gaulle's ideas for armour, and he could see that through mechanized mobility the enemy's command could be completely paralysed by a blow sudden and swift enough to smash his front. Guderian was a well-read general; he knew that Arminius, Gustavus, Turenne, Marlborough, Frederick, and above all the Spartan generals, such as Cleomenes, Leonidas, Pausanias,[3] Agis, and Agesilaus, and also Napoleon, Sherman, some of the Southern generals of the American Civil War, and Moltke had used mobility as a psychological weapon. Guderian planned 'ultimate' mobility – to confuse, distract, dismay, and finally to terrify. He wanted a war-strike so fast that no enemy operating on conventional methods could possibly keep track of what was happening on their front, flanks, or rear. And he achieved it. Largely owing to Guderian the North-west Europe campaign of 1940 was one of the most successful in history.

3 Regent to King Pleistarchus, not Pausanias, second Spartan king.

Since the nineteen-twenties the Japanese Army Staff also had been studying the history of war. Previously they had known little about it, but, applying themselves to its study as assiduously as they worked at copying Western industrial methods, they translated into Japanese Clausewitz and many other military writers and set about imbibing foreign philosophy and practice. The generals saw their nation as a great military country in the German mould, but they set their sights too high – nothing less than the most ambitious scheme of military conquest yet known – and they blatantly copied the Germans in practically every detail, even to trying to imitate the goose-step.

Their initial stroke – on Pearl Harbor – a copy of the Nazis' attacks on Warsaw, Rotterdam, and elsewhere – was bold and successful. But the Japanese had not read history deeply enough. One bold, violent military stroke is just like one bold, violent blow on the nose; it makes the recipient angry. As the Germans knew, an attack must be sustained, followed up by one sledge-hammer blow after another. For many reasons the Japanese were incapable of delivering these blows against their major enemy, the United States.

Generally, the Germans and Japanese were the only ones to show any sense of 'future' in warfare, by both their material and their psychological approach to it. By their bombing of Pearl Harbor the Japanese showed that they had a true Arminius-like appreciation of the purpose of warfare. Their attack has been labelled 'treacherous', 'vicious', 'cunning', 'foul', and many other things. Vicious and cunning it was, for war largely depends on both, but treacherous it was not. War is not a game played to rules like cricket or football. It would have been absurd for the Japanese to give notice of their intentions and so let their prey escape.[4]

It was difficult to select a battle from the second Great War of modern times to illustrate facets of the sequence of leadership. So many great and successful campaigns or battles occurred: the

4 The author should point out that he has a healthy dislike for the Japanese and a loathing for their treatment of their prisoners. He could never forgive them for the way they ill-treated and murdered Army nursing sisters they captured. As an infantryman he fought against the Japanese and has no respect for them as men, but he considers them efficient soldiers.

German capture of Fort Eben-Emael, their overrunning of Europe, their capture of Greece and Crete, and their great battles in the early days of the war with Russia, such as Vyazma-Briansk in October 1941, their magnificent defence of Monte Cassino in 1943–4.

The Australians' defence and retaking of New Guinea; their remarkable defence of Tobruk and their campaign in Syria; the American battles in the Pacific, such as those for Tarawa or Okinawa or Iwo Jima. The battle of Alamein, of Tunisia, of Sicily, Anzio, Kohima; the D-day landings and the battle for Normandy; 'the Battle of the Bulge'. The many German-Russian battles on the Eastern Front, of which Stalingrad is the prime example. In the end, for reasons which I hope will become apparent, I chose the battle of Alamein, October-November 1942.

However, as we have seen, no great battle has occurred without preliminaries, and in the case of Alamein the preliminaries were protracted and complex. We must go back to Wavell, who commanded the British forces in the Middle East 1939–41, to understand the situation which came to exist in October 1942.

One day Wavell's capabilities as a general will be appreciated. He was the first British commander in the Second World War to understand the lessons of the German campaigns in Poland and France and to apply them to desert fighting. He was the first British commander efficiently to co-ordinate British land, air, and sea forces in a single campaign. Most outstandingly he welded an army of several nationalities into a first-rate fighting force, and with it in 1940 won some of the cheapest victories in British military history.

Wavell's army won these campaigns because it was superior in leadership and in the quality of its fighting troops. In every other respect the enemy was vastly superior, although he himself gave a different picture in an order to his army:

> In everything but numbers we are superior to the enemy. We are more highly trained; we shoot straighter; we have better weapons and equipment. Above all, we have stouter hearts and greater traditions, and we are fighting in a worthier cause.

It was a good order, but it was too flat, too self-conscious – especially when delivered to the Australians and New Zealanders who formed the infantry fighting backbone of his army. Wavell was a close student of Allenby, whom he admired tremendously – enough to write a biography of him. During two years in Palestine he learned many of Allenby's methods of command, observed his handling of the polyglot British army and his methods of maintaining discipline and morale. 'He saw a military mind of real magnitude . . . resort to ancient stratagems of war and receive and destroy an enemy.'[5]

Wavell also learned from Allenby that a commander could get the most out of his subordinates if he gave them freedom of action to the limit of their abilities. Wavell, who lectured and wrote about soldiers and soldiering more than most other generals have done, likened the relationship between the general and the army to that between a horse and a rider. 'The horse (the army) should be cared for (training and maintenance) in the stable as if he were worth £500. But he should be ridden in the field as if he were not worth half-a-crown.'

Wavell, in 1939, felt it was a mistake for the British Army to spend its time studying the characteristics of foreign soldiers, but in this he was wrong and was merely echoing the narrow sentiments of third-rate generals, to which group Wavell did *not* belong. He changed his mind, for two years later it was largely his study of Italian military morale in North Africa which induced him to launch his pursuit-offensive against the retreating Italians.

Many military critics believed it was impossible to surprise an enemy on a bare coastal plain,[6] but Wavell saw – and was probably the first British general to see – that the desert could be used like the sea to ship men and equipment to any decisive point – if a commander had adequate mechanical equipment and absolute mastery of the air.

His preparation for his big attack against the Italians in December 1940 amounted to an elaborate feint, and he used as a model Allenby's Gaze manoeuvre of November 1917. Using camouflage imaginatively, he built dummy emplacements, a fake

5 H.A. de Weerd, *Famous British Generals.*
6 But Chauvel, under Allenby's command, achieved it on a bare plain with his Australians at Beersheba in 1917.

aerodrome, and a great counterfeit tank park in such positions as to lead the Italians to expect a conventional frontal attack on Sidi Barrani. In fact, Wavell's force struck from the south-west and surprise was complete.

The few months that followed were history-making. In one of the most brilliantly bold operations of war Wavell sent the 7th Armoured Division cross-country to cut off the retreat of General Tellera's forces south of Benghazi. They caught the column and fought and bluffed it into surrender – 112 tanks, 216 guns, 1,500 trucks, and 20,000 men. All this was blitzkrieg pattern, even if it was not accomplished with blitzkrieg speed.

Because of his victories Wavell became, overnight, 'the most famous British general', but Wavell himself would have admitted – he was one of the most honest, forthright soldiers ever – that Allenby was at his shoulder during his campaigns.

It is no slight on Wavell to say that the Italian commander, Graziani, helped the British victories. Graziani was still imbued with First World War philosophy – that is, he fought battles for territory instead of trying to destroy his enemy's army.

Poor Wavell. Rommel retook Libya, and Wavell was suddenly transferred to the command of India. It is wrong to judge a commander by the extent or number of his victories. Wavell certainly had some disasters – but at a time when nobody else could have done any better.

TWENTY-TWO

MONTGOMERY AND ROMMEL; A RETURN TO THE 'PERSONALITY' GENERAL

It has become a cliche that the North African desert is a paradise for the tactician and a nightmare for the quartermaster. It is relatively easy here to lead armies, much more difficult to feed them even in static positions, but much of the warfare was now mobile and armoured, and the British, though they had pioneered tank warfare, were now inferior to the Germans. A tactical device practised by Rommel had much to do with one defeat after another inflicted on the British. When counter-attacked he would form a hidden screen of strong, efficient anti-tank artillery and try to lure British tanks into fire from short range.

Right through to Alamein the Axis methods were sound enough and reflected the sober and reasoned German approach to previous experience and to history. They would make several well-spaced probing attacks to find a weak spot. But, in any attack, the moment the leading tanks were knocked out the attack would become static. The Germans had long since learned that to drive against stiff resistance was sheer suicide. The British and the Americans learned from the German methods.

After Wavell's transfer to India the British Eighth Army suffered several serious and assorted setbacks. One of them, the death of Lieutenant-General W.H.E. Gott when his transport aircraft was shot down, brought about Churchill's appointment of General B.L. Montgomery as commander of the Eighth Army, under General Alexander as Commander-in-Chief, Middle East. The Italians and Germans were at El Alamein, the Army's fortunes were at their lowest ebb, and everything hung in the balance – or so it appeared.

When an historian praises a contemporary figure he runs the risk of being accused of being blinded by that figure's personality and reputation, so I must here make clear that I am no blind disciple of Field-Marshal Montgomery. In some ways he must have been insufferable. One can be forgiven for thinking of him as conceited, dictatorial, immoderate in his statements, high-handed in his actions, and lacking in discretion.

But after giving all proper credit to O'Connor, Wavell, Auchinleck, Cunningham, and Ritchie, generals upon whose foundations his victory was laid, I still think that he was the outstanding senior Allied general of the Second World War, although inferior to Gustavus, Turenne, and Napoleon.

Montgomery had always been a capable soldier, but after the death of his wife in 1937 he studied war as never before, not only delving into military history but probing the psychology of command in large armies.

But when he took over the Eighth Army in 1942 the Germans could not have been particularly perturbed. Rommel, 'the Desert Fox', was at this time the best-known general in the world; the British and Commonwealth troops in the Middle East regarded him with a sort of veneration. Even the Australians, noted for their irreverent, caustic, and loudly voiced opinions of generals, conceded that Rommel was 'a good bloke'. Possibly by a combination of accident and design Rommel had become a legend. If you were up against Rommel you had little chance of winning – this is what most soldiers thought, despite the way Morshead's Australians had kept him out of Tobruk. The Rommel complex was the German's not-so-secret weapon, and his personality was felt as much as had been that of Hannibal of Caesar, Wellington or Napoleon.

Montgomery's first battle was to outshine Rommel, and as he was public relations conscious and as he had a natural ability to project himself – as had Hannibal, Caesar, Charles Martel, Charlemagne, Condé, Napoleon and most of his marshals, Allenby in Palestine, and Orde Wingate in Burma – this was not too difficult for him to *want* to do.

Nevertheless, under modern conditions of war it is difficult for a commander to project his personality and to use it as a driving force.[1] He has advantages that generals of other ages had not, such as radio and high-speed transport, but his men are much more numerous and they are generally scattered over a great area. Also, the commander has so much 'office work' to do that he cannot hope to move around among his troops and be seen by virtually every man as were generals of other eras.

Montgomery's success in becoming a 'character' was outstanding. The only Allied leaders who had comparable success during the Second World War were Orde Wingate, 'Blood and Guts' Patton, and, to a lesser extent, 'Tiny' Freyberg. Others – Eisenhower, MacArthur, Blamey, Wavell, Slim, to name a few – had personalities strong enough to be felt at some distance, but they were not 'characters'. The make-up of the German and Russian soldiers and of the German and Russian armies and political structures made it impossible for any of their generals to be 'characters', but Rommel came nearest to being one in the German Army and Zhukov in the Russian. Nearly every German general had a powerful personality – an inheritance of command from Frederick.

Correlli Barnett says of Montgomery's public-relations activities in his book *The Desert Generals*: 'All this would have been profoundly distasteful, even had it been necessary, to any man not abnormally vain.' But distasteful to whom? To more orthodox generals perhaps. To Mr Barnett assuredly. But not to thousands of men who made up the Eighth Army – and they were the men whose reactions counted.

Soldiers love a character, whether he happens to be their platoon commander, C.O., or commander-in-chief. Montgomery was a genuine character, a born exhibitionist with a sense of the dramatic and with tremendous confidence in himself. Such a man can be inspiring.

Not necessary? It was vitally necessary for Montgomery to project his personality, to make a splash. Barnett, *inter alia*,

1 Elsewhere during the Second World War the 'personality cult' was less successful. In 1944 Marshal of the RAF Lord Tedder advised the Supreme Commander, General Eisenhower, to get rid of Montgomery, and Eisenhower very nearly did so.

roundly and justifiably condemns orthodoxy and its dreadful results and then rebukes the one man who most successfully broke away from it.[2] From a purely practical point of view drastic action was necessary: in the previous six months prior to Alam Halfa the Army had suffered more than 100,000 casualties.

Montgomery cleverly built up his own personality. He adopted the Australian slouch hat, covered with various hat badges. He wore it square on his head, as no Australian ever did, but it had the desired effect. Later he exchanged the hat for a black beret of the Royal Tank Regiment, and on it wore their cap badge as well as his own badge or rank.

His habits disturbed many of his officers, they even distressed some. He neither drank nor smoked; he prayed and quoted scripture. He disliked needless noise, and before conferences, which he was apt to call at inconvenient times, he set aside two-minute periods for coughing. His inspection trips were whirlwind-like, and he had his nickname, 'Monty', painted on his personal reconnaissance tank.

Yet Montgomery was no mere martinet and could be tolerant – especially when he knew he had to be. If this appears to be a back-handed compliment it is not meant to be; the ability to show tolerance and latitude when it is not inwardly felt is a talent that only gifted commanders possess. When Montgomery first visited the New Zealanders he said to General Freyberg, 'I notice your soldiers don't salute.' Freyberg replied, 'Wave to them, sir, and they'll wave back.' Montgomery tried it – and it worked.

Yet the picture of Montgomery as a hell-for-leather, impetuous general is false. He spoke with bravado but acted with caution. 'I am proud to be with you,' he told his army. 'You have made this army what it is. You have made its name a household word. . . .You and I will see this thing through together.' He spoke playfully about 'hitting the enemy for six right out of Africa' and piously referred to 'the Lord Mighty in Battle', as Cromwell had often done. But generally the picture was of Napoleon and his 'Mes enfants' all over again.

2 Some of Barnett's dislike of Montgomery may be due to the impression that an order is a basis for discussion. Neither Montgomery nor any other great captain would tolerate such an attitude towards an order.

A German staff officer, von Mellenthin, noted: 'the fighting efficiency of the British improved vastly under the new leadership and, for the first time, Eighth Army had a commander who really made his presence felt throughout the whole force.'

In fact, his first order made the Army sit up and take notice. He said that all withdrawal plans were to be burnt. 'We will fight the enemy where we now stand; there will be no withdrawal and no surrender. We stay here alive or we stay here dead.' The words were Montgomery's, but the instructions came from Alexander. This was immaterial; Montgomery was the man on the spot, and within a few weeks everybody in the Eighth Army knew him.

One historian has written that Montgomery introduced something new into British military history – army *esprit de corps*. 'There has been regimental *esprit de corps* before but not a spirit that distinguished a whole army.' The Eighth Army was indeed unique in the Second World War, but it is too much to claim that Montgomery introduced army *esprit de corps*. This was at least as old as Marlborough. 'Monty' had several things in common with 'Corporal John'; one was that both were aged fifty-four at the time of their most famous victories.

Montgomery had the best group of subordinate commanders since Napoleon selected his marshals. In de Guingand Montgomery had a Chief of Staff as able as Napoleon's Berthier. Among his armoured and infantry commanders were Gatehouse, Lumsden, Briggs, Horrocks, Leese, Morshead, Wimberley, Tuker, and Freyberg.

His programme of training was so severe that an American officer is supposed to have said, 'Montgomery put an army that was already supposed to be veteran through a physical conditioning programme equal to that of the commandos.' The historians who have criticized Montgomery as a general have perhaps not realized that his methods were more French and Napoleonic than British, or perhaps, knowing this, they resented it. I will discuss Montgomery's Napoleonic make-up at greater length after an account of the battle.

On the other side of the Alamein position was one of history's most formidable soldiers, even if he was not quite the wizard that legend has made him out to be. Vibrant in Erwin Rommel was the whole spirit, theory, and practice of hundreds of years of German military craft.

'Let it be quite clear,' Rommel once told his officers, 'that there is no such thing as 'Direction Front', but only 'Direction Enemy'!' In this he crystallized the creed of every great German general since Arminius and especially of Frederick and those who reformed the Prussian Army after Jena.

'The final decision of any struggle if the enemy attacks will probably rest with the Panzers and motorized units behind the line. Where this decision is reached is immaterial. A battle is won when the enemy is destroyed. Remember this one thing – every individual position must hold. . . .' This too was Frederician. The infantry must stand firm while the cavalry dealt the *coup de grace*.

Long before Alamein, Rommel had said, 'Whoever has the greatest mobility, through efficient motorization and efficient lines of supply, can compel his opponent to act according to his wishes.' It was his misfortune at Alamein that because of shortage of petrol he did not possess enough of any of these three prerequisites.

Rommel was one of the few generals of the Second World War to exercise personal control over a battle; the Germans said he was too often in his command vehicle and too frequently absent from his headquarters. He gave practically all his orders by radio as the occasion demanded.

Montgomery regarded Rommel with respect but not with awe; he had a tendency to repeat his tactics, and that was proof that he was human and vulnerable. For his part, Rommel had an open mind about Montgomery.

Montgomery took over a 40-mile line that extended from the Qattara Depression north to El Alamein. Its main features were Himeimat, Deir El Munassib, Ruweisat Ridge, the Hill of Jesus (the so-called Double 24 feature), and Thompson's Post near to the Mediterranean.

The most important general feature of this position was its unattackable flanks, a position strongly reminiscent of Miltiades' front at Marathon.

On the British side were some concrete pill-boxes, with extensive wire entanglements and minefields, covered by well-concealed artillery. On his first visit to the front Montgomery saw the strategic importance – as his predecessor, Auchinleck, had done – of Alam Halfa, an undefended ridge of high ground in the rear of the Alamein position. Montgomery reasoned that Rommel would make Alam Halfa his main objective, and he prepared an elaborate trap for the German armour. More than this, he let false maps fall into Rommel's hands – maps which showed that a soft and sandy approach to Alam Halfa was firm ground. In the defensive battle which Montgomery fought here between August 30 and September 7 1942, Rommel, for whom the battle was a desperate gamble, did everything that Montgomery wanted him to.

Rommel had some bad luck, however. General von Bismarck, commander of the 21st Panzer Division, was killed by a mine, and the Afrika Korps commander, General Nehring, was severely wounded. Rommel himself was so sick that he had to leave his command truck, a disaster for the Germans because Rommel was another Charles XII – though a much more stable one – in that he depended more on personal observation and decision than on a preconceived plan.

The victory at Alam Halfa was a fine spur to the Eighth Army's morale, as Montgomery had known it would be.

The Germans lost 49 tanks, 55 guns, 395 vehicles, and 2,901 men; the British casualties amounted to 1,750 men and 67 tanks, although only half of these were total losses.

This battle over, Montgomery turned his attention to assault. From study, Montgomery noticed that whenever Ritchie, his predecessor, fought a battle of confusion against Rommel the Eighth Army was beaten. Montgomery wanted a simple plan with a simple intention: once action was joined the initiative must never be allowed to pass to the enemy.

Nevertheless, Alamein was not the simple slam-bang-bust-through battle that many people suppose, but a complex operation of many phases and movements, and not the least of Montgomery's achievements was his masterly handling of the complexities.

Montgomery's plan aimed at maximum surprise and deception. The 4th Indian Division would feint at Ruweisat Ridge, the 44th and 50th would feint near Deir El Munassib, and the 7th Armoured south of Himeimat. The Australians would pin down three divisions along the coast. The real attack would come in the north at Tel el Eisa, where infantry and engineers would create a gap for the Armoured Corps – a specially formed striking force. Significantly, Montgomery was deliberately striking at the strongest part of the German front, but the Germans were expecting the main assault at Ruweisat Ridge, farther south.

To strike in the north was common sense, because a breakthrough here would automatically cut off the enemy troops to the south; a break-through on the south would merely force them back on their lines of communication.

Montgomery, too, had learned from Allenby's deception at Gaza in 1917. Montgomery formed a truck park in the rear of the break-through point. Each day German scout planes watched the training area of the 10th Armoured Corps far behind the lines, but each night squadrons of tanks disguised as trucks were moved into the truck park and an equal number of trucks were withdrawn. Until the invasion of Normandy the preparations for Alamein comprised the most elaborate fake undertaken with dummy huts, tanks, vehicles, dumps, gun-emplacements, water tanks, and even a fake pipeline. The blow was being readied.

The Axis line at Alamein was very strong, with minefields five miles deep in places, but the overall defences were not nearly deep enough if a British attack in strength was anticipated – and this must have been the case. Still, the guns were well sited, and tanks had been dug in to serve as strong-points, a sign that Rommel was on the defensive and was not contemplating an attack.

In his forward minefields alone – 'the Devil's Gardens' the Germans called them – Rommel had used 500,000 mines, plus great quantities of captured British bombs and shells made into mines were of German, Italian, French, and Egyptian manufacture, all with their own peculiarities. The most notorious was the German Teller, a difficult one to deal with. Most mines were intended to cripple tanks, but the S-mine was aimed at infantry-men. When a soldier trod on the horns of the S-mine a charge shot a cylinder into the air about stomach-high, where it burst, with a spread of shrapnel bullets. Trip-wires were connected with S-mines and with the large aircraft bombs, which when exploded killed men in scores.

Across the trap-strewn desert the British infantry would have to walk, accepting casualties. However, on Montgomery's order a special school was set up where methods of mine-detection and -lifting were evolved so efficiently that mines could be dealt with even by night. To explode mines harmlessly, a small number of Matilda tanks was fitted with 'the Scorpion' – a contraption of whirling chains.

The situation, with unattackable flanks and both sides with powerful defences, was piquantly, even alarmingly similar on the static lines of 1914–18, and everybody knew that battle on a large scale was inevitable.

'War is a simple thing,' Montgomery said, 'the ABC of modern war is common sense.' And he showed his own common sense by insisting that every man was to know the plan for Alamein. I think it likely that the men in the ranks knew more about the plan of battle than any other private soldiers in history engaged in a major fight. His decision to make his plans generally known proved that he had studied his Australian and New Zealand fighting-men, for they above all others have always fought even better when they were 'in the picture'.

It also proved that he had studied Rommel, for he was now 'one up' on his opponent. The British forces knew what they were doing right from the start; the Germans and Italians had to wait for a succession of orders and were never fully informed about their commander's intentions.

In September Rommel flew to Berlin, leaving von Stumme in command of the Afrika Korps. Stumme divided his armour, sending some of it south so that if the British stab came where expected Stumme could crush it by bringing his armour together like great jaws.

On October 23, with Rommel still absent, the Allied forces comprised 220,476 men, 939 tanks fit for action, 892 guns, 1,451 anti-tank guns, and 530 aircraft. The Axis had 108,000 men, including 53,736 Germans, 548 tanks, 1,063 anti-tank guns, 350 aircraft. Another 18,000 Germans landed just before and during the battle, while another 77,000 Italians were in the rear areas. Montgomery had physical superiority.

In the days of Turenne and Cromwell, of Marlborough and Napoleon, no commander would have considered giving or accepting battle voluntarily unless he had first managed, by art or subterfuge, to gain numerical superiority. In modern war generals had acquired the unprofessional habit of engaging battle regardless of their prospects – in short, they gambled. Montgomery was no gambler, though he was prepared to take caculated risks.

TWENTY-THREE

ALAMEIN, A BATTLE WON, A PURSUIT LOST; NAPOLEON–MONTGOMERY

On the eve of battle Montgomery issued a famous order:

> When I assumed command of the Eighth Army I said that the mandate was to destroy Rommel and his army, and that it would be done as soon as we were ready. We are ready now. The battle which is now about to begin will be one of the decisive battles of history. It will be the turning-point of the war.

This was unequivocal, pure Cromwellian stuff. There was no loophole such as *'If every man does his duty we will win through'*. Even Napoleon never claimed that he was about to fight one of the decisive battles of history. But, Montgomery added, twelve days of bitter fighting lay ahead.

A bombardment gives warning of an imminent attack, but Montgomery did not make the mistake of the generals of the First World War. At the battles of the Somme and Third Ypres the bombardment lasted several days, and though they did much material and moral damage, the Germans were able to reinforce and to reorganize. At Alamein Montgomery limited his initial bombardment to thirty minutes. At 11.30 p.m. on Friday, October 23, the British artillery barrage – 450 guns on a six-mile front – struck the Axis positions, and so began the battle which some historians have called a 'generals' battle', while others have labelled it a 'soldiers' battle'. Few victories in history were so much dependent both on a commander's capabilities and soldiers' skill.

The artillery battered the command-posts and cut communications. Under cover of this bombardment, which stunned even the veteran Germans by its violence, infantry and engineer patrols advanced half an hour later to clear mines and barriers, so that infantry could advance in strength. The RAF was vastly superior to the Luftwaffe, and its fighters and bombers made a sustained and heavy attack on Axis positions.

After that, except for ten minutes' rest each hour to cool the gun, the guns fired for five and a half hours – 600 rounds per gun. And they had orders that if they came under fire themselves they must not pause or take cover.

The extraordinary aspect of the battle is that infantry and engineers – *men* – were used to clear laborious tracks through minefields for *armour*. No army had previously faced such a complex and dangerous mine-lifting and 'de-lousing' task, and no doubt the lessons learned at Alamein will one day be put to use by future commanders. The task took twelve days. Had enough armoured minesweepers been used they could well have cleared the way in as many hours. The British Tank Corps had invented minesweepers in 1917 and had used them most effectively. Montgomery had no minesweepers, so he used men, but somebody bungled badly in not providing him with minesweepers, especially as it was well known that the Axis were using mines in hundreds of thousands.

This infantry-leading-armour pattern of attack was entirely that of the French attack of 1916–17 when the infantry captured enemy trenches and put ramps across them so that the small Renault tanks could follow up and cross them.

Despite really tough opposition the Australians secured most of their final objective by 5.30 a.m. and the New Zealanders most of theirs. The Axis outpost troops fought magnificently, but, owing to the smashed network of communications, command was practically paralysed.

On October 24 von Stumme died of a heart-attack. Ritter von Thoma took over and desperately tried to concentrate his armour for the enemy break-through attack he knew must come. Rommel overshadowed von Thoma as Montgomery overshadowed his generals, yet without von Thoma Rommel might not have been so successful, for this tall, courageous man, wounded twenty times, was one of the great masters of tank-warfare – perhaps the greatest master. He had fought in Spain, Poland, Russia, and France and was as able a tactician as ever Germany sent to war.

Perhaps had Rommel himself been present from the beginning the battle might have had a different twist, but not a different ending. Napoleon, I think, would have recognized a breakthrough as inevitable and would have prepared accordingly – that is, he would have lined the corridor along which the British thrust must pass and raked it as it ran the gauntlet. Or he would have pulled back earlier and allowed the British to beat the air. Only an inspirational, opportunist general could have had a chance of stopping Montgomery's attack dead – and then only with his army's morale equal to that of the Eighth Army.

On October 25 Rommel, who had been in hospital, took off for North Africa, at Hitler's urgent request, and that evening was in command again. He learned from von Thoma of the desperate shortage of petrol and of ammunition. Casualties in men and machines had been very high, but the Axis defence was still formidable, and at one time Montgomery was forced to assume a temporary defensive. Up till the evening of the 25th Axis losses were no more than 3,700, very much less than the British losses.

Fighting was spirited and sustained, for rarely have two armies been so well matched in battle discipline. On the 7th, in one epic fight within the main battle, 300 riflemen, gunners, and sappers – from, respectively, the 2nd Battalion Rifle Brigade, 76th Anti-Tank Regiment, and 7th Field Squadron – became a garrison outpost at a position known as 'Snipe' and were isolated during a determined German-Italian counter attack. In quivering desert heat they resisted with such spirit and became such a nuisance to Rommel that an all-out effort was made to wipe out the post. By one of those mistakes that can so easily happen in the heat of battle, other British tank units also tried to wipe it out.

The Axis tanks made repeated attempts to crush the post, and at times came within 100 yards before they were hit and wrecked by the defenders' 6-pounders. The action gained such fame that a Committee of Investigation was set up to examine it critically. The committee concluded that the minimum number of tanks burnt and totally destroyed was 32 – 21 German and 11 Italian – plus 5 self-propelled guns. Perhaps another 20 tanks had been knocked out but dragged away by the enemy. Other miscellaneous vehicles had also been destroyed. British losses were 72 riflemen and gunners killed or wounded. This remarkable defence divorced from the major action going on around it, was remarkably reminiscent of the defence of Rorke's Drift in the Zulu War of 1879, and was one of Rommel's major setbacks at Alamein.

Tradition made possible the magnificent stand at 'Snipe' – tradition sown at Crécy and Agincourt, nourished at Blenheim, Quebec, and Waterloo, in the defence of Lucknow in 1857–8 and Kandahar in 1880, and brought to flower at Le Cateau in 1914 and elsewhwere. The link of leadership in junior ranks never showed itself more clearly than at 'Snipe', where the senior officer, Lieutenant-Colonel V.B. Turner of the Rifle Brigade, won the V.C.

I accept the risk of being accused of bias when I say that I believe that only British, Australian, New Zealand, or other German troops could have held out at 'Snipe'. French troops certainly could not have done so, for the Napoleonic legend and spirit had crumbled to dust in 1871.[1]

With the intelligent leading of his senior officers and the gallantry of the soldiers, Montgomery imposed on Rommel a type of battle to which he was not accustomed and in which he would probably react faultily. If Montgomery strengthened one link in the chain of command which is stronger than the others, this is it. By a combination of means he imposed his will on his opponent – and he has left a clear pattern to be followed in the future.

'As long as you can make a German commander dance to your tune, you have nothing to fear; but once you allow the initiative to pass into his hands you are liable to have plenty of trouble,' Montgomery said. I hope future British commanders will

---

1 Men of the Free French garrison of Bir Hacheim defended this fortress magnificently in May and June 1942, but it *did* fall. 'Snipe' and Rorke's Drift did not. General Koenig, commander of Bir Hacheim, so favoured evacuation that he refused to accept supplies. To answer those apologists for the French who point to successful defences carried out by the French Foreign Legion, it is only necessary to say that Germans predominated in the Legion's ranks.

remember this; for the time will come when they will have a chance to test this tenet against German leaders.

At last, on the 29th, Rommel began to make preparations for withdrawal to Fuka – a decision he should have made days before. But while he made these advance preparations he realized that Montgomery had switched his main thrust along the coast road. This thrust was savage and bloody and was carried out by the already battle-scarred and casualty-depleted Australians. Rommel reinforced his positions across the road, especially at Thompson's Post, where some of the most violent fighting of the entire battle took place.

Montgomery, at his H.Q. beside the Mediterranean, studied Rommel's tactics, which showed obviously that Rommel knew the main threat was along the road. Accordingly at 11 a.m. on the 29th Montgomery changed his own plan. He would make his final blow not along the road, after all, but six miles south of it and break Rommel's powerful defences on the Rahman Track. Nevertheless, the Australians would resume their road-axis attack to keep Rommel distracted.

Their attack was so savage, so typically Australian, that Rommel reacted exactly as Montgomery wanted him to. He threw in everything he could spare – and much that he could not spare – to hold the northern pocket. The Australians had obsessed him at Tobruk; they obsessed him again now.

Rommel began to lose the battle the moment he attempted his battering-ram counter-offensives, for his armour was as much at the mercy of the British anti-tank guns as British armour was to his guns.

He tried four times to throw back the Australian infantry and British tanks, and the pocket was an inferno of dust, heat, noise, and combat. But, as everywhere along the line, Montgomery had chosen the right men for the right place, and, as General Alexander said, the Australians 'fought the enemy to a standstill'. They suffered 22 per cent of the British casualties in the battle.

To lead the final assault, on November 2 Operation Supercharge, Montgomery chose Freyberg, who evolved an artillery preparation of an intensity not seen since 1918. A total of 360 guns from five divisions were put under command of just one young commander, Major-General S.C.E. Weir, the New Zealand artillery commander. This centralized control of artillery has been called 'revolutionary'. It was as old as Mahomet, from whom Gustavus learned how to use it, from whom Napoleon had inherited gunnery ideas. In a way it was a return to 1914–18, with the infantry advancing behind a creeping barrage, the shells in which would fall 12 to 25 yards apart. But this was a creeping barrage in depth – four curtains of it at least – and it was preceded by a heavy aerial bombardment. It lasted four and a half hours, and 15,000 shells were fired.

This old-fashioned attack was the prelude to a dashing thrust by the 9th Armoured Brigade (Brigadier J. Currie), 123 tanks, many of them in battered condition; few were fully efficient. Because of heavy enemy fire, mines, and accidents 29 failed to arrive at the starting-line on time. It was a desperate venture, and every man knew it. Freyberg had told them that Montgomery was prepared to accept 100 per cent casualties, a psychological spur as old as leadership itself.

The attack by the 9th Armoured Brigade – the 3rd Hussars, the Wiltshire Yeomanry, and the Warwickshire Yeomanry – might better be termed a charge, for the spirit which pervaded the men who made it and the dash with which it was mounted and sustained were entirely cavalry in character. The spirit of the Scots Greys, of the Death and Glory Boys, of thousands of long-dead dragoons, hussars, and lancers rode with the 9th Brigade in its charge. This is no mere romanticism. In 1942 the men who served in armoured units still thought of themselves as 'cav' and were very conscious of the cavalry spirit. Tradition brought victory to the 9th Armoured. Colourful Currie himself was a product of the Royal Horse Artillery, and two of his C.O.s were masters of hounds.

Currie stood upright on the outside of his tank, some commanders sat on top behind the turret, the others, with their turrets open, stood up with head and shoulders outside. Pennants flying, the tanks carried all before them, crushing enemy soldiers bewildered and dazed by the barrage, rolling inevitably over dead and wounded. But as night brightened into dawn the tanks became silhouetted and the German gunners and infantry hit back savagely. Tank after tank was knocked out and casualties mounted. The whole cold, dusty dawn was a thunderous, vicious scream of noise, and into it the Hussars and Yeomanry drove, Currie, always erect, charged right in among the enemy guns, and in places, the enemy were surprised and battered into early defeat at point-blank range.

But a counter-attack column of the 21st Panzer Division came up in the dust and did great damage to the brigade, as did potent 88s sited farther back or on a flank. In some of the fierce actions only two or three tanks in a British squadron survived. The 2nd Armoured Brigade was supposed to appear about this time on the heels of the 9th, but it did not arrive. Nevertheless, the few remaining tanks of the 9th extricated themselves and, with all the discipline of fine cavalry, re-formed and continued the fight. The 3rd Hussars had started the battle with 35 tanks; they now had 8. Twelve officers of the regiment had been killed and only 4 remained alive and unwounded. The Wiltshires lost practically every tank. The brigade's total tank losses for the whole night's operation were 103, and their casualties in men were well over 50 per cent.

But within 100 yards of their burnt-out tanks were 35 wrecked enemy guns, some entangled with the tanks which had knocked them out. The gun crews had been shot down at their posts, just as cavalry had sabred gunners in a thousand earlier actions. The brigade had taken 300 prisoners, and could have taken many more had infantry been available to collect them.

Freyberg said: 'It was a grim and gallant battle right in the enemy gun-line. Although the 9th Brigade did not reach its objective and had heavy casualties the action was a success as the enemy gun-line was smashed.' Montgomery told the brigade's survivors that their exploit had ensured the success of the operation.

It had also ensured the brigade a place in history, for their action was unique – a cavalry-style tank charge against emplaced guns. In fact, it was the ultimate in cavalry actions. The slow process of evolution that had begun at the end of the sixth century when horsemen were first equipped with spurs completed its cycle at Alamein.

It may be argued, as Freyberg admitted, that armour was used incorrectly in this battle, but as an instance of evolutional fulfilment it was superb. Nevertheless, the charge proved that armour cannot attack concealed or semi-concealed guns in a good position, such as behind a crest, and hope to succeed. Tanks, whether British or German, could no more advance against well-manned anti-tank guns than cavalry could against machine-guns.

Rommel himself came to the conclusion that in general 'there is little chance of success in a tank attack over country where the enemy has been able to take up defensive positions.' The anti-tank gun and the mine dominated the battle of Alamein, and because of them the defenders were in a much stronger position than the attackers.

It is not possible to win battles with tanks unless they have close anti-tank support, as the Russians learned from the Germans on the Eastern Front. The Germans repeatedly smashed Russian armour, not with tanks alone, but with tanks aided by mobile tank-attack guns.

The charge by the 9th Brigade was the prelude to a much larger battle, Tel el Aqqaqir, a tank duel on a divisional scale, with both sides supported by intense artillery and anti-tank fire and by air action. In this vital battle, over and over British tanks ran out of ammunition, and 'ammo trucks' drove out across the shell-swept battlefield to supply them. Montgomery's armour fought the panzers and the Italian tanks to a standstill; by the end of the day Rommel's tank strength had fallen by 117, of which 77 were German. But though British artillery destroyed many enemy battles and the British tanks outclassed Rommel's, the Axis tanks nevertheless brought their enemies to a halt and stopped all penetration; but Rommel knew the battle was lost. The Afrika Korps had only 35 serviceable tanks left, von Thoma had been captured, and the supply position was, as Rommel wrote, 'absolutely desperate'.

He was not yet beaten; perhaps he did not yet realize that he was out-generalled. Rommel had been called the supreme opportunist general, but Montgomery had a mind twice as agile. He knew how to exploit success and had the rare courage – seen only in genuinely great captains – to press on with a new action before waiting to see the result of the one before. He did this now. Before the Tel el Aqqaqir battle was well under way Montgomery decided to strike southward from what was known as 'the New Zealand funnel' – a corridor driven into the Axis lines. Two minor and completely successful operations were made, thus widening the funnel and giving new ground for further exploitation. This day was the beginning of the end for Rommel, and he abandoned any idea of a counter-attack. All he could hope to do was to build some kind of barrier behind which he could withdraw in good order, though in this he was hindered by air raid after air raid.

But on that eleventh day of battle very few men in the Eighth Army could foresee a decisive victory. Montgomery still exuded confidence, but his officers were far too exhausted to soak up any of it. Troops were scarce, and already base areas and hospitals had been scoured for men fit for action. Montgomery had warned everybody that the battle would be vicious and unremitting for twelve days. One day to go.

That night Montgomery had enough evidence to show that Rommel was on the verge of a general retirement, and he reasoned that his opponent would plan a stand on the scarp near Fuka. He gave instant orders for further exploitation – a larger funnel through which he could launch the New Zealanders and the 7th Armoured Division in a great south-north sweep in an attempt to cut off the enemy's retreat. This decision was a brilliant conception and, again, reveals a first-class military brain. In his ability to come to a decision, to give instant effect to it, Montgomery was equalled only by Alexander the Great, Frederick, and Napoleon among the really great commanders. The attack on the night of November 3 and the fights on November 4 ended the battle – twelve days after it had begun. Montgomery's forecast had been right.

Rommel was already withdrawing, but Hitler told him on November 3 'not to yield a yard of ground'. Rommel sent his A.D.C. to Hitler to say that to stand fast meant annihilation. This resulted in Field-Marshal Kesselring's arrival at Rommel's H.Q. on November 4. According to Rommel, he reaffirmed Hitler's decision, but Kesselring was to write that he advised Rommel to ignore Hitler and accepted full responsibility for a retreat. Rommel, to save what he could of his army, ordered withdrawal.

Casualty figures vary. According to Alexander between October 23 and November 7 the Axis armies lost 10,000 killed, 15,000 wounded, and about 30,000 prisoners.

Barnett quotes German losses at 180 tanks, 1,000 dead and 8,000 prisoners, the Italians losses at 1,000 dead and 16,000 prisoners.

Total British casualties were 13,600 killed, wounded, or missing – and missing usually meant dead.

The German retreat from Alamein was magnificently conducted. Montgomery had won the battle, but he can be accused of having lost the pursuit. He was hesitant in getting it started and over-cautious in the actual movement. He must have known that the Axis defences were smashed, that they had little armour and were running out of petrol, yet Rommel was able to withdraw much of his force. By re-grouping for pursuit on November 5 Montgomery gave Rommel eighteen vital hours during which the Axis troops never stopped moving.

Rommel, though in great difficulties from lack of everything, held his command together by the strength of his own personality and by the innate steadiness of his men. He fought some splendid rearguard actions, and when he couldn't fight he bluffed. That he was able to hold Montgomery down to such a slow rate of advance despite British numerical and material superiority attested to his stability. Montgomery had, at times, 450 tanks to Rommel's 50, yet he took three months to reach Tripoli from Alamein. Montgomery, the established-front, semi-static-battle general, was no pursuit general.

C.E. Lucas Phillips, another defender of Montgomery and author of an admirable book about the battle, *Alamein*, states that the 'German division had been reduced to skeletons' and that 'the Italians had been broken to bits', and on the following page claims that the 'resounding victory' was the beginning of 'the no less victorious pursuit'. There is no victory in a pursuit which could average only thirty miles a day for the first sixteen days against a 'skeleton' and 'broken to bits' enemy. This is the only point of Lucas Phillips's assessment of Alamein with which I disagree.

The withdrawl was Rommel's victory. It was as competent as that of Moore to Corunna in 1808–9, of the Russian rearguard actions under Rosen during the Russian retreat in 1812 and similar actions under Ney when the French, in turn, were retreating. It was as well co-ordinated as the British retreat from Mons in 1914. But, most of all, it was startlingly similar to the intriguing series of rearguard actions fought by the Confederate General Johnston when he held Sherman down in his march from Chattanooga to Atlanta to an advance of a mere hundred miles in seventy-two days. Clever enough not to remain too long in one position, Johnston invariably took precautions to secure his retreat

– just as Rommel did. And, in final praise, let it be said Xenophon would have been proud of Rommel.

I have said that Montgomery was Napoleonic in many ways. Anybody who has analysed the writings of both men will have seen the marked similarities in style and in personal evaluation. Also, Montgomery closely followed some of Napoleon's strongest maxims.

'I see only one thing – the enemy's main army', Napoleon said. Montgomery followed this precept. On the northern flank his troops surrounded a large force of Germans, but Montgomery refused to be drawn into a decisive action at that point. He continued to concentrate his spearhead against the German main force – the panzer divisions.

Montgomery was positively imbued with the following Napoleonic maxims:

'Glory and military honour is the first duty a general should consider when he is going to fight; the safety and preservation of his men is secondary; but this very boldness and tenacity ensures the safety and economy of life.'

'Nothing is more important in war than unity in command; thus . . . there should be but one army acting on one line and led by one chief.'

'In war the leader alone understands the importance of certain things, and he may alone, of his own will and superior wisdom, conquer and overcome all difficulties.'[2]

'In battle . . . art is shown in directing fire from many quarters on one point; when the fight is once begun, a leader skilful enough to bring to bear on one point an unexpected mass of artillery is sure to carry the day.'

'The first quality of a commander is a cool head,' Napoleon wrote. And Montgomery echoed, 'Never worry.'

2 De Gaulle, in 1934, in *The Army of the Future*, showed his profound appreciation of this point: 'In order to secure distinguishing characteristics for military formation the leaders must stamp their own images on them. They must be allowed the right to do that.'

After the war Mongtomery said: 'I call high morale the greatest single factor in war. A high morale is based on discipline, self-respect and confidence of the soldier in his commanders, in his weapons and in himself. Without high morale no success can be achieved.'[3] Napoleon had said this before him, as had a dozen other great captains or military writers over the centuries, for the chain of command is a living thing.

3 True, but the victor in nearly every case has been superior in weapons.

TWENTY-FOUR

FULL CIRCLE AND THE FUTURE

For a few days each century destiny dominates a battlefield – I use the term in its widest sense to include, as it now must, Whitehall, the Pentagon, and the Kremlin. On these few days the judgement, discretion, education, outlook, and authority of commanders, which depend mostly on the intellectual and moral reflexes acquired during their whole career, are tested by fire.

Peace is merely the incubation period of war; the type of war – 'hot' or 'cold' – makes no difference. In practice the war is usually won by the nation and the commanders who most determinedly prepare for it in peace.[1] The defeat of the Germans in 1945 does not invalidate this principle. They won everywhere during the early years of the war. They lost in the end for a variety of reasons, chief of which were the aerial devastation of the German homeland, the drain of fighting on several fronts at once, Hitler's interference with his generals, and the generals' failure to stand up for their own military principles.

The British appreciation of the scientific aspects of war is shown by the three-month course at the Royal Military College of Science at Shrivenham, now attended by all British officers before their year's training at the Staff College. The commandant of the college, Major-General R.W. Ewbank, wrote in 1964:

> Whether we like it or not, the Army today lives, moves and has its being in a scientific environment, and one which is becoming more so every year. I believe that an officer today,

1 'If you want peace, prepare for war.' Roman proverb.

whatever his arm, cannot but increase his efficiency – and that means his ability to lead men in battle as well as to equip and prepare them for battle – if he makes a real effort to try to understand what is going on in the world around him.

It is even more encouraging to find a senior lecturer at the college writing:

If there are lessons from history we must know them; if there are lessons from science we must know these, too . . . there is a basic foundation of knowledge drawn from many fields which is a common requirement for all of us.

Such statements, coming from key officers, are encouraging, for science can improve the accuracy of predictions about the future. It takes about ten years to bring a new weapon system into service, so planners must predict at a range of fifteen years and upward. The environment of a nuclear battlefield will be vastly different from all previous military experience. It will call for greater dispersion, but at the same time much more rapid effective command and control. Consequently, commanders must have or must develop an imaginative adjustment for the future.

However, some generals still want to fight a war with strategy and tactics more suitable for the weapons and methods of ten or twenty years or even half a century before. It is the leader who can adapt himself most rapidly to change who wins battles; this is why it is wrong to give high command to an elderly soldier. No man is so rigid in thought as an old soldier, and the few exceptions, such as Turenne and Blücher, only prove the point that younger senior officers are the most effective ones. Most Governments now realize this and put their Service chiefs out to grass at a comparatively early age.[2]

A purely professional environment is extremely dangerous, and the higher the rank of the commander and the longer his length of service the greater the danger. He becomes rigid in outlook and

2 Had young and vital Captain John Moore of the 32nd Regiment been in command at Cawnpore in 1857 instead of doddering, indecisive General Wheeler there would have been no frightful massacre.

develops an inability to appreciate anybody else's opinion; this happened to several German and Japanese generals, to Hitler, and to Douglas MacArthur. MacArthur's frame of mind became so very dangerous that the President had to remove him from command.

Paradoxically, many professional soldiers of all ranks know very little about war, even if they are well informed about the mechanism of armies.[3] There is still an impression – fortunately it is fading – that a general automatically knows all there is to know and that it would be offensive to a senior officer to expect him to undergo serious training. Somehow or other, by his very elevation to high rank he is supposed to become imbued with profound knowledge.

In Britain, at least, high-ranking officers no longer merely pontificate and are not confined within a purely professional environment. It is encouraging to find that their education has regular injections of information not directly connected with warfare but of vital concern to an officer whose interests must be global and catholic.

Brigadiers who attended a representative course heard lectures on the following subjects: The Far East and Malaysia; The Economic Future of Britain and the Commonwealth in its World Setting; Britain and the United States; the Future of Australia and New Zealand; Russian Foreign Policy; People and Power in the Middle East; 'Victory' or Co-existence?: The American Dilemma; Crisis in Africa; The Congo Impasse and the Communist Threat to Tanzania; Problems of Western Europe.

Courses of this kind are held in the United States and in the NATO countries, with the result that senior officers become much more widely informed, and hence their minds stay more elastic. Mental elasticity is vital, for the modern commander has multiple interests; battle is not his sole existence and end.

Even so, soldiers are profoundly conservative and more prone to resist change than the members of any other profession. Even the great military innovators were slow in bringing in their innovations. Hundreds of military disasters or near disasters and the deaths of millions of soldiers can be laid at the feet of

3 An observation made also by Liddell Hart, in *Thoughts on War.*

conservatism, but the military hierarchy has never been permanently cured of it.

One of the earliest examples of conservatism concerned the Roman defensive system, which under the Emperor Augustus had no central reserve – always a paramount and fundamental necessity. Nearly 300 years elapsed before Diocletian, during the last ten years of the third century AD, partly remedied this by establishing the *comitatenses* – a field army under the direct command of the emperor. Even then Roman tactics remained wedded to the belief that infantry was the decisive arm, and not until 351 was the cavalry able to prove itself the decisive arm – at the battle of Mursa, the first victory won in the West by newly raised Roman heavy cavalry.

It would be frustrating to list the many examples of military conservatism. It was the morass of helplessness and hopelessness in which 24,000 British soldiers died of illness and exposure in the Crimea.

It was the pig-headedness before the 1914–18 war when most leaders, especially the British, refused to see the potential use of aircraft and mechanization in battle. It was the wall against which the tank pioneers beat their heads in vain for years. It was the criminal stupidity which sent human bodies charging against sheets of machine-gun bullets.

Even some of those who say most emphatically that the missile now dominates the battlefield, persist as obstinately as others in their belief in close-quarter action. Tank soldiers – I have spoken to many of them – persist in their determination to rush at the enemy and deal with him at close quarters, which is as brainless as it is gallant.

The need for younger generals with more flexible minds increases in urgency proportionately to the increase in speed and destructiveness of modern warfare. The capable commander needs to be aware of the need for physical and mental fitness as modern war, especially guerrilla warfare, places increasing strain on the body and mind of the soldier.

Primarily, any general who aspires to be a great captain of the future must decide on his attitude towards destruction. The approach commanders have towards war, and in particular to the lengths they may justifiably go to bring an enemy to his knees, has its progressive chain. It is true that in the history of war there are always commanders who wage it with less ferocity than others. According to the accident of the existence of such men the behaviour of commanders and armies fluctuates from war to war, but generally the trend is towards greater barbarity and greater destructiveness, even if most armies have succeeded in curbing indiscriminate rape and plunder. As commanders have found greater power in their hands they have naturally used that power, and nearly always under the guise of 'military necessity'. At Agincourt Henry V ordered all prisoners to be killed, but this was an almost innocuous act compared with the sack of Magdeburg in 1631, when more than 40,000 people perished. And this was a minor atrocity compared with the destruction of Warsaw or Dresden or Hiroshima.

By their intensive bombing of Germany, carried out without warning and with complete disregard for the life and property of non-combatants, the British, Americans, and Russians fulfilled to the letter Clausewitz's philosophy of defeat and total destruction. Superb irony.

They also obeyed a maxim propounded by Lenin, who said that the 'soundest strategy in war is to postpone operations until the moral disintegration of the enemy renders the delivery of the mortal blow both possible and easy.' America was not following this maxim when she struck her mortal blow against Japan.

The evolution of weapons has had much to do with the sequence of leadership. Thousands of years ago David showed that with a missile a soldier could deliver a fatal blow without taking a chance of receiving one. Gradually the expert archer improved on this principle. The breech-loading rifle added to the range of the blow and the probability of a hit, and the machine-gun made hitting a near certainty, without seriously increasing exposure.

The trouble is that war has not yet recovered from the state of convulsive evolution into which firearms threw it. Thousands of types of muskets, rifles, and guns have come and gone. The sword and lance had been nothing more than extension of the human limbs, but firearms possessed characteristics quite independent of the skill and bravery of the soldier.

Progressively their range, rate of fire, stopping power, penetrating effect, quantity of ammunition required, and so on governed the choice of formations, place and time of combat. The volume of fire increased. In his later battles Napoleon usually began by silencing the whole of the enemy's artillery by means of his massed artillery fire: he aimed at having 4 guns for each 1,000 men. Many later commanders tried to follow this principle, with varying success.

Combatant armies fought, usually, at greater distance from each other, and troops, under dangerous fire, had to take cover. The commander found observation and control much more difficult. Two things happened simultaneously: technical ability and knowledge became more important; the commander's direct action on the man who was carrying out his orders decreased from war to war, battle to battle.

Astute generals, realizing that they could not be seen by all their men at any one time, deliberately set out to infuse great *esprit de corps*, and at appropriate times and places they appeared in person, and often dramatically. Condé, Hoche, Napoleon, Rommel, and Montgomery were generals of this type.

Moltke was the high priest of technical ability and knowledge. Before the war of 1870, by studying the French railway system, Moltke was able to forecast with absolute accuracy the direction of Napoleon III's advance, the distribution of his forces, and the extent of the front they would occupy. Moltke was grimly materialist, and by 1914 material elements began to reach towards the ultimate.

The power of weapons reduced warfare pretty much to a matter of mathematics. Vast and complex calculations and numerous specialists to make them were required before a commander could indulge in the luxury of what some called martial inspiration, but was nothing more than painful deliberation. He had to weigh the detailed proposals of his assistants, and when, after all the preliminary staff work was completed – and it could take months – all he saw of the battle itself was its plotting on a map. There was no longer much scope for genius or even for individualism, except under a few unconventional and enterprising generals.

It was once possible to choose between two kinds of strategy – those of annihilation and exhaustion. It is now highly improbable that a major *conventional* war could last long enough to exhaust a nation by famine or in any other way, so that again history has turned full circle, and battles of annihilation, as practised in ancient times, will once more confront the world. The only difference is that not only armies but whole communities will be annihilated, thanks to the conscription of science into the ranks of combatants, for David's sling-shot has become a long-distance nuclear missile.

The delivery of blows without exposure is the very essence of missile fighting and is the true source of modern military power. In this respect the Polaris missile – fired from under water by a submarine which cannot be tracked – can hardly be bettered as a defensive-offensive weapon. Should intercontinental ballistic missile warfare develop the aim will be largely Napoleonic in theory – to knock out the enemy's 'artillery' before he has much chance to use it.

The significant point is how the missile will be delivered – if it is delivered. I have already pointed out that most great victories have been won by the strategy of indirect approach. But surprisingly the direct approach has always been the accepted form of strategy. Many a general has adopted the indirect as a last, desperate resource. When it worked, as it so often did – even when the general concerned had been previously military weakened – he apparently did not realize its significance. The most consistently successful leaders, facing a powerful enemy, rarely attacked him directly; Alexander is the only exception. Marlborough made only one direct attack – and paid for it. Caesar erred several times – and also paid for his errors.

A competent commander should do anything rather than commit himself to a direct approach. He will cut loose from his communications – as Hannibal, Genghiz Khan, Napoleon, Grant, Sherman, von Lettow-Vorbeck, and Salmond did – he will cross deserts, mountains, and swamps and suffer the inevitable hardships. A direct approach causes a stalemate which becomes more insoluble war by war, if only because such an approach consolidates and stabilizes the enemy on his own base. Far from being caught off balance, he is ready to fight.[4]

4 'The art of the indirect approach can only be mastered and its full scope appreciated by study of and reflection upon the whole history of war.' Liddell Hart, *The Strategy of Indirect Approach*.

General 'Stonewall' Jackson's motto during the American Civil War was 'Mystify, mislead, and surprise' – the du Guesclin theory. As a strategical and tactical principle it is unexcelled for present-day warfare. The power of striking like 'a bolt from the blue' has the greatest possible value, as Colonel Henderson observed in his book published in 1905. 'The first thought, and the last, of the great general is to outwit his adversary and to strike where he is least expected.'

From the time of Waterloo there has existed the belief that superiority in numbers is decisive – and increasingly decisive. This is a dangerously false doctrine. There is only one major factor in today's war – surprise backed by continous action. The victor in the next great war is the side which strikes first – without declaration of war, without even a hint that it is about to strike. This is the true and ultimate nature of war, and it amounts to paralysis by destruction. But – surprise is becoming increasingly difficult to achieve.

One major problem – that of supply – which bedevilled commanders more and more as warfare become increasingly complex, has been largely solved, but the scope and extravagance of its solution may be the undoing of the nation which has most noticeably mastered it – the USA.

The Americans' success in solving the problems of supply followed directly on their experiences in the Civil War, with later lessons from other wars. But this success has had a hampering effect on the US armies, which use a vast amount of transport to carry iced drinks, comic books, hot-water bottles, over comfortable bedding, and an array of 'amenities' which would make the ancient commanders roar with laughter – and their soldiers too. During the Korean War the roads were cluttered with non-essential transport which became a danger to the fighting troops. The nation which can most nearly reproduce Spartanism in its army in peace as well as in war will be best prepared to meet the challenges of the future. An army which places too much stress on its material comforts and in which the men are merely looking foward to their retirement pension does not deserve the name of army.

It is significant that in the American Army for every 18,000 men in the forward zone there are another 50,000 in the rear areas of the theatre of war; the Russian Army needs only two behind the forward zone to support one in the zone. An American-type division needs 600–800 tons of supplies a day; a Soviet-type division 150 tons.

Despite scientific and technological improvements, by a curious paradoxical reaction machine warfare has reached the stage where leadership in the real sense is again paramount. Fire has caught up with movement, but never again could a front become static in the sense of 1914–18 because there is no front, or, to put it another way, it is a 360-degree front with a depth extending to the homes of the soldiers at home. Speed has reached such a climatic pitch that leaders of all ranks will have to make decisions and implement them in minutes or seconds.

The quality of audacity is fostered by subsidized 'adventure training' in deserts, mountains, and even in Arctic regions. This is an enlightened aspect of Army planning.

The added responsibility which faces more junior officers in war does not mean that the High Command or the General Staff is out of a job. On the contrary, never has planning and forethought been so necessary. For now war, though undeclared, is perpetual, and the General Staff must have its plans ready to the minute. Prussian war plans, as evolved by Moltke, were elaborate and far-reaching, but in comparison with today's requirements they are crude.

In some circumstances, following the necessity for dispersion, infantry warfare could easily assume a form of 'regular guerrilla' fighting. The infantry would always give way to opposing mechanized columns, then would return when the armour had moved on. At the same time enemy rear areas and bases would be nuclear-attacked. This combination could easily exhaust mechanized forces before they could reach their decisive strategic objectives.

I think it very likely that nuclear warfare, instead of leading to more intensive mechanized warfare, would bring about a type of action in which infantry would again predominate, if only because the complicated and expensive war engines of all types are painfully dependent on complex supply services, which would certainly be thrown out of gear by base-area nuclear-attack.

We are going to need a type of really tough light infantry after the style of General Moore's creation. Between 1939 and 1945 the Germans and Russians produced infantry that could march 30–35 miles a day, and were so reliable that they often arrived at an objective before long motorized columns which had left the departure point at the same time. Paratroops will be needed too, though much more in non-European theatres of war, such as in Asia, where air and radar cover will be more scattered.

Future wars – at least those fought on this planet – seem bound to be ideological. Wars have for so long been fought for territory that we tend to forget that in various eras wars have been fought in an attempt to impose a religion or a political system on an enemy people. In the twentieth century we have come full circle. But ideological wars require ideological armies – and such armies are not created overnight. Iron Curtain and Asiatic countries have given close attention to psychological and political problems of existing and future armies. Because of the very democratic principles they seek to defend, the Western countries lag far behind in indoctrinating and disciplining their troops to the iron standards required.

It would be difficult to overemphasize the importance and threat of guerrilla warfare, which is in itself a type of indirect strategic and tactical approach, especially in Vietnam. Ever since 1945, without cessation, it has been taking place in one country or another – in Palestine, Greece, Cyprus, Cuba, Malaya, Vietnam, Laos, Borneo, Algeria, Kenya, to mention just a few theatres of operation. Between 1945 and 1965 no fewer than 40 wars occurred.[5] More than a quarter of the world is subject to or threatened by guerrilla warfare. Occasionally, there has been a more or less conventional action, of which the Korean War was the prime example. The world is confronted with two vastly different weapons threatening its peace – the megaton hydrogen bomb and a nail in a piece of wood buried in a rice paddy. A remarkable contrast. There will be more guerrilla warfare, much more, because the fearsome deterrents leave combatant powers no stronger form of war, as President Kennedy pointed out. Should conventional warfare break out there would be an ever-present and increasing risk of its getting out of hand to the point where nuclear weapons might be used. Nuclear weapons, however, are virtually useless in guerrilla warfare.

5 In the 5,560 years to 1965 a total of 14,531 wars occurred – 2.6 a year.

Some races are natural guerrilla fighters; some countries have natural guerrilla terrain. In some places guerrilla warfare has become a way of life, as in Vietnam, where Americans expect it to continue until the end of the century and possibly beyond that. They say that only an all-out war with massive forces on both sides would bring about an earlier decision. We may well find that guerrilla warfare is 'conventional' warfare and that warfare formerly regarded as conventional is now unorthodox.

For armies of the more conventional Western or Westernized countries the mission is obvious: their soldiers must learn to master the guerrilla and to evolve counter-guerrilla tactics. To do this they must know the enemy intimately, his character and mentality, his methods, tactics, techniques, strengths, weaknesses. They must themselves be versatile, enterprising, and tough. More than that, as Lieutenant-Colonel T.G. Greene, editor of the *United States Marine Corps Journal* points out, 'to beat the guerrilla means to fight not in the sharp black and white of formal combat, but in a grey, fuzzy obscurity where politics affects tactics and economics influence strategy. The soldier must fuse with the statesman, the private turn politician.' This is the doctrine of Clausewitz all over again – that war is a continuation of politics. The foundation of the United Nations, of the North Atlantic Treaty Organization, and of the South-East Asia Treaty Organization are just such continuations.

It is not possible for the Western countries to give too much attention to counter-guerrilla training; we shall be living with guerrilla warfare for many years. The British have learned much, but only the United States seems to have found the correct mental approach to the problem, and even here the Marine Corps has evolved the best techniques. The Americans realize that they themselves cannot become guerrillas – not unless they intend to fight in California or New England. Guerrillas have to blend with the local population; they must look, speak, act, and think like natives of the troubled area. Neither the British in Borneo nor the Americans in Vietnam can do this.

Career politicians, whose interference in war reached unhappy heights between 1939 and 1945, will not have time to interfere in nuclear warfare. A president, a prime minister, or a dictator might give the order to press the button, but after that he must keep out of the way. A commander's initiative will again become almost absolute, in the Caesarian-Gustavian-Napoleonic way.

I say this despite the sophistication of computer controls, which – so the Americans say – leaves practically nothing to chance or to human error. In the new Combat Operations Centre of the North American Air Defence Command built deep inside Cheyenne Mountain, Colorado, and opened in April 1966, are no fewer than 13 computers and a vast amount of other complex equipment. By simply pressing buttons, NORAD officers can electronically scan the entire North American continent and its distant approaches. A single operations panel can call up 12 million pieces of computerized information. But beyond the electronic logic of the computers there is always a human brain which must make the final decisions. The United States and Russia are engaged in a race for the armed domination of space, a state of affairs that is almost unnoticed by the world at large. Already the two nations are doing a good deal of spying from unmanned satellites.

Despite all scientific advance, and perhaps in part because of it, leadership is turning full circle.

The great commander will restore personal contact with his men. His armies are bigger, but he has the means to travel around them. He could not hope to do this during battle, except on brief occasions, any more than the great commanders of the past did so. But he must do so beforehand and with great assiduity and dedication. In any case, while senior commanders must remain with their maps and telephones and computers in relative safety there should be field generals capable of once again leading from the front and prepared also to head the casualty lists as in the days of old and as so many German generals did during 1939–45.

The commander's personality must be developed again and 'developed as a Law', as de Gaulle advised in *The Army of the Future*.

To exercise imagination, judgement and decision, not in a certain direction, but for their own sake and with no other aim than to make them strong and free, will be the philosophy of training of leaders. The real school of leadership is general culture. . . . Through it the mind learns to . . . educate itself to a level where the whole can be appreciated without prejudice to the shades of difference within it. There has been no illustrious captain who did not possess taste and feeling for the heritage of the human mind. At the root of Alexander's victories one will always find Aristotle.

No poetic hyperbole this, for Aristotle was the young Alexander's tutor for three years. And how many people know that Xenophon and Socrates were close friends? Did *philosophers* teachings make such great *soldiers*?

So has the chain been formed, so will it be lengthened, by the brotherhood of men with a hunger for glory and a taste for martial immortality. But remember this – those who will win the strongest links will be those most willing and able to snatch lessons from the womb of time by an analysis of the birthpangs of the past and to father their application to the present – whenever the present might be.

APPENDIX: SUN TZŬ

The reader has encountered many military maxims and proverbs throughout this book. He may be interested to read a few of those propounded by Sun Tzŭ 2,500 years ago and to reflect on the similarity between them and the maxims and practice of much more recent times:

It is a military axiom not to advance uphill against the enemy, nor to oppose him when he comes downhill.

An army should be always ready but never used.

Attacking does not merely consist in assaulting walled cities or striking at an army in battle array; it must include the art of assailing the enemy's mental equilibrium.

Attack is the secret of defence; defence is the planning of an attack.

The commander stands for the virtues of wisdom, sincerity, benevolence, courage, and strictness. [The five cardinal virtues of the Chinese are humanity or benevolence, uprightness of mind, self-respect or self-control, wisdom, sincerity or good faith.]

To secure ourselves against defeat is in our own hands, but the opportunity of defeating the enemy is provided by the enemy himself.

If you know the enemy and know yourself you need not fear the result of a hundred battles. If you know yourself but not the enemy for every victory gained you will suffer a defeat.

To fight and conquer in all your battles is not supreme excellence; supreme excellence consists in breaking the enemy's resistance without fighting.

Without harmony in the State no military expedition can be undertaken; without harmony in the army no battle array can be formed.

Avoid what is strong and strike at what is weak . . . the soldier works out his victory in relation to the foe whom he is facing. . . . He who can modify his tactics in relation to his opponent and thereby succeed in winning may be called a heaven-sent captain.

With a superior force, make for easy ground; with an inferior one, make for difficult ground.

Do not repeat the tactics that have gained you one victory, but let your methods be regulated by the infinite variety of circumstances.

Only the side that gets more men will win.

BIBLIOGRAPHY

Barnett, Correlli: *The Desert Generals* (William Kimber, 1960).

Battles of the 19th Century (Cassell, 7 vols, 1900).

Baynes, Norman: *The Byzantine Empire* (Oxford University Press, 1925).

Boutell, Charles: *Arms and Armour in Antiquity and the Middle Ages* (Reeves and Turner, 1874).

Burne, Lieut.-Colonel Alfred H.: *The Art of War on Land* (Methuen, 1944).

Churchill, Winston S.: *The World Crisis* (Odhams, 1919).

Clausewitz, Karl von: *Vom Kriege (On War)*, German edition of 1840.

Crane, Stephen: *Great Battles of the World* (Bell and Sons, 1901).

Creasy, Sir Edward: *The Fifteen Decisive Battles of the World* (Macmillan, 1902).

Dane, Edmund: *Trench Warfare* (United Newspapers, 1915).

Denison, Colonel G.T.: *A History of Cavalry* (Macmillan, 1913).

Dodge, Colonel T.A.: *Gustavus Adolphus* (Houghton Mifflin, 1895).

Dunant, J. Henri: *A Memory of Solferino* (Cassell, 1947).

Eady, Major H.G.: *Historical Illustrations to Field Service Regulations, Operation, 1929* (Sifton Praed, 1930).

Falls, Captain C.: *The Art of War* (Oxford University Press, 1961).

Farrer, J.A.: *Military Manners and Customs* (Chatto and Windus, 1885).

Fuller, Major-General J.F.C.: *The Conduct of War 1789–1961* (Eyre and Spottiswoode, 1961).

—— *Decisive Battles of the Western World* (3 vols, Eyre and Spottiswoode, 1954–56).

—— *Armament and History* (Eyre and Spottiswoode, 1946).

—— 'Machine Warfare' (*The Infantry Journal*, Washington, 1943).

Gardiner, S.R.: *History of the Great Civil War, 1642–49* (2 vols, Longmans, 1886–89).

Gaulle, General de: *The Army of the Future* (1934).

Guibert, Jacques de: *Essai general de tactique* (2 vols, 1775).

BIBLIOGRAPHY

Hansen, Harry: *The Civil War* (New American Library, 1961).

Harbottle, T.B.: *Dictionary of Battles* (Swan Sonnenschein, 1904).

Hart, Captain Sir B.H. Liddell: *Thoughts on War* (Faber and Faber, 1944).

Hart, George H.: *Great Soldiers* (Grant Richards, 1911).

Henderson, Colonel G.F.R.: *The Science of War* (Longmans, 1905).

Henry, Professor L.E.: *Napoleon's War Maxims* (Gale and Polden, 1899).

Jackson, Robert: *Formation, Discipline and Economy of Armies* (Military Library, 1845).

James, Charles: *Military Dictionary* (Military Library, 1810).

Laffin, John: *Digger: Story of the Australian Soldier* (Cassell, 1959).

—— *Scotland the Brave: Story of the Scottish Soldier* (Cassell, 1963).

—— *The Face of War* (Abelard-Schuman, 1963).

—— *Swifter Than Eagles: Biography of Marshall of the RAF Sir John Salmond* (Blackwood, 1964).

—— *Jackboot: Story of the German Soldier* (Cassell, 1965).

Morley, John: *Oliver Cromwell* (Macmillan, 1900).

Nicolai, Dr G.F.: *The Biology of War* (Dent, 1919).

Parker, Barrett (editor): *Famous British Generals* (Nicholson and Watson, 1951).

Phillips, C.E. Lucas: *Alamein* (Heinemann, 1962).

Portway, Lieut.-Colonel Donald: *Military Science Today* (Oxford University Press, 1940).

Reide, Thomas: *Military Discipline* (Military Library, 1795).

Rogniat, H.: *Sur l'art de la Guerre* (1817).

Rose, J. Holland: *The Indecisiveness of Modern War* (Bell, 1927).

Sheppard, Major E.W.: *The Study of Military History* (Gale and Polden, 1953).

Stocqueler, J.H.: *The Military Encyclopaedia* (W.H. Allen, 1853).

Tillotson, J.: *Stories of the Wars, 1574–1658* (Ward Lock, 1899).

Vagts, Alfred: *A History of Militarism* (Hollis and Carter, 1960).

Wars of the 19th Century (Cambridge University Press, 1914).

Wavell, Field-Marshal Earl: *Soldiers and Soldiering* (Jonathan Cape, 1953).

—— *The Good Soldier* (Macmillan, 1948).

—— *Allenby: Soldier and Statesman* (Harrap, 1946).

Whitman, Captain J.E.A.: *How Wars Are Fought* (Oxford University Press, 1941).

Other reference works are mentioned in the text.

I have also referred to various issues of the *Army Quarterly*, the *British Army Review*, the *Royal United Services Institution Journal*, the *Swiss Military Review*, and other foreign official Service magazines.

INDEX

Ranks shown are mostly those held at the time of an action or campaign. However, where no rank is given in the text the final rank of the soldier concerned, where known, is given in the index.

Austerlitz, battle of, 1, 43,
    156–74, 195, 217
Austria, Crown Prince of, 207,
    208

Bacon, Roger, 90
Bagration, Prince, 164, 169,
    170
Bard, capture of, 151
Barnett, Correlli, 234–5, 249
Bazaine, Marshal, 210
Beck, Colonel-General Ludwig,
    143
Behrenhorst, Georg von, 175
Belisarius, Byzantine general,
    66
Benedek, General, 200, 207
Beresford, Marshal, 17
Bernadotte, Marshal, 157, 158,
    162, 169, 170, 172, 173,
    176
Berthier, Marshal, 158, 159,
    236
Berwick, Duke of, 150
Bir Hacheim, battle of, 4, 244n
Bismarck, General von, 238
Bismarck, Otto von, 206, 207,
    208
Bittenfeld, General von, 207
Black Prince, 83
Blamey, Field-Marshal Sir T., 234
Blenheim, battle of, 4, 52, 116,
    117, 129, 244
Bloch, M., 215, 217
Blücher, Field-Marshal, 180,
    187, 254
Bonaparte, Napoleon, 1, 3, 4,
    8, 10, 11, 13, 16, 17, 18,
    19, 20, 22, 24, 40, 43, 55,

65, 89, 92, 113, 117, 118,
    131, 142, 143–55, 156–74,
    175, 176, 180, 185, 186,
    187, 188, 191, 192, 194,
    198, 205, 206, 208, 209,
    211, 216, 217, 220, 227,
    233, 235, 236, 240, 241,
    243, 244, 246, 249, 251,
    258, 259, 264
Bonnal, General, 217
Bouquet, Brigadier-General
    Henry, 136
Bourcet, Pierre de, 144, 146–7
Boyen, Major, 179
Braddock, General E., 136
Brandenburg, Elector of, 112
Breitenfeld, battle of, 98, 117
Briggs, Major-General R., 236
Brunswick, Duke of, 139, 140,
    141, 142
Buller, General Sir R., 117
Bülow, Dietrich von, 175
Buxhöwden, General, 170, 173
Byzantines, 68, 69

Caedicius, Lucius, 60
Caesar, Julius, 16, 17, 18, 24,
    54, 55, 57, 58, 91, 98, 99,
    149, 151, 185, 223, 233,
    259, 264
Caffarelli, General, 169, 170
Calcabellos, action at, 13
Callimachus, Greek leader,
    31–2, 33, 38
Cannae, battle of, 1, 43–4, 44,
    119, 133, 156, 216, 226
Canrobert, Marshal, 196, 210
Carnot, French minister, 147,
    157

Narses, conqueror of Gothic
Italy, 66
Naseby, battle of, 104–9
Nehring, General, 238
Nero, Claudius, 11, 41, 45,
46–7, 48, 50–1, 52, 116,
171n
New Model Army, 101–4, 110
Ney, Marshal, 13–14, 17, 158,
176, 187, 250
Niel, Marshal, 196, 197, 201
Nightingale, Florence, 203
Normandy, Duke of, 81
Northampton, Earl of, 83, 85
Nostitz, General, 128

O'Connor, General Sir Richard,
233
Okey, Colonel, 104, 106, 107
Oman, Carola, 185
Orléans, battle of, 91
Orsini, Italian assassin, 191
Othman ben abi Neza, 70
Oudenarde, battle of, 5, 116n
Oudinot, Marshal, 159, 160,
164
Oxford, Earl of, 83

Parker, Captain Robert, 116
Paterculus, Velleius, 61
Patton, George, 17, 234
Paullus, Aemilus, 14
Pausanias, Spartan general,
227
Pax Dei ('Peace of God'), 76
Pearl Harbor, 228
Pepin II, 70
Perseus, 14
Persian Army, 33, 34

Peter the Great, 117
Philip of France, 82, 83, 84,
85
Phillips, C.E. Lucas, 250
Physical fitness in modern
armies, 40
Pitt, William, Prime Minister,
174
Placentia, 46
Plassey, battle of, 134
Plevna, battle of, 20
Polaris submarines, 11, 259
Poltava, battle of, 117
Polyaenus, 21
Polybius, 44
Ponitz, C. E., 189
Porcius, L., Roman consul, 47,
48, 50
Praetorian Guard, 16
Pydna, battle of, 14

Rapp, General, 172
Retzow, General, 128, 130
Ritchie, Major-General N., 233,
238
Roberts, Field-Marshal Lord,
220
Rogniat, General, 24
Rommel, Field-Marshal Erwin,
14, 16, 19, 231, 232–40,
241–52, 258
Roon, Count von, 208
Rorke's Drift, 244
Rosen, General, 250
Rossbach, battle of, 126
Rundstedt, Field-Marshal von,
1
Rupert, Prince, 100, 102, 104,
105, 106, 107, 108